THE VALUE OF HAWAI'I

2

ANCESTRAL ROOTS,
OCEANIC VISIONS

BIOGRAPHY MONOGRAPHS

The Center for Biographical Research of the University of Hawai'i at Mānoa is dedicated to the interdisciplinary and multicultural study of life writing through teaching, publication, and outreach activities.

In addition to *Biography: An Interdisciplinary Quarterly,* published since 1978, the Center sponsors the Biography Monograph series; a chronological list of previous monographs follows.

Anthony Friedson, ed. *New Directions in Biography* (1981).

Gloria Fromm, ed. *Essaying Biography: A Celebration for Leon Edel* (1986).

Frank Novak, Jr. *The Autobiographical Writings of Lewis Mumford: A Study in Literary Audacity* (1988).

Mari Matsuda, ed. *Called from Within: Early Women Lawyers of Hawaii* (1992).

Alice M. Beechert and Edward D. Beechert, eds. *John Reinecke: The Autobiography of a Gentle Activist* (1993).

Donald J. Winslow. *Life-Writing: A Glossary of Terms in Biography* (2nd ed., 1995).

Koji Ariyoshi. *From Kona to Yenan: The Political Memoirs of Koji Ariyoshi.* Ed. Alice M. Beechert and Edward D. Beechert (2000).

Leon Edel. *The Visitable Past: A Wartime Memoir* (2000).

Ruth Nadelhaft, with Victoria Bonebakker, eds. *Imagine What It's Like: A Literature and Medicine Anthology* (2008).

Michi Kodama-Nishimoto, Warren S. Nishimoto, and Cynthia A. Oshiro, eds. *Talking Hawai'i's Story: Oral Histories of an Island People* (2009).

Philippe Lejeune. *On Diary.* Ed. Jeremy D. Popkin and Julie Rak (2009).

Craig Howes and Jonathan Kay Kamakawiwo'ole Osorio, eds. *The Value of Hawai'i: Knowing the Past, Shaping the Future* (2010).

Maureen Perkins, ed. *Locating Life Stories: Beyond East-West Binaries in (Auto)Biographical Studies* (2012).

For further information about the Center or its publications, contact the Center for Biographical Research, University of Hawai'i at Mānoa, Honolulu, Hawai'i 96822 USA; telephone/fax: 808 956-3774; biograph@hawaii.edu; www.hawaii.edu/biograph.

The Value of Hawai'i
2

Ancestral Roots, Oceanic Visions

EDITED BY

AIKO YAMASHIRO

&

NOELANI GOODYEAR-KA'ŌPUA

A BIOGRAPHY MONOGRAPH

PUBLISHED FOR THE BIOGRAPHICAL RESEARCH CENTER
BY THE UNIVERSITY OF HAWAI'I PRESS
2014

19   18   17   16   15   14   6   5   4   3   2   1

Library of Congress Cataloging-in-Publication Data

The value of Hawai'i 2 : ancestral roots, oceanic visions / edited by Aiko
Yamashiro and Noelani Goodyear-Ka'opua.
    pages cm — (A biography monograph)
    Autobiographical essays.
    Includes bibliographical references and index.
    ISBN 978-0-8248-3975-8 (pbk : alk. paper)
1. Hawaii—Social conditions.   2. Hawaii—Economic conditions—1959–
3. Hawaii—Politics and government—1959–   4. Quality of life—Hawaii.
I. Yamashiro, Aiko, 1984– editor of compilation.   II. Goodyear-Ka'opua,
Noelani, editor of compilation.   III. Series: Biography monograph.
    DU627.8.V36 2014
    996.9—dc23

                                                    2013040573

University of Hawai'i Press books are printed on acid-free paper
and meet the guidelines for permanence and durability of
the Council on Library Resources.

Print-ready files provided by Biographical Research Center.

Printed by Sheridan Books, Inc.

contents

HOW TO USE THIS BOOK

This book is by no means a definitive or all-encompassing collection of everything we value about Hawai'i. We hope you take this collection as a starting point for more wonderful and inspiring ideas, projects, conversations. For more possibilities.

For curriculum materials, events, additional stories, and videos related to this book and the first *The Value of Hawai'i*, visit our website, at

http://thevalueofhawaii.com.

This book can be read from cover to cover, or one can jump around, heeding the call of whatever title beckons. Here are some suggestions for alternative clusters of essays (listed by author's name), if you are looking for writings on particular topics:

HEALTH

Elise Leimomi Dela Cruz-Talbert
Joseph Keawe'aimoku Kaholokula
Cheryse Julitta Kauikeolani Sana
Mark Patterson
Dawn Mahi

RELATIONSHIPS WITH ELDERS

Kamanamaikalani Beamer
Jeffrey Tangonon Acido
Derek Kurisu
Bonnie Kahape'a-Tanner
Kainani Kahaunaele
Dawn Mahi
Sania Fa'amaile Betty P. Ickes
Cade Watanabe

FOOD

Derek Kurisu
Cheryse Julitta Kauikeolani Sana
Hi'ilei Kawelo
Elise Leimomi Dela Cruz-Talbert
Dean Itsuji Saranillio
Hunter Heaivilin

A NOTE ON THE TEXT

All glosses and translations included in this collection have been generously provided by the authors of each individual essay. In light of the interpretive nature of translation and the historically damaging effects it has sometimes had in the Pacific, we suggest you take each gloss and translation as an opportunity to do further research or to approach other Pacific or Hawaiian-language specialists to supplement the interpretations our authors have provided.

We acknowledge the fluidity of the Internet, but all the web sites and links cited in these essays were live on September 17, 2013.

ACKNOWLEDGMENTS

When we were given the responsibility and privilege of carrying this project into a new book, we knew a passionate and creative planning hui would be a crucial first step. Mahalo nui for the guidance of Nancy Aleck, Lehua Kaʻuhane, Dawn Mahi, Brandy Nālani McDougall, Craig Santos Perez, Lyz Soto, Melvin Won Pat-Borja, and Aubrey Morgan Yee. Our gratitude to Craig and Brandy for helping select and edit the beautiful poems that grace this book. Thank you also to Nāʻālehu Anthony, Christine Costales, Jim Di-Carlo, Trisha Lagaso Goldberg, Kaleikoa Kaeo, Kekuewa Kikiloi, Matthew Lynch, Makana Paris, Hōkūao Pellegrino, and Jojo Peter for their time and insight into this project.

For the stunning cover image and cover design, mahalo nui to Prime, Eric Agarijo, and Mark Guillermo. Prime, we will never forget sitting in 808Urban with you and listening to the depth of stories, emotions, and relationships that produced the images in the mural that is the basis of this cover. Mark, we will never forget how your first design struck us, inspired us to breathe deeper, made the book real for the first time. Mahalo for all these gifts.

We are deeply grateful to artist and aloha ʻāina Haley Kailiehu for providing the beautiful images gracing the pages that open each of the six sections of the book. Your thoughtfulness in considering each contributor's story is not forgotten. We can't thank you enough for taking on this project on such short notice and still giving it so much care and creative power.

Thank you to Claire Gearen and David Goldberg for their unwavering support in imagining and creating curriculum for *The Value of Hawaiʻi*, for inspiring teachers and students to be bold and creative.

This second book wouldn't exist without the passion and love of all the contributors to the first volume. You are our teachers and friends, and we are grateful for that. We would especially like to mahalo Craig Howes and Jon Osorio for their fearless leadership, for their great heart, and for their faith in us.

We are so blessed to have taken this journey with the most amazing contributors! You all are the breath and life of this book. We are grateful for the relationships we've built with you and so honored to help carry your stories to more and more people in Hawaiʻi and the world.

Aiko: Mahalo nui to the 'āina, wind, and rain of Pālolo, Mānoa, and Kalihi for caring for me and sustaining me throughout this project. To the waves at Barber's Point for teaching me patience and resilience, to the ocean for her powerful generosity. To my amazing co-editor, Noe, I would not have dared something so fantastic without your brave and brilliant spirit. To my family for teaching me love; to my dear friends for late-night poetry and drinks, for long talks, for the grip of strong, loving hands. And to Bryan, my forever home.

Noe: My deepest aloha and mahalo to nā kai 'ewalu and the waters of the great ocean that inspire, carry, and connect. I cannot give enough thanks to the contributors and to my co-editor, Aiko, for opening themselves and their stories to me. This vulnerability and mana has given me great hope for our shared futures. Mahalo nui to 'Imai, Hina, and La'i for sharing me with this project and letting it have some of our precious moments together.

— *Aiko Yamashiro and Noelani Goodyear-Ka'ōpua*

* * * * *

We gratefully acknowledge the authors' permissions to include these previously published works:

No'u Revilla's "Ceremony" was previously published in *Capitalism Nature Socialism* 24.3 (2013).

Darlene Rodrigues's "Eve" was previously published in a program for the 2012 "Distinctive Women of Hawai'i" Conference.

Emelihter Kihleng's "Micronesian Diaspora(s)" was previously published in *Xcp: Cross-Cultural Poetics* 14 (2004) and in her poetry collection *My Urohs* (Honolulu: Kahuaomānoa, 2008).

Brandy Nālani McDougall's "The Second Gift" was previously published in *Hawai'i Review* 79 (Winter 2013).

Jill Yamasawa's "Sedilia" was previously published in *Tinfish* 18½ (2008) and in her poetry collection *Aftermath* (Honolulu: Kahuaomānoa, 2010).

Kathy Jetnil-Kijiner's "Tell Them" was previously published in *Kurungabaa* 4.1 (2012), and recorded by Studio Revolt at the Poetry Parnassus at Southbank Centre for London, 2012.

WE ARE ISLANDERS

AIKO YAMASHIRO & NOELANI GOODYEAR-KAʻŌPUA

The majestic female figure on the cover of this book is artist John "Prime" Hina's depiction of Pele, the fiery deity who currently resides at Halemaʻumaʻu on Hawaiʻi Island. In his rendering, Pele holds an ʻumeke—a bowl typically used for containing food—on her right hip. The ʻumeke poi is an important symbol in Hawaiian culture. In many families across the islands, the ʻumeke has traditionally been the center of any shared meal. Once the ʻumeke is uncovered no harsh or injurious words are to be spoken, as the poi will soak up that negative energy and transfer to those who consume it. Traditionally, the bowl was never emptied. Any remaining poi from a meal would be saved. Later, fresh poi would be mixed into the existing contents, so that the food always contained some of the beneficial microorganisms that develop in the fermentation process. An intergenerational mixture of probiotic flora.

Here, Pele does not hold an ʻumeke poi, but rather a bowl overflowing with lava and steam. Fire, earth, air, water: all the elements that create land are loosed. Having opened the calabash, this image creates the space for conversations and interactions about the well-being and the futures of Hawaiʻi. The words offered within this book are similarly intended to open space for productive discussion about how to protect, enhance, and create value in our islands. Unlike poi, the lava does not keep us from sharing critical opinions or hashing out difficult and contentious issues. The lava does remind us, however, that such conversations can be both destructive and creative. Powerful.

When telling us, the editors, about this image, Prime explained that he intended the bowl to symbolize a kind of social contract. This "different kind of contract," or perhaps, *compact* of mutual obligation contrasts sharply with the *contracts* that have allowed the (over)development of urban, suburban, and resort construction in ways that do not typically balance social, environmental, cultural, and spiritual impacts against the financial bottom line. One way to see this ʻumeke is as an agreement between land and people to care for one another. By placing her at the center, the artist reminds us that our compact with Pele, with the earth herself, is always present whether we choose to see it and honor it or not. One thing this book argues is that if we do not do better at balancing our human needs and desires with the natural resources and forces of these islands, the ʻāina will hold us accountable. And we love her for it.

BACKGROUND

Like the book you hold in your hands, the first volume, *The Value of Hawaiʻi: Knowing the Past, Shaping the Future* (U of Hawaiʻi P, 2010), was a collection of short essays written for a general Hawaiʻi audience, on issues ranging from education to prisons, agriculture to the military, the economy to climate change, and more. That first volume set out to help readers understand the current state of the islands through a firm understanding of history. "How did we get here?" the contributors asked. This volume takes that foundation as a point of departure for a new central question: How can more of us protect and enhance what is precious about Hawaiʻi for coming generations? How will we feed ourselves? Take care of one another? Negotiate and celebrate differences? Share resources?

Craig Howes and Jon Osorio, editors of the first volume, asked passionate experts in each field to bring these wide-ranging issues together to provoke and ground public conversations about what we value, where we are headed, and what we need to do to change course. As part of this commitment to conversation and change, a copy of the book was given to every sitting State Legislator in 2010. The book was taught widely at various campuses of the University of Hawaiʻi, Chaminade University, and Hawaiʻi Pacific University, as well as in various public and private high school classes. A visual debate card game was developed with the help of Mililani High School students, asking youth to create images and arguments about how to work across issues to solve problems they saw in Hawaiʻi. And with kōkua from innumerable individuals and community groups, dozens of talk-story events were organized in 2010 and 2011.

The voices gathered in this second volume are hopeful about the future, and they urge us toward changes in perspective. On the cover of volume one, Kamehameha looks to George Washington. However, when we are locked in a gaze toward the US continent (what so many still call "the *main*land"), we tend to see our islands, our unique cultural knowledges, and even ourselves as small, inconsequential, disempowered, and inferior. This view of Hawaiʻi as an isolated US outpost has been both perpetuated and resisted by a generation or two raised in the late territorial and early statehood eras: the post-WWII "baby boomers."

This volume turns our gaze in a different direction. Instead of toward Washington, imagine Kamehameha looking out across the channels that connect our island archipelago, and even further, across the vast oceans that connect us to the watery world of Oceania—a body that comprises half of the Earth's surface. It is in these directions that the writers of this volume beckon you. As Bonnie Kahapeʻa-Tanner—captain of the educational sailing canoe *Kānehūnāmoku*—puts it in her contribution to this volume: "We are the people of the Pacific, Moananuiākea, connected infinitely by the waters that touch each of our shores and flow through our veins" (180).

Most of the essays in this volume, *The Value of Hawaiʻi 2: Ancestral Roots, Oceanic Visions*, were written by authors who were raised after the twilight of the sugar and pineapple plantations. We grew up in the midst and the aftermath of a massive urban, suburban, and resort development boom. We have experienced the ways the costs and profits of the industries that replaced sugar and pineapple have not been distributed equally or fairly. We are ʻŌiwi and settlers who have benefitted from the Hawaiian renaissance, and still we see so many unfulfilled promises and obligations to the Hawaiian people and nation. We know that our children and grandchildren will carry the full weight of ecological and social problems, such as climate change, growing economic inequality, and erosion of public safety net services, which have been left to us to address.

Whether Kanaka ʻŌiwi or recent immigrant, whether from Honolulu or Hanalei, one thing that binds all of us who live in Hawaiʻi is that we are islanders. The islands mark us, just as we mark them. Our island world makes the ecological and social challenges that are facing most people in the world today more immediate and apparent. In this second decade of the twenty-first century, we are already witnessing a heightening of the problems of ecosystems degradation, fewer available agricultural lands, overtaxed fisheries, and a widening gap between haves and have-nots. With the measureable impacts of global warming already upon us; with the promises of the Hawaiʻi Clean Energy Initiative and decisions about major development and transit projects hanging over us; with maxed-out landfills beneath us; and yet with the wisdom of our respective gods, ancestors, and neighbors still around us, the contributors to this book present a distinct sense of urgency, and potential. The current and coming generations will have to execute huge shifts in the ways we live, if we are to preserve and enhance what is precious and of value in our islands.

The contributors to this book do not labor under the illusion that such transformation is entirely possible within a single lifetime. (The City and County of Honolulu hasn't even been able to pass a ban on plastic shopping bags, for goodness sakes.) But we know that if we do not start to plan for and move toward significant changes in the ways we live on and relate to these lands and waters that support us, the horizons of possibility will be significantly narrowed for future generations. The voices here open up new conversations, guided by aloha, hopefulness, and creativity.

The original title of Dean Saranillio's essay for this volume was "Another Hawai'i is Possible," and that could have been a fitting title for the whole book. The contributors to this volume were invited because each one of them is already working to create the conditions of possibility for major shifts in the ways we produce and consume energy, deal with "waste," design urban space, grow food, cultivate healthy eating habits, educate our youth, build community, tell stories, promote land-based subsistence practices, care for and pray for one another, and much more.

HUAKA'I: OCEANIC FLOWS, DEPARTURES, AND RETURNS

"Nā kai 'ewalu" is a Hawaiian way to name our archipelago. The eight seas. Rather than focusing on the landmasses, this moniker refers to the channels that connect our islands, pathways to one another. Similarly, along the lines of flows, the voices gathered in this book are not content to stay isolated on islands unto themselves—government, health, agriculture, Hawaiian issues, and so on. In fact, they recognize that to meet the onslaught of challenges that we face, we need to think and work across fields and vocations. And so in this volume, we see how sustainable food production flows into leadership development; how the revitalization of fishpond technologies can go hand in hand with ecosystem restoration (rather than the way conservation is often pitted against food production); how urban arts can be a basis for entrepreneurial training.

The table of contents is organized to help readers navigate these flows. Because most of the essays are built around personal stories and the experiences of the authors, the lead title for each piece evokes the central storyline. The subtitle, listed as a separate line in the table of contents, helps to place the essay by indicating its topical focus, such as agriculture, alternative futures, video production, music, public education, energy, or island-style activism. Because we value creativity as an important source of our ability to flow and connect, poems by Hawai'i and Pacific poets are seeded throughout this book, adding additional voices, emotions, and possibilities to each topic. The essays and poems are grouped into the following thematic sections, which emerged organically only after all the individual pieces had been collected together. We invite you to read each piece as a stand-alone story, but also to think about how they are working together in important and complex conversation:

• Moʻolelo. We quickly saw storytelling as a main theme throughout many of these essays, and as a first and foundational step in connecting people together to make change. Through stories, we understand ourselves, this place, and each other. These essays find personal and community strength in storytelling, and in telling the stories that are not heard. We place ourselves within genealogies and find the courage to create the next verses.

• Kuleana and Developing Hawaiʻi Responsibly. This section challenges and expands dominant understandings of "development" in Hawaiʻi, bringing together topics like energy and public health with labor and art. Here we seek to reimagine critically concepts like urban and rural, and begin to come to terms with all we've inherited from the choices of past generations. These essays argue for deep wells of community wealth that overflow narrow understandings of development and progress. Kuleana emerges as a guiding ethical framework for what a renewed sense of development might mean.

• Huakaʻi. We live on islands connected by a vast and powerful ocean. The seas inhabit us, just as we inhabit them, and as islanders, we have long and beautiful traditions of voyaging. This section poses difficult questions about migration and militarism, about how common understandings of globalization and wealth dehumanize and devalue our knowledges and our power to move. These essays chart new ways of navigating our identities and kuleana, of connecting Hawaiʻi to the world and to other movements for cultural revitalization, health, and dignity.

• Puʻuhonua. Critical to revaluing ourselves and our stories, to healing the pain within ourselves and communities, are concerted efforts to honor and create sacred and safe spaces. Puʻuhonua, or sanctuaries, are not limited to religious buildings. A person, a community, or a natural landform can be a puʻuhonua. In this section, the authors urge us to find and nurture puʻuhonua in unexpected places—in our food, our prisons, our schools, our cities, and our mountains. By renewing sacred connections between the health of the land and the health of our bodies we can create a safer and more resilient world for our children.

• Aloha. The two essays that begin and end this collection remind us of the central importance of aloha. Kamana Beamer shares the wisdom of his tūtū, Auntie Nona Beamer: "It's just aloha, dear." Seems simple, no? But aloha ʻāina—the kind of deep and committed love for land and all who dwell upon it; the kind of love that affirms the importance of independence and interdependence; the kind of love that demands action, ingenuity, creativity, and memory—is not easy, even if it is elegantly simple in principle. The essays that begin and end this collection remind us that we are going in dangerous directions if our actions are not guided by great love for this place and each other. What does it mean to reject the ways aloha is commercialized, exploited, and disconnected from its profound meanings? How can we instead cultivate a rigorous practice of grounded and revolutionary aloha? These essays provide a starting point for those conversations.

WHEN YOU ASK PEOPLE FOR PERSONAL STORIES, WHAT WILL THAT BRING?

In birthing this project, the editors and authors labored together not only to produce a book, but to create and renew relationships. We have come to believe that such relationship-building, establishing trust through vulnerability, is essential to realizing preferred futures. When we set out as co-editors, we encouraged our authors to write creatively, openly, and autobiographically, knowing that sharing life stories would be a powerful way to help readers connect their lives to these issues, and to these lives. At the beginning of this project, we did not fully understand the enormity of this request.

Many of the contributors to this book would not consider themselves writers. Although the essays are relatively short, they were difficult to write, even for those who write professionally. Each of the authors is talented and powerful, with important things to say. They each have years of experience in their respective fields. But how do you write about your whole life, about your dedication and passion, about everything you deeply care about, in 3,000 words? How do you write at a young age, when you doubt you have the authority or the wisdom to speak? The contributing writers wrestled with these issues and opened themselves to our thoughts, feelings, pushes, and pulls. We opened ourselves to them, and struggled to listen carefully with our minds, bodies, and naʻau. Some of the essays you are holding in your hands were born from hours-long meetings, from drinking and writing-together sessions, or from recording stories on cell phones. We cried and laughed together. We confronted fears and insecurities in ourselves and in our work. This collection is a record of that speaking and listening.

This process has convinced us that personal storytelling and listening are crucial to meaningful social change, to creating sincere connections between our communities and between seemingly separate issues. The very process of telling our personal stories within larger contexts is transformative. It asks us to believe in each other in ways necessary to building social movements. It takes courage and faith to let someone else into the middle of your story, and sometimes to help you tell it.

In a mid-week meeting at Point Panics that laid the foundation for Bonnie Kahapeʻa-Tanner's essay, stories were like the waves pumping through the break and crashing onto the stone shoreline. As bodysurfers shot through the tube and then disappeared into the white wash, Kahapeʻa recounted to co-editor Noe some of the little known hardships that one of her teachers, Mau Piailug, and his family endured while he supported the Hawaiian rediscovery of our long-distance sailing heritage: "We don't consider the sacrifices that others have lived with so that we in Hawaiʻi could have the opportunity to revitalize our voyaging traditions. But now that we know more of the story, it's our kuleana to ask ourselves how we are going to live differently because of it." Like the waves crashing in front of us that day, stories are powerful. They can pick us up, move us, and energize us. They can also be crushing and oppressive. Stories are so powerful, in part, because they have material consequences. Surging upon the shore, they change the landscape even if only for a time. After that meeting, Noe wrote:

> Both Kahapeʻa and I grew up alongside Kāneʻohe Bay—the largest sheltered body of water in our archipelago and home to one of Hawaiʻi's only barrier reefs. As a child playing in the shallows of the bay, I was flanked by two different stories about the value of Hawaiʻi. Frequently, over the sounds of my dog's paws splashing through the water as she bounded after tiny fish, we would hear military jets flying overhead or revving their engines at sea level. With my back to the Koʻolau mountains behind me, I would look to the right and see the distant silhouettes of structures on Kāneʻohe Marine Corps base. Hawaiian land valued as a strategic US military outpost. In contrast, to my left sat one of the largest remaining fishponds in the islands, built over 600 years ago and used continuously until the 20th century to provide for easy access to fish. Hawaiian land valued as a basis for sustainable food production. By the late 1970s, when I was a small child, the massive pond's mile-long outer rock wall was so overgrown with mangrove that I could not even tell what it was. Stories of the role this pond played in feeding the people of my community in earlier generations had been so silenced that I did not even know the loko iʻa existed, even when we stumbled through the tangled hedge onto it. Today, I am grateful that my own children can say otherwise. Now that they know and can become part of the story of this fishpond's revival, how will they live differently?

When we are brave enough to let people into the middle of our stories, we see points of connection, where our grief and hopes and fears and loves are shared. Stories can become vessels that help us to navigate the waves that pick us up and move us. In a morning meeting at Yogurstory, Jojo Peter explained to co-editor Aiko how, in Chuuk, the word for "canoe," "waa," is the same as the word for blood vessel. He gestured to his arm, to the horizon. We are vessels, each of us, going forth into storied places to bring back space and hope to those we love. This is our power as canoe people. This is absolutely necessary for our survival. He was speaking about his people, about those voyaging far from their homes in Micronesia, seeking health for themselves, their elders, their children. Shortly after this meeting, Aiko wrote:

> These words spoke to me too, struggling with a smaller vessel. It is very, very hard to see our parents suffering. Seeing their health steadily deteriorate—diabetes, drinking, chronic pain, heart disease, stroke, depression. Feeling helpless as their health and hope are entangled, and futures seem landlocked. They've always taken care of me. How can I, their child, now a young woman, have any power to transform their lives, or my own? Shouldering the weight of the complicated, and well-meaning,

choices of our parents and elders, it's easy to feel like there's nothing we can do. At 28 years old, this is a deep and growing fear I have. But Jojo's story pushed me to remember that our individual actions live within much longer genealogies. That even when we feel we are very small vessels, there is still something so powerful in our motion back and forth, between islands; to go and return, to always return. We can move in the rhythm of forgiveness and hope, even when we don't have the words for these yet. Even when we don't quite know what to do. And by understanding how we are connected by currents much larger than us—currents of colonialism, oppression, global greed, but also currents of ancestral, cultural, and spiritual knowledge of how to live as island people—we can begin to help each other find a way.

This book's focus on life stories asks us to think about how our lives are tangled, and how to be patient enough to work through these knotty interconnections. For example, how do we bring together Hawaiian sovereignty and labor movements, or immigrant- or gender-focused movements for justice and safety? How do we ally in meaningful ways, and what will "solidarity" actually require? This book does not provide simple answers to these questions, but its writers invite you to consider personal stories as ways to begin, to travel toward one another and to think about how to enter someone else's waters with reverence and respect. The stories collected here call us to ask ourselves, how will we live differently, value Hawai'i and each other differently, once we have heard them?

The Value of Hawai'i 2: Ancestral Roots, Oceanic Visions brings together a diversity of voices, not to celebrate blissfully the "happy melting pot" of Hawai'i, but to commit truly to imagine and practice less fearful or judgmental ways of being together. In this book, you will read the perspectives of people from Native Hawaiian, Japanese, Filipino, Tokelauan, Korean, Chinese, Chuukese, Marshallese, Okinawan, Haole, and other ethnic backgrounds. You will hear from settlers who are productively working through their ambivalences about wanting, on the one hand, to remain connected to these islands as home, and on the other, to respect that Kānaka Maoli have a much deeper genealogical relationship with this place and have suffered distinct harms that other groups have not. You will hear from Kānaka who feel compelled to share with and kōkua groups who have arrived upon our shores as a result of various forms of violence and displacement, and who still face discrimination and marginalization in these islands. This book carries stories of people reaching out across a diversity of histories, genders, spiritual beliefs, sexual orientations, classes, ages, and professions to imagine radically different futures. There are already innumerable cracks in the walls that keep us from feeling each other's pain and beauty, if we know where to look. We are islanders. In our differences and interdependencies, we hope this book binds us by our aloha for each other and for Hawai'i nei.

ALOHA

HALEY KAILIEHU

TŪTŪ'S ALOHA 'ĀINA GRACE

It may be a uniquely Hawaiian relationship celebrated in moʻolelo like Kamapuaʻa, Laʻanuimamao, and Kamiki, which illustrate the pilina paʻa mau (enduring love) of a tūtū wahine (grandmother) and moʻopuna kāne (grandson). In each of these moʻolelo, the kūpunahine are a fundamental part of the moʻolelo as a foundation, mentor, and even akua to their moʻopuna kāne once the kūpuna have passed into pō (the realm of spirits). In fact, as I came to better understand these moʻolelo, I also better understood why many Hawaiian men today often recall their relationship with their tūtū as being one of the most important. In ways similar to this pilina, my grandmother had always been my champion. She had a vigor and determination that were not easily matched. Her name was Winona Kapuailohiamanonokalani Desha Beamer. Throughout her life she served both Hawaiʻi and my ʻohana in more ways than I could express in this essay; some of those roles included being a single mother, kumu hula, educator, composer, and activist. She was affectionately known as "Aunty Nona."[1]

My great-grandparents traveled from Nāpoʻopoʻo in South Kona to Honolulu so that she could be born at Kapiʻolani hospital. Born on August 15th, 1923, she was the eldest of five children and was the first moʻopuna and punahele of her grandmother, Helen Kapuailohia Desha Beamer. Almost from birth, she learned our family traditions of music and hula. It was this foundation that she drew upon and promoted throughout her life. She came of age in a time that would be nearly unrecognizable to many keiki today. Most of Hawaiʻi was relatively undeveloped, with many ʻohana thriving from the abundance of the ʻāina, with intimate knowledge of their places and fisheries. At the same time, institutionalized racism and systemic oppression of Hawaiian culture and language were in full force.

In 1937, Kamehameha Schools administrators expelled her for performing standing hula and chanting. I can recall her telling me how an administrator had told her she was to be expelled because Princess Bernice Pauahi Bishop had written in her will that students at Kamehameha were not to speak or practice things Hawaiian. When my grandmother requested to see that section in the will, administrators refused to allow her to access it, likely because they were being dishonest and no such content existed in the will. When she left the office that day, she slammed the door behind her with enough force to break the door pane, and she heard the shards of glass crash behind her. Suffering through outrage and public humiliation, she later returned to graduate from the school, and years later, in 1949, was hired as an instructor of Hawaiian music and culture at Kamehameha.

Her courses provided a safe space for many students at Kamehameha to better understand Hawaiian music and culture, and simply to *be* Hawaiian. She was a tireless advocate of things Hawaiian. Alongside others, she systematically fought for the inclusion and valuing of things Hawaiian at Kamehameha and in the broader Hawaiian community. She would compose mele as a means to show the children their special connection to Hawai‘i, their genealogy, and place, while teaching personal compositions such as "Pūpū-hinuhinu" to countless school children while conducting workshops in public and private schools across Hawai‘i.

Her love for nā mea Hawai‘i and Kamehameha Schools did not cease following her retirement in the 1980s. In the late 1990s, she risked much when, as a kupuna, she publically challenged Kamehameha trustees, catalyzing a movement that led to changes in leadership and direction at Kamehameha. I had recently graduated from Kamehameha in 1996, when she called me to discuss the climate of the school and the morale of students. Structures that I thought immovable and forces that seemed all-powerful to an adolescent, she confronted with courage, grace, and aloha. As a former employee of Kamehameha and current professor at the University of Hawai‘i at Mānoa, when I reflect on the positive change that she helped to create for Hawai‘i, and in particular its children, her legacy is awe-inspiring. While being her only mo‘opuna is simply humbling.

EXTRAORDINARY ALOHA

"It's just aloha, dear," my tūtū told me after spending time with the Dalai Lama during his first visit to Maui in April of 2007. My grandmother had moved to Maui following a long stay in Queen' hospital. She had regained her strength amidst complications from diabetes that included heart surgery and fights with renal failure. I remember feeling less than fulfilled with her summary of her meeting with this global figure, the Tibetan religious leader who managed to frame the story of his exile from his homeland and the plights of his people into global discourse. I didn't understand how she could characterize their meeting with the simple phrase—*it's just aloha, dear.*

My grandmother is no longer here for me to seek clarification. To be completely honest, I feel as if I am still coming to know the depth of her phrase. My essay will discuss my thoughts on what she was trying to convey by reminding me, "it's just aloha, dear," and the ways in which this phrase relates to Aloha ʻĀina as a movement for a better island world. I will discuss Aloha ʻĀina as a movement for social, cultural, and ecological justice in Hawaiʻi while highlighting its uniqueness and value for the world.

I was in my truck on the mauka road winding my way from my home in Waimea to Kona. As I was nearing Puʻuwaʻawaʻa, I gazed at the utter beauty of Mauna Kea, Mauna Loa, and Hualālai. It was an amazingly clear, trade-wind day, and I felt nearly overwhelmed at the privilege to see and feel the beauty of this place. It was at that moment that I began to think about the ways that we use the word aloha, and was struck that we use this word to express what in English seem to be very distinct kinds of relationships. How is it that we use the word "aloha" to express the feeling a grandchild has for a grandmother, a husband for a wife, a father for his daughter, the empathy for a sick child, and the relationship between a person and the land?

THE FULLNESS OF ALOHA

The concept of Aloha ʻĀina is quite holistic. While environmentalists and conservationists often advocate for nature as an entity distinct and separated from human culture, and social justice movements are not usually concerned with ecological health, Aloha ʻĀina links social, cultural, and ecological justice.

The renowned Hawaiian scholar David Malo notes that "ma ka noho ana a kanaka, ua kapa ia he aina ka inoa"[2] [it is because people live and interact with a place that it is called ʻāina]. Unlike the Euro-American concept of nature, "ʻāina" is interconnected with people. Given that one literal translation of ʻāina is "that which feeds," one can begin to see how a movement built on the principles of Aloha ʻĀina would distinguish itself in crucial ways from a movement focused on conserving nature as distinct from human interaction. This becomes even clearer when one looks to Hawaiian origins and genealogies that make islands, coral, plants, birds, and fish the elder siblings of kānaka.

I am often fearful of my work being lumped with or boxed into categories that end with the suffix -ist. However, I think I could find some level of comfort with being boxed into a group called ʻāina-ist or aloha ʻāina-ist, where the concept of Aloha ʻĀina was defined as a movement toward the *union of culture and ecosystem.* This was the true beauty and utter genius of the resource and economic system of Hawaiʻi prior to the arrival of Cook. Language, culture, social structure, resource management, and land tenure were entirely embedded in and organized to be in harmony with ecosystems. Agricultural systems like loʻi (wetland taro fields) complemented systems of aquaculture, while culture and social systems recognized the uniqueness of place and environment. Distinct resource management systems were refined for place, like the food systems of Waipiʻo on Hawaiʻi Island that maximized stream-fed water resources. These systems differed from those in dryland field systems in places like leeward Kohala and Kona.

As I type this essay on my MacBook Pro 2013, I also understand that with all of our tools and modern technologies it is a sobering realization to know that these elder systems, and labor systems that relied on tools made of stone and natural materials, fed more people on every island from their local resources than the systems we have today. It is also empowering to know that we can do better than we do today; the knowledge and resource practices of the elder systems remain, and of course, we have access to better tools. Large physical remnants of ʻOiwi land tenure systems and vast resources still exist to help us understand indigenous resource management practices that are island and place specific. The archival records which document specific Hawaiian land divisions such as moku, ahupuaʻa, ʻili, moʻo, and so on, should not be seen as capturing ancient relics of the Hawaiian land system, but rather, as *living models* for today. How can we reorganize our living conditions and social structures to make use of these divisions of resource and place? Hawaiʻi's quest for sustainability and Aloha ʻĀina has the advantage of building on an earlier successful structure. Much work needs to be done, however, to create the political will and leadership that embody the values of Aloha ʻĀina, to bring closer the union of culture and ecosystem.

THE UNIQUENESS OF ALOHA

"Many parts of the world would long to have the same acceptance of others, you know, the diversity of people that you have," uttered Archbishop Desmond Tutu during a visit to Honolulu in August of 2012.[3] The United States occupation of Hawaiʻi can be compared to the Chinese occupation of Tibet. The systemic oppression of Hawaiian culture and language after the US-backed overthrow of the Hawaiian Kingdom can be compared to similar policies enforced in colonial Africa. However, the ethnic diversity and continued strength of Hawaiians makes our situation unique. My grandmother would often begin a public speech by saying she was French, Scottish, English, German, and *all* Hawaiian. Today, there are many examples of members of the lāhui (genealogically Native Hawaiian) who, according to US racial classifications and stereotypes, appear to be white, black, Asian, or Hispanic. The ethnic diversity of Native Hawaiians can challenge US racial classifications that demand we pick just one way to be, or divide our bodies by percentages. It is powerful that we can be so ethnically diverse while at the same time hold common sets of values and cultural affiliation, which are largely centered around aloha, the collective, and the 'āina.

There are differing levels of violence against culture and the environment inherent in imperialism, colonial settlement, and occupations. It would be foolish to try to measure or compare the degrees of evil inflicted on the populations of Tibet, South Africa, or Hawai'i, or to try and measure the difference between the murdering of humans and the bombing of a mountain that is an ancestor, or the creation of a gated community where there once existed a communal fishing village. However, there may be nothing that speaks more directly to the Hawaiian situation from the lessons of the South Africans and Tibetans than the idea that it takes love, compassion, and fearlessness to endure your way out of an occupation. Perhaps the fact that the Hawaiian movement has been peaceful while also being incredibly fearless and ethnically diverse might make it unique to the world while giving it the strength to endure. As other places around the world will only become more ethnically diverse while also struggling to maintain natural resources and quality of life, Hawai'i and Aloha 'Āina will be able to offer solutions.

THE FUTURE OF ALOHA

"The word aloha is very simple but the real meaning is quite vast. You need a lot of effort to implement the real meaning of aloha," said the Dalai Lama on a subsequent visit to Hawai'i in April of 2012.[4] Aloha isn't easy. In fact, people like Kekuaokalani, Manono, Boki, Liholiho, Eddie Aikau, George Helm, Kimo Mitchell, and countless others have given their lives for Aloha 'Āina in Hawai'i. The aforementioned people have exhibited important qualities of aloha: to be fearless and unwavering when one's values and 'āina are threatened. Aloha requires one to speak and act out in the face of injustice. Aloha is active and something that needs to be put into practice, not something that is a state of being. The problems around social, cultural, and ecological justice in Hawai'i are not insignificant, nor are they something that we can will away through selfless compassion.

The social and environmental issues are serious, though often it takes a few additional steps to recognize them. One such issue is that of the "ceded lands." One of my favorite shirts, created by the Hawaiian Force in Hilo, reads "Live Aloha/Return Stolen Lands." This slogan highlights the active parts of aloha as well as the links between social and ecological justice. By the reign of Queen Lili'uokalani, the Hawaiian Kingdom managed roughly 1.8 million acres of government and Crown lands that held the specific reservation of being "koe na'e ke kuleana o nā a kanaka," or, "subject to the rights of Native Hawaiians." These lands are some of the most culturally and environmentally important lands in Hawai'i, and have fed generations of Native Hawaiians. Following the US-backed overthrow of the Hawaiian Kingdom government, these lands were confiscated, renamed the "Public Lands," and the constitutionally vested rights of Native Hawaiians to these lands were hidden behind nomenclature that suggests they were owned by the general "public." The renaming of these lands was a deliberate attempt to sever genealogical connections to Native Hawaiians. This has also caused confusion for those who do not know Hawai'i's social and political history, and has been a powerful tool to mask the United States history of injustice in Hawai'i. People who move to Hawai'i from another place and hear the phrase "Public Lands," often are confused as to why Native Hawaiians suggest a special connection to and ownership of them. However, future Aloha 'Āina will one day regain control of our 'āina. Of course it will not be enough to solve this social justice issue alone. Once stolen lands are regained, these lands also must be managed differently in ways that seek to bring a union to culture and ecosystem.

My tūtū fought for Aloha 'Āina until her passing in 2010. Following her recovery from triple bypass heart surgery, renal failure, and constant complications with diabetes, she found the strength to compose and deliver a protest to the "President and Congressmen of the UNITED STATES OF AMERICA," which sought to rid Hawai'i of future United States military installations, and declared, among other things, that the United States must:

> Give heed to our voices. We have extended aloha to you, and you seek to extinguish our very being. Respect us; be aware that we were once a sovereign international nation. We are descendants of a mighty civilization and deserve to be listened to in our own homeland.

Aloha 'Āina is a powerful ideology, one that I believe can transcend race, culture, and environment. I know if I can be a better aloha 'āina, if I can live with aloha and wiwo'ole (fearlessness) as did my kūpuna before me, and mentor those who come in my path to stand on a similar foundation, I can create a better island world for my keiki. I, however, will never let them forget, *it's just aloha.*

NOTES

1. See the "Resources" of this essay for more stories about Nona Beamer.
2. Davida Malo, *Ka Mo'olelo Hawai'i* (Honolulu: First People's Productions, 2006): 11.

3. Sarah Zoellick, "Tutu embraces island life," *Honolulu Star-Advertiser,* August 3, 2012: A-19.

4. Audrey McAvoy, "Dalai Lama: Real effort needed to implement aloha," *The Maui News* April 17, 2012, available at http://www.mauinews.com/page/content.detail/id/560258/Dalai-Lama-Real-effort-needed-to-implement-aloha.html?nav=5031.

RESOURCES FOR FURTHER INFORMATION AND INSPIRATION

1. Nona Beamer, *Nā Mele Hula: Hawaiian Hula Rituals and Chants,* Vols. 1–3 (Honolulu: U of Hawaiʻi P, 1987).

2. Nona Beamer, *Talking Story with Nona Beamer: Stories of a Hawaiian Family* (Honolulu: Bess, 1984).

3. Winona Beamer, *Nā Hula o Hawaiʻi: The Songs and Dances of the Beamer Family* (Norfolk Island, Australia: Island Heritage, 1976).

4. George S. Kanahele and John Berger, eds., *Hawaiian Music and Musicians: An Encyclopedic History* (Rev. ed., Honolulu: Mutual, 2012).

5. Jon Van Dyke, *Who Owns the Crown Lands of Hawaiʻi?* (Honolulu: U of Hawaiʻi P, 2008).

MOTHER

FAITH PASCUA

At night in my house when everyone should be sleeping, eyes closed, minds drifting towards wonderland,

She's still awake in the living room, flipping through memories of what used to be,

She's crying wishing her storied scrapbook past was reality again.

She reminisces over pages of smiles; compiled accomplishments enough to fill miles of trophy cases.

She was the original Dust Buster Dirt Devil housekeeper, Winner of the 2006 Housekeeper of the Year award.

She remembers wanting to vacuum the red carpet something majestic;

Floors so shiny, you could see your inner child in the reflection. She idolizes perfection.

That hotel was her home away from home, her fortress of solitude, and it has been for over 16 years.

She cleans hotel rooms; finds the history in dirty laundry, closet skeletons, and linens.

Knows what happens in honeymoon suites, and capable to clean the fuck out of them.

She knows that business trips are filled with more personal endeavors anyway,

Seeing infidelity with the mistake of forgetting the Do Not Disturb sign on the doorknob; she has seen it all.

Until last fall when my brother and I watched her crumble under the fall of the economy,

The uncertainty placed her waiting by the phone.

She's on-call for work now. Today she's number 4 but they didn't even make it to 3 . . .

This job is her first baby, 16 years in the making, not having the experience quite yet,

(New to baby bottles and cleaning products) at first this job was just to pay the bills, just for now, just until . . .

It became her passion, found sanctuary in her pink-flowered uniform, and comfort-gelled shoes

She's my mother, sobbing solo under the single light in the living room,

Resisting to open her scrapbook, trying to not find a reason to be angry at the supernatural, because she's losing faith. Like a flickering candle . . .

When she thinks no one is around, she still tries her uniform on; this is her battle suit.

Her idle hands turn to iron and from Wonder Woman to wondering woman, she feels like she lost her super powers.

My mother is an aglet, found at the tip of shoelaces, she's capable of keeping your sole in place,

She will tell you she loves you by just being there . . . but she's forgotten.

Her paycheck is the only way she remembers her value, that coming home without one renders her useless.

Mommy, you are not an ATM, not an automated teller machine,

Worth is not measured in money; your amount balance will never be zero to me.

See no one remembers what an aglet is. No one cares about the life of the housekeeper who cleaned their hotel room. But mom, you are more than a source of income.

You're my monster-in-the-closet inspector, and the detector of sorrow and sobbing anywhere.

And when the shake of the money problem earthquake leaves our home, I want you to know:

I love you more than a laid-off full-time housekeeper, but my full-time mother.

Assuring you that even if your faith fades away, I will always be here.

MOʻOLELO: STORIES AND STORYTELLING

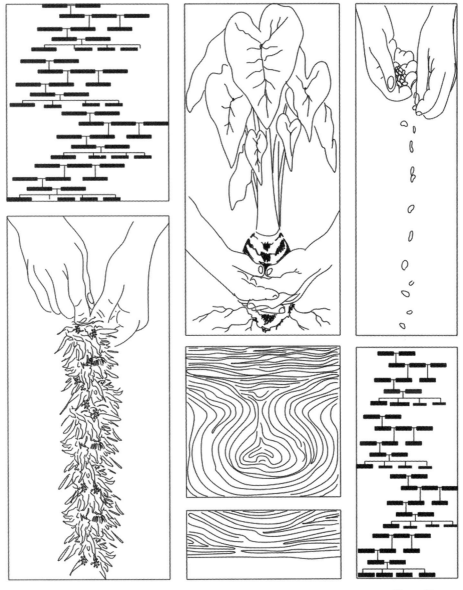

HALEY KAILIEHU

SO LISTEN TO ME

LYZ SOTO

Slam poetry is a competitive form of spoken word started in the 1980s in Chicago by Marc Smith, a poet and construction worker, who was looking for a way to get everyday people excited about poetry. At its most basic, slam poetry is an open mic event with rules and a time limit. In Hawai'i, it has often developed a separate sense of place defined by a desire for cultural self-definition within colonial realities that resist this type of exploration. In other words, the poems written and performed by youth from Hawai'i can be quite different from those heard in the continental United States. Yes, our youth are still teenagers, and much of their writing reflects the concerns of stereotypical American teenagers, and yet Hawai'i's youth reflect this place: an ethnically diverse community overlayed with American decorations, on top of an indigenous population that continues to fight for breathing room in their own homeland. Slam has given space to these voices, offering articulations of life in Hawai'i that run counter to those represented in popular media, like *Hawai'i 5-0*, *Magnum P.I.*, and *Pearl Harbor*.

For the last eight years, I have been a mentor with Youth Speaks Hawai'i (YSH), which was founded by Melvin Won Pat-Borja, Travis Ka'ululā'au Thompson, and Kealoha (Wong) in 2005 with the help of Jason Mateo and Michelle Lee from Youth Speaks, Inc. (Bay Area).[1] YSH works towards facilitating youth in finding their own voice through slam poetry and spoken word. Our guiding principle is that young people have important things to say, but they may need some help in discovering *how* to say them. Our standardized-test-obsessed educational system often mimics an industrial conveyor belt complex that restricts and/or silences those voices that step outside the mainstream box. Youth existing outside this box make up a large portion of the young people served by YSH, where we give them the latitude to find their own opinions and approaches, with mentors who will work with them for years rather than months.

To evaluate the current status and future of slam poetry and spoken word in Hawai'i, we need to reexamine complex intercultural relationships and political situations steeped in histories that, through much of the twentieth century, have been sidestepped or silenced. For example, why do we not offer Hawaiian as a language option in all of our high schools? Why are we rarely taught the stories of place that predate European contact? Why do we have to work so hard to maintain cultural ties that look in any direction other than east, towards the US continent? Why are we not working harder to erradicate the systemic culture of bullying in our schools? Why don't we have more discussions on the impact of historical events on today's social disparities? Why are we "trouble makers" or "crazy activists" when we suggest solutions that are less about consumer growth and more about sustainable plans for a substantial future? When can we begin to imagine beyond our current social and political gridlock and start pronouncing the directions we would like to travel in the future—futures that are as daring as they are spectacular?

Slam poetry from Hawai'i offers us two opportunities: the chance to commune with those who share our life experiences, and the possibility of advocating our positions to those who are unfamiliar with Hawai'i. Spoken word and slam poetry will continue to offer spaces for the developing voice and the story that needs to be heard. In this essay, I will be trying to stitch together multiple conversational threads that include looking at slam poetry and spoken word as points of identity exploration, personal and cultural testimony, and political activism.

SAFE SPACES: TURNING SILENCE INTO WORDS

Spoken word, more particularly slam poetry, was already fairly well-established on the island of O'ahu when I stumbled into its wake in January of 2006, at the Hawaiian Hut in the Ala Moana Hotel. On a fluke, I went with a friend to see Hawai'i Slam's First Thursday. There were hundreds of people in attendance and they were all there to hear and see poetry. We had to wait in line for more than twenty minutes to get in to a large open room offering cabaret-style seating with a rather odd backdrop of pan-Polynesian decor. All of the voices that night were beguiling in their immediacy, but the voice that really caught and held my attention belonged to a thirteen-year-old boy, named Ittai Wong, who could barely reach the microphone. He lit up the stage. That light appeared internal, as if his silence would leave us in darkness, and his voice offered a luminscent haven. This was passion. This was declaration. This was life changing.

Did I say life changing?

I did.

I felt silly writing it and then I wrote it again and found it could not be erased, because that first encounter with slam poetry did change my life. It came to me when I was experiencing a difficult time as a newly minted single parent, and I desparately wanted to redirect my attention towards anything but self-reflection. A YSH mentor came up to me and said I should drop by a Wednesday writing workshop at the ARTS at Marks Garage, so I did, and then I never left. YSH became an artistic and intellectual home, where the standards were shifted from the western educational canon to personal expectations that were actually achievable. Workshop facilitators continue to baldly state that participating writers should not compare themselves or their work to literary superstars or even to each other, because these kinds of comparisons can create fairly monumental writer's block.

These workshop spaces were and continue to be inviting, stimulating, and most importantly, safe. Attending youth will not be harrassed because of who they are, where they come from, or what they have experienced. They can openly talk about what we, as adults, like to pretend that people under the age of twenty do not understand, much less experience. They talk about prejudice and bullying in their schools or at home. They write about homelessness, parental alcoholism and drug addiction, or familial mental illness. They talk about the consequences of economic disparities and cultural bigotry. In these workshops, they can turn feelings of ostracism and alienation into declaration, then into testimony, and finally into performance.

My own experience with this form of catharsis and validation was writing a poem about having to tell my four-year-old son that his father would not be returning home. That poem, deeply personal and emotionally difficult, had to be written and performed. It was a compulsion, and releasing that poem into the world acted as an unexpected purgation, but the real surprise lay in how audiences responded to that piece. After performing, I was regularly approached by children of single parents and single parents, thanking me for putting their experience into words, saying it made them feel better. So herein lies one un-standardized gift from the testimonial possibilities of slam poetry. However, I say this with a word of caution about pressuring repeated performances of trauma for the sake of communal catharsis when it might come at the expense of individual health. I stopped performing that piece about my son. It was too painful. Once we had moved beyond that space of heartbreak, performing that poem demanded returning to a path I no longer wanted to tread.

TALKING BACK TO THE AMERICAN DREAM

Much of the teamwork done by youth in YSH from 2007 and 2008 was directed toward creating poems that offered identities that moved beyond stereotypical portrayals of people from Hawai'i. The decision to create these kinds of poems was largely dictated by our annual participation in the Brave New Voices International Poetry Slam Festival (BNV). This audience, comprised almost entirely of youth from across the continental United States, knew nothing of Hawai'i and its people, so these poems became an important introduction.[2]

This introduction became even more important when, in 2008, YSH was selected by Youth Speaks, Inc., to participate in *Brave New Voices* by HBO Documentary Films. This broadened our audience at home here in Hawai'i and in the continental United States, and to a larger international audience. The YSH slam team of 2008 created several poems telling a historical and contemporary experience of Hawai'i that interrupted the often bizarre stereotypes of Hawai'i as an exotic paradise filled with beautiful, easygoing brown savages, and willing women with extraordinary breasts

"Kaona," written by Jamaica Osorio and Ittai Wong, and performed by Osorio, Wong, William Giles, and Alaka'i Kotrys, worked to introduce the recent colonial history of Kānaka Maoli in Hawai'i to a continental US audience. The poem begins:

Ua ola ka 'ōlelo i ka ho'oili 'ana o nā pua

Our language survived through the passing of flowers

In 1896, the last reigning monarch of Hawai'i,

Queen Lili'uokalani

Was held prisoner in her own palace

Communication with the outside world was prohibited

Thus newspapers were snuck into her room

Wrapped around flowers

For months our Queen and her people wrote songs and stories

hidden in Hawaiian, so as to converse without

the Overthrowing Provisional Government knowing

It is because of this we know our history

the language of Hidden meanings

Kaona[3]

This is a Kanaka Maoli story written and spoken by Kanaka Maoli youth, countering stories of the overthrow that suggest indigenous indifference or a lack of initiative or agency. In "Kaona," a strong people resisted the overthrow of their government, and actively protested the actions of the provisional authorities and the eventual annexation of Hawai'i to the United States. "Kaona" also attests to the ways Kānaka Maoli held on to their cultural practices, especially language. This is just one example of indigenous youth using the genre of slam poetry as a method for reclaiming and announcing identity.

"Kaona" was also written by two youth who were and continue to be passionate about storytelling. Remember Ittai Wong from the beginning of this essay? Ittai was the reason I first got involved with Youth Speaks Hawai'i. He was the first of now many youth (whom I did not actually give birth to) to call me "Mom." In the five years I worked with Ittai, I was given the extraordinary opportunity to watch him grow from a child to a young man. I was also given the special privilege of being a mentor to Ittai's developing voice as a poet and a performer. I got to witness his stories shift from re-tooling Dr. Suess tales, to re-telling an important part of Hawai'i's history, to remembering his own particular mana'o. I witnessed a boy who loved hearing stories grow into a young man who loves telling stories.

Jamaica Osorio, who wrote "Kaona" with Ittai, first came to YSH when she was fifteen years old. I remember her as passionate, charismatic, intelligent, committed, and wordy. I say that last bit with a bit of wink and a nudge, but I doubt Jamaica will deny that part of our mentorial relationship was initially defined by editing. Jamaica would write reems of paper that were then honed down to two pages. This was an excruciating process that she embraced and fought with simultaneously. Having said that, I have watched Jamaica go on to represent her people in spectacular ways, from the White House to Holland. I have seen her refine her writing and embrace the revisioning process, and in turn I have learned social commitment and intellectual activism from her.

SPEAK, POET: WHEN THE PERSONAL BECOMES POLITICAL

In the same year Wong and Osorio wrote "Kaona," William Giles wrote a poem he entitled "Prayer Forms," inspired by his experiences of seeing multiple friends and family members enlist with the US military and then get posted to war-torn regions. Will's extraordinary gift for performance electrified the audience at the 2008 YSH Grand Slam Final. His commitment to speaking truth and performing the moment inspires fellow poets to work with a similar passion. In this poem, he begins by setting the scene of his cousin's deployment:

I will claim that I have never felt as helpless as the day

I saw my cousin . . .

go to war

[. . .]

See we had stood in this line before

when he went to boot camp

A group of us all saying "Don't change!" and promising to write

All pretending it was just like another football camp

Another harmless training session to a game that was going to earn him

a scholarship and pay for his future

[. . .]

A proud son of Sāmoa:

The group of native islands annexed off

in accords of world wars, split

down the middle as if the land mass

were just a bag of marbles auctioned off

between two kids on an elementary school playground

Now off he goes to fight for the one of two that still withholds

independence: The United States[4]

In this excerpt, the listener is given the oportunity of seeing how an intensely personal story gives voice to a larger, often unspoken, political situation. CNN rarely discusses the unincorporated territories of the United States, particularly those in the Pacific region. Most people outside of the Pacifc do not even realize Sāmoa is a divided archipelago, or that a disproportionate number of Sāmoans enlist in the American military. Will tells this story through the windowed view of his familial experience, and we, as an audience, are invited to bear witness.

"Kaona" and "Prayer Forms" are examples of spoken word poems that straddle artistic and activist situations that demand personal truth telling and emotional commitment. Spoken word introduces large and complex social issues through personal story. These stories can range from telling the experiences of cultural oppression, to the loss of a loved one, to the injustices of racial and economic prejudices, to the joy of first love, and to the heartache of gender-based discrimination, which is far more common than we like to imagine. Our youth write about all of these experiences. Their poems are beautifully crafted and intimately performed, giving us access to the stories that belong to us and the stories that we might never have known, but needed to hear.

A CHECKLIST TOWARDS KEEPING THE SPOKEN ARTS A VIBRANT PART OF HAWAI'I

Poets love lists, and I am no exception, so:

1. Great Venues and Stable Funding: For nearly a decade, slam poetry events on O'ahu have regularly attracted hundreds of audience members, and slam poets are in high demand as guest lecturers/performers in classrooms and community performance venues. While the demand for our work and our pedagogical approaches is growing exponentially, we artists and educators continue to receive the bare minimum of financial support. Ready access to affordable performance and workshop spaces would go a long way towards keeping this movement alive. In addition, many who work and mentor youth in writing and spoken arts volunteer their time. Consistent funding would go a long way towards offering these people a living wage for the important work they do in our community. Long-term educational relationships define Youth Speaks Hawai'i programming, built on the idea that sustained mentorial relationships are crucial to the work we do.

2. Evaluating Our Influence: The work of Youth Speaks Hawai'i didn't really gain significant traction until we were spotlighted on a national stage. Why? Why did it take national attention to gain attention at home? Why do we so frequently look first to the United States continent for our sphere of influence?

3. Say the Future: We in the spoken word community are really good at pointing out the current fractures in our societies and the inequalities of our pasts, but we often fall short of envisioning and articulating better possibilities for our communities. Let us begin speaking the future into action.

4. It's Just a Gimmick: Slam has been a major mechanism for popularizing spoken word, but it is important we do not allow stagnation by limiting our repertoire to the competitive three-minute format. A spoken art piece could be thirty seconds. It could be an hour and a half. It could always be revolutionary.

5. Engage the Pacific: Our work with Pacific communities has taught us that engagement and communication across "our sea of islands" is necessary to the health and sustainability of our societies. Youth Speaks Hawai'i has recently become a program under Pacific Tongues, which expands its mission of working with youth in Hawai'i to creating spoken arts opportunities that are multigenerational and cross-cultural in and around the Pacific.

SO LISTEN TO ME

We, as a multigenerational community, need access to a spoken catharsis. Since its inception, many YSH performances have moved audiences with spoken word poems that demanded emotional responses to issues that have often been so intellectualized as to become inaccessible to many members of our community—not because of a lack of understanding, but rather through a lack of heart. The brain tells us how to get things done, but the heart tells us why we should do them. The best moments of spoken word join these two together and move the audience to acknowledgment and action, because at its core, spoken word poetry in Hawai'i invokes the practice of call and response. Each recitation says, "I am here. I am speaking. Do you hear me?" with the audience responding, "Yes, we are here, and yes, we hear you." And in these spaces, the act of listening is as important as the act of being heard.

NOTES

1. We get asked this a lot, so here's a preemptive answer: Kealoha continues to run Hawai'i Slam, but ended his active participation with YSH in 2008. Melvin Won-Pat Borja and Travis Thompson continue to contribute to YSH programming.

2. BNV is an annual festival that brings together youth poetry slam teams from across the United States, as well as teams from Guåhan, England, and Bermuda to compete in a poetry slam. Because this is currently one of the few events of its kind created exclusively for youth, BNV also becomes an opportunity for young people from extremely diverse backgrounds to share important pieces of their culture and their personal experiences with each other. I remember one participant saying that going to a youth poetry slam was another way of going to church.

3. Jamaica Osorio and Ittai Wong, "Kaona," *Hāpai nā Leo,* ed. Bill Teter and Sage U'ilani Takehiro (Honolulu: Curriculum Research and Development Group, U of Hawai'i, 2010): 227–29.

4. This poem is printed with the gracious permission of the poet.

SUGGESTED SOURCES FOR FURTHER INFORMATION AND INSPIRATION

1. Youth Speaks Hawai'i YouTube channel, at http://www.youtube.com/user/YouthSpeaks Hawaii.
2. Youth Speaks YouTube channel, at http://www.youtube.com/user/YOUTHSPEAKS.
3. Spoken word by Patricia Smith, Andrea Gibson, Anis Mojani, Ishle Yi Park, and Tonya Ingram. Google them!
4. Youth Speaks Hawai'i facilitates a weekly writing workshop at The ARTS at Marks Garage at 1159 Nu'uanu Avenue, from 4:30 to 6:00 every Wednesday. The workshop is free and open to all youth between the ages of 13 and 19.
5. YSH also hosts The YSH Second Saturday Slam, at The ARTS at Marks Garage, which runs from 3:00 to 5:30 pm, every second Saturday of the month.
6. YSH helps facilitate after-school workshops and poetry clubs at many high schools across the island of O'ahu, and hopes to help establish more in high schools on neighbor islands. If you are interested in participating or if you have a particular interest in having us in your school, please contact us at our website at http://pacifictongues.org, our Facebook at facebook.com/youthspeakshawaii, or on email at info@pacifictongues.org.

NO SEED LEFT UNTURNED

JAMAICA HEOLIMELEIKALANI OSORIO

1.

The day my mother promised me the gravity
of the moon was the day i found my body
was meant to be an ocean
but was only a hollow shark skin drum
only pillars of stories that never stuck,
a belly that would never swell, tides
that never pulled, kuahiwi
i couldn't conjure, scars
where hips should have been, beauty
was the lie our mothers told to us in tradition
and truth was a story that left
      a bitter taste
like sour poi, on our tongue

WHAT THEY CANNOT SEE: HE MELE NO HŌPOE

i saw you dance in the distance
pulling my glance with the diction of your stance
gliding over the land like water
over itself

If the saying is true, that "history is recorded by the victor," women of color are history's biggest losers. Racism, colonization, sexism, and the controlled institutionalized nature of education has developed a culture of silencing any threats to the scripted hegemonic, colonial narrative. That is to say, communities of power control what is "normal" by undermining the very existence of alternative narratives.

Imagine then, the potential power we might wield by harnessing our moʻolelo and using them as a weapon against this single-sided writing of history. Hawaiians have long been constrained to one-dimensional, lackluster, and often disrespectful caricatures. There are many images we must first overcome to reclaim our wonderful bodies. Our intention must be to work to overpower the images of our Queen, Liliʻuokalani, depicted as a monkey in nineteenth-century political cartoons. We should show our disgust that the producers of the 2009 film, *Princess Kaʻiulani*, had the audacity to first propose the name "Barbarian Princess," as their title. And ultimately, we strive to outshine generations of literature and films inspired by the nauseating oversimplification of the kanaka maoli kino (body) as primitive, as in the 1966 George Roy Hill film, *Hawaii*. We need only gloss over the many films and images depicting Hawaiʻi to realize that nearly the entire corpus of industrialized Hawaiian filmography and imagery was created without kanaka maoli participation and authority. The result is that the kanaka maoli kino is often represented, to its detriment, by a set of rules and images that have been constructed without the powerful influence of kanaka maoli voices.

With a name that speaks too much of your magic
Nānāhuki,
too heavy for the diphthong of my tongue
instead, let me call you Hōpoe
i have seen you gathering parts of yourself in the form of
yellow lehua there
i have been with you from the beginning
only waiting for the pahu to sound for our haʻa to begin

You created of this stranger in me
a lover
let me cover your body in the sacred skin of this nahele
plant you a fortress of rumbling lehua trees
each blossom a promise to return.
my love
to move your rhythm again
for your hā to find home in my mele

Can you see those strange men
watching from beyond the page
see the way they have drawn us naked and grown
how they miss your skin feathered with yellow lehua

They write us into stillness   into silence
it seems through them,
we have been forgotten

i wonder how it is they cannot see
i wonder
what has made them so blind

We must fight to reclaim our right to reveal and tell our own stories in meaningful and positive ways, toward healing and honoring our kino. If we can heal and take ownership over the presentation of our bodies and stories, we can build a nation. With this in mind, I offer you my own moʻolelo, which is a story of uncovering what has been hidden, of calling that which has been spackled over to the surface. In this moʻolelo, I imagine a new telling of the Hiʻiakapoliopele epic, through the voice of Hiʻiaka, in poem and song composed out of love for her Hōpoe.

The first time I read *Ka Moʻolelo o Hiʻiakapoliopele* (Awaiaulu, 2007), I was in college. I had heard bits and pieces of the story throughout my childhood but never read any version of the story for myself. It is important to note that the nature of moʻolelo and Hawaiʻi's oral literary tradition has allowed for many versions and ways of telling our stories. The Hiʻiaka epic alone has been published upwards of thirteen times within our Hawaiian-language nūpepa (newspapers). Beyond those written publications, storytellers and other historical figures tell these moʻolelo orally, or through dance, and attach specific details to moʻolelo that may not exist in other versions. I chose this published version, translated and compiled by Awaiaulu Press, because of the process in which it was translated. The project was envisioned to train new translators with the intention that more kānaka maoli would be prepared to take ownership over the translation of our historical texts. I also chose this particular text because of the way it highlighted hundreds of mele and oli that specifically gave voice to the wāhine in the moʻolelo.

WHILE I LEAVE YOU, LOVE

i will sing for you
only one song
in my departure
only one promise in this severing
that leaving
with you behind
will be my truest sign of aloha
nothing will ever eclipse
the shadow that shakes from this lehua
the way the yellow of it
stills the chill settling in our koko

you and i never were
ʻaʻole
we always are
chose instead of the still of past
the shiver found in this forest
threw every part of these temporary bodies into this home
this valley crater that grows us
in every direction

e kuʻu ipo,
watch the parts of us as we feather into flowers
your lips
how they fold into this soil
how you are every part of this home i love
and fear to leave
watch the way growth happens all around
and how the birth of us turns me to song
turns you to dance
turns us both
together

Immersing myself in this text allowed me a unique perspective and opportunity while researching and writing a thesis focused on wāhine in Hawaiian literature. I was painfully unprepared and blissfully ignorant to what such a project would uncover. I found that the more I read and looked into myself, the less I wanted to write, analyze, and theorize. I wished to breathe these moʻolelo in—to become the moʻolelo and allow them to become me.

2.

Everything was brown when i was born
family was a gradient ocean that was too wide to understand
but by age 6
my eyes learned to polarize and measure
i learned the difference between mother and father
was a continent
and 15 points on a chromatic scale
i knew then
i would spend the rest of my life
trying to fit into the craters crumbling between them

forget that i am leaving
forget that there is more beyond the walls of this ʻāina
this ahu
extending into sky
remember the calm of this movement
the forever of this voice
and know
that i will return
in body
spirit
and song
so that our dance
shall never end

Getting to know Hiʻiaka pushed me to become more acquainted with my own body. For the first time in my life, I imagined a picture of womanhood that stretched far beyond any definition I had previously understood. I saw so much of myself in Hiʻiaka's spirit, tenacity, adventure, and deep commitment to love. I found myself comforted by the way she loved. Mostly, I identified with the way her aloha inspired growth in herself and her environment. I came to see myself as a piece of Hiʻiaka, that I was one of the many magnificent realities born from her aloha. I believed our stories were the same, that the both of us were two small women fighting our way through the page, trying with all our might to scream something between the lines. We were fighting for the strength to tell our own story. Hoping we might reach someone enough that they would carry us, the way I have learned to carry Hiʻiaka, in the body.

My relationship with Hiʻiaka is evolving every day. I cannot tell you where it will take me but I can pinpoint its beginning. There is a moment in the moʻolelo when Hiʻiaka learns that the origin of Nānāhuki's (Hōpoe) name comes from her love of gathering lehua at Hōpoe. In learning this, Hiʻiaka offers what I believe to be one of the grandest gestures of aloha I have ever encountered: a lehua grove—grown entirely out of her love for Hōpoe. In this moment, Hōpoe herself becomes the lehua that Hiʻiaka will carry with her and draw inspiration from throughout her journey and life.

PAE KA LEO O KE KAI

i arrive to find the kapu man dead
sending songs into the ʻāina before me
scripture composed to the rhythm of your pahu
they land on the ears of friendly hosts
they claim i am the deity of their dance
the akua they marvel to for this movement
and yet,
they are ignorant to the source of my mele

They forget you
do not see the shadows your palms left
pressed against my hips
don't feel the cool brush of wind to the sweat collected
between our skin
they know nothing of the way you fed me your body
how i drank of you until every step
every twist was an instinct to praise you
every kāhea
a song strung from the shift your kino pressed into papa
how you became a kumu only by allowing your body to be
lāʻau lehua planted in earth
so that you may dance every time the Moaniani Lehua wind
blows

They are stranger to you
and our song
and i wonder
how they might call themselves dancers
and not know your name
not have felt the pressure of your poho to their hips
not the whisper of your voice saying, "pēlā" against their
chests

When I read Hiʻiaka I did not find the story I had been told so many times before—a story of a young girl traveling off to Kauaʻi to fetch a lover for her sister. ʻAʻole. Instead I found a young woman who was changed forever by a love so pure and tangible that it not only changed the path of these two women, it transformed the physical landscape of their home. In that moment, I was so captured by the ability of this love, so far beyond my own understanding, to birth life in ʻāina and body, reminding all of us that the two (earth and body) are the same. Hiʻiaka's aloha for Hōpoe inspired creation—whether it was the composition of mele, oli, hula, or in this case, a forest. We see Hiʻiaka's power to give life through aloha, and in seeing such a love we are inspired to love and create in the same way.

I honor Hiʻiaka for sharing a moʻolelo of two women, so fiercely enchanted by each other that the universe around them could not help but grow in their presence. Their love was expressed in nature in a way that we are unable to ignore; through the whisper of the Moaniani Lehua wind, or the dancing of lehua at Hōpoe, to the pōhaku that remain strong for generations to show the sacrifice of love.

they know not how all of this became the dance i would
compose to the rhythm of your breath
only that i have been singing the same song ever since

They call me their akua
their kumu
all i can do is wonder
as a haumana of your haʻa
as a student of this bend at the knees praise
if i have spent enough time in your arms
in the center of your swaying scripture
if i have made a home permanent enough in your body
to give mana to this ʻami
of this curve and hinge of the hips

i send my voice to you over the ocean
praying for reply

                    Pae ka leo o ke kai

the voice of the sea sings

            Haʻa ka wahine

the female bends

         ʻAmi i kai o Nānāhuki

she turns the sea of nānāhuki

reminding me
i have much still to learn of your body

The aloha between Hiʻiaka and Hōpoe exists beyond the human body and is projected tangibly as an extension of the personal kino to the body of our ʻāina. How magnificent must a love be that everything it touched, brushed against, or breathed upon would be changed, forever? I truly believe that this aloha is the story Hiʻiaka is fighting to tell—a story that shows the depth and possibility of love to transform all. A story that certainly has the mana to transform the narrative that surrounds our bodies. This is something I have experienced personally.

Getting to know Hiʻiaka allowed me to start to understand myself through a new vocabulary. I learned that Mana Wahine meant, to me, that I too could identify wholly as a wahine through my intimate relationship with this ʻāina, without sacrificing any bit of my sexuality, or masculinity. I learned that to do so allowed me to come to a fuller, more fantastic understanding of the manifestation of womanhood. This understanding fully transformed the way I would come to see, imagine, and approach my own body. Hiʻiaka allowed me to marvel at my body for my ability to live inspired by the past and still create for myself and others in the present and future.

To further the self-discovery of identity and kanaka maoli culture, I urge kānaka to return to the intimate study of our moʻolelo. It is imperative that we also continue to engage with moʻolelo and literature in new ways, specifically through the acts of composition and storytelling. Our moʻolelo provide a framework and an outline that can assist in the initial finding of the body, but it is only through original composition and performance that the kanaka maoli voice lives.

NO SEED LEFT UNTURNED

When attempting to lull a foreign body
leave no seed unturned
scatter language over skin
let every song that resists to be put to tongue
come to life in the shake of hips
conjure wahine Hōpoe
sweet lehua nectar that
insists on being remembered

As you pass through, in danger
make wind of metaphor to brush chill against the nape of
his neck
let him not forget the sharp sting of the ʻŪkiu rain
make sure the seeds will stick

Sing your way through valley and cliff's edge
bring vision to places you've come to in darkness
that your kaona may be memorialized in pōhaku's
premonition
insure that women will repeat the words you have written
that you will be remembered
as the wahine

who left Hōpoe's lehua grove
but never forgot the taste
of sweet nectar on your tongue
a seed that insists to flower

Uncovering, translating, and re-visioning our existing moʻolelo is only the first step in a process of re-occupying the kanaka voice and body. The second, and I argue, more significant step in this nation-building movement is that we begin to create for ourselves with the inspiration and guidance of the past. It is our kuleana to create, to name, and to live these moʻolelo—to bring life to our culture. We can unlock our greatest potential if we can dedicate ourselves to becoming primary sources of ʻike for our moʻopuna, just as our kūpuna are for us.

It is also increasingly important that our fellow residents and visitors to Hawaiʻi take an interest in these moʻolelo. These stories, whether historical or cotemporary, are the script to this ʻāina. Not only do these moʻolelo tell the story of the birth and flourishing of the kanaka maoli ancestry, they tell the story of the birth of the ʻāina itself. To live in Hawaiʻi and benefit from all her wonder without seeking an intimate understanding of what created her, of how kānaka maoli cared for her and lived in harmony with her, is to wholly misunderstand the kuleana that comes with calling Hawaiʻi home.

HŌPOE I KA POLI O HIʻIAKA

Many men have told my story
have uttered your name into speech
some have carved it into pōhaku and pepa
a part of you and
i live forever
in the margins between sound and solid

But the hua we shared
those parts of us were held in kino
in leo
stay carved in the creases of my poho
so that every part of
this earth i hold has a moment
to know your touch

ʻAe,
maybe our words are best kept for two
but the manner in which you glided over and danced with
Papa deserves to be shouted from my hallowed hands

So i will resist
the letting go of the ocean that tries to fall through
even when i am tempted to destroy this temple
allow feelings to rise like tides
swell the fractures at the base of my ʻōpū
hallow a crater once full of fire
transform Kīlauea's heat into a forgotten story
instead i choose to
hold so tight these hua
our only pua

The future of Hawaiʻi is a moʻolelo we must write together. As I continue to grow and create, it is my hope to give other wāhine the opportunity to find themselves between the lines of our shared stories. In that pursuit I offer these poems, as a gift, something I have created out of love for you all. I hope you will see my contribution to our moʻolelo as a grand gesture of aloha that may bring you closer to understanding and identifying with your own kino and ʻāina and all its outstanding potential.

Aloha nō.

that they may lay
in the center
of my poli
a place once reserved for aliʻi
but ahi and ʻā have left me
an open cavity
for your memory
i promise
that those parts of you we shared in quiet
they will not spill open

It is right that only this earth knows of the words we
planted
that they lie rooted in the kumu of our moʻo
only my gift of lehua can ever claim our love

It is right
even if they too
are gone
now

3.

Our skin tone kept us
quiet
from questioning these bodies
wondering which parts were broken
we learned to be
complacent in our difference
while we soaked in the silence
let the salt seep into our skeleton
leave its mark
make us feel like we belonged to the ocean.

RESOURCES FOR FURTHER INFORMATION AND INSPIRATION

1. Haunani-Kay Trask, "Writing in Captivity," *Inside Out: Literature, Cultural Politics, and Identity in the New Pacific*, ed. Vilsoni Hereniko and Rob Wilson (Lanham: Rowman and Littlefield, 1999): 17–26.

2. Albert Wendt, "Towards a New Oceania," rpt. in *Seaweeds and Constructions* 7 (1976): 71–85.

3. kuʻualoha hoʻomanawanui, "Mana Wahine, Education and Nation-building: Lessons from the Epic of Pele and Hiʻiaka for Kanaka Maoli Today," *Multicultural Perspectives* 12.4 (2010): 206–212.

4. Noenoe K. Silva, "Pele, Hiʻiaka, and Haumea: Women and Power in Two Hawaiian Moʻolelo," *Pacific Studies* 30.1–2 (March 2007): 159–81.

5. Steven Edmund Winduo, "Unwriting Oceania: The Repositioning of the Pacific Writer Scholars Within a Folk Narrative Space," *New Literary History* 31.3 (Summer 2000): 599–613.

WE, THE STAR KEEPERS

RYAN OISHI

For the past two years, I have found myself in a perfect storm of weddings. At the age of thirty, the biological clocks of my high school friends seem to have aligned with the certainty of a tidal chart. Upon this nuptial tempest, I have been cast to the shores of Boston and San Francisco, Richmond and the North Shore of Oʻahu, and nearly every hotel in Waikīkī.

These weddings are a time of reconnecting. Stories from our high school days at Punahou are dusted off and trotted out with great relish. And they are also a time of looking towards the future: blossoming new families, promising new careers. Because I am one of the few of us still living in Hawaiʻi, my friends frequently ask me questions about home. And because I work at Kamehameha Schools, sometimes these conversations turn to Hawaiian-related issues (as if my employment has somehow vested me with expertise in Hawaiian-related things). A month ago, I found myself walking down a bustling Vancouver street with my soon-to-be-married friend when the topic of Hawaiian sovereignty came up. My heart sank when I saw in his eyes that sovereignty was not even a possibility in his imagination.

My heart sank because my friends, in most situations, are very intelligent individuals. They were successful students in high school and college. Many are now entering respectable professions as doctors and lawyers, engineers and businessmen; some will return to Hawaiʻi and become future leaders in our communities. And yet, when it comes to the issues closest to home, to issues like sovereignty or GMOs or food sustainability or rail or the building of a new telescope on Mauna Kea, I've noticed a certain lack of foundational knowledge, the prerequisite of healthy debate. I worry when I hear my friends rely on reductive and sometimes inaccurate narratives of Hawaiʻi's history, narratives that have been promoted by our tourism industry and tacitly supported by our educational system.[1]

As a high school teacher at Kamehameha Schools, these conversations caused me to reflect on my role as a teacher in providing that foundation. What responsibilities do we have in preparing the next generation of servant leaders, many of whom will be nurtured in our private schools? What foundations of knowledge do our students need to face the challenges of Hawaiʻi's future?

MY JOURNEY

I thought back to my own education at Punahou: the many wonderful teachers I had, and the wealth of resources and opportunities available to my friends and me. It was an incredible privilege to attend Punahou, and I was reminded of that fact by my father, who in response to a generous financial aid package, dragged me one Saturday morning down to Middle Field with a pick and bucket to pull weeds. "This is a small way for us to pay back the school," he said (oddly, I was equally proud of my father as I was embarrassed at being seen by my classmates).

And yet, for all the opportunities and doors that were opened for me at Punahou, I don't remember taking a single Hawaiian history class in my four years of high school. In English, I had the opportunity to read *Hamlet* and *The Great Gatsby* and dozens of other novels and poems and plays, but not a single Hawaiian moʻolelo. In my senior year in 2000, the Hawaiian language program was just starting as an elective class. None of my friends took Hawaiian; it didn't count towards graduation requirements. For all the valuable things I learned at Punahou, from Japanese to calculus to European history, I left knowing little about the contemporary issues facing Hawaiʻi, and the dynamic history that has shaped our present.[2]

It was only in college at the University of Southern California—through a postcolonial literature class that exposed me to Irish and Caribbean writers like W. B. Yeats, Derek Walcott, and Kamau Brathwaite's rhythm of the hurricane—that I arrived at Doheny Library, searching for Cathy Song and Haunani-Kay Trask's *Light in the Crevice Never Seen*. I also found *Bamboo Ridge* on those shelves. What a revelation it was to read Darrell Lum's "Beer Can Hat" for the first time!

This led me back to Hawaiʻi to pursue a Masters degree in English at the University of Hawaiʻi at Mānoa. There, I was exposed to a rich and ever-expanding body of literature written by Hawaiian and local writers, grounded in the complex and contested history of this place. Not only were these inspiring writers writing in the familiar voices of Hawaiʻi's people, but using literature to engage in the difficult problems facing our community. Although many of these stories came from a generation prior, they spoke to problems that I recognized. I began to see the web of connections between yesterday and today, between the health of the land and the health of the people, between stories and our storied lives. When I read Eric Chock's "Poem for

George Helm, Aloha Week 1980," I was introduced to George Helm and the concept of Aloha ʻĀina. When I heard George Helm sing "Kuʻu Pua i Paoakalani," my heart trembled with love and anger. His story took me to Queen Liliʻuokalani's *Hawaiʻi's Story by Hawaii's Queen*: a Queen who had once been for me simply the composer of beautiful melodies at the time of the overthrow became a light of wisdom, courage, and forgiveness (I cannot listen to the "Queen's Prayer" without tearing up). I began to feel the tension within our state motto, "Ua Mau ke Ea o ka ʻĀina i ka Pono," to trace the scars of Hawaiʻi's colonial history, to see the connections between the 1970s struggles in Waiāhole-Waikāne and the struggle against GMOs today. I began to notice how agro-chemical multinationals like Monsanto and Syngenta were modern-day mutations of global capitalism, the reincarnations of the sugar plantations that brought my great-grandfathers to ʻOlaʻa and Puʻunēnē.

Through this foundation of knowledge, the connections between literature and my own life became more real and direct. When I read Alani Apio's *Kāmau*, I was working as a busboy at the Princess Kaʻiulani hotel. I began to notice unsettling juxtapositions—newspaper headlines disparaging rising homelessness besides announcements of new luxury condominiums—and better understood the struggle to protect the iwi kupuna from golf courses and telescopes and rail developments. These observations sparked a curiosity that moved from literature to history: I desired to know how these issues of land tenure flowed from the Māhele and the Democratic Revolution of 1954, and turned to books like Gavan Daws and George Cooper's *Land and Power in Hawaii* and Lilikalā Kameʻeleihiwa's *Native Land and Foreign Desires* for greater perspective.

Above all, in these stories I found inspiring tales of solidarity and compassion, overflowing with the dignity of Hawaiʻi's people—my neighbors, my friends, my heroes, who came together time and again to confront Malo's big fish from the dark ocean.[3] Their victories and defeats inspired me to write my own poems, to add my own voice to this unfolding story.

MAKING SPACE FOR MOʻOLELO

When I graduated from UH and began teaching in the English Department at Kamehameha Schools, I was exposed to more and more traditional moʻolelo, stories that stretched back countless generations before the stories I had read in college. Even with my newly-minted graduate degree, I felt I had jumped into the deep end of the pool. On top of being a new teacher, here was a whole new literary tradition in which I had no expertise. I dipped my toes tentatively into the waters of this new literature, but stuck to the more familiar terrain of contemporary Hawaiian and local texts.

My greatest fear in approaching these moʻolelo was not doing them justice. These fears, I imagine, were shared by others in my department. Fortunately, our chair, Kaʻimi Kaiwi, gave us the freedom to move at our own pace: in my first year, she gently nudged us forward with the goal of incorporating at least one piece of Hawaiian literature into our curriculum by the end of the school year. We were encouraged to learn as we went along, to take risks, to make mistakes, and to grow in our understanding of these texts.[4]

Through the commitment and leadership of teachers like Kaʻimi, Richard Hamasaki, and many others, our English Department has collectively arrived at a place where moʻolelo have assumed their rightful stature alongside Homer and Shakespeare in our curriculum. This comparative approach has provided a rich intellectual vista for our students, where they can ground themselves in the stories of Hawaiʻi while reaching out to the wisdom of other literary traditions. In addition to the traditional Western and World canons, it is possible for a student who has passed through our high school to have read major texts such as *The True Story of Kaluaikoʻolau, The Wind Gourd of Laʻamaomao; Lāʻieikawai,* and *A Legendary Tradition of Kamapuaʻa,* as well as excerpts from longer works like *The Epic of Hiʻiakaikapoliopele, Kamehameha and his Warrior Kekūhaupiʻo,* and *Ruling Chiefs of Hawaii,* among others. These works are supplemented by a vibrant body of contemporary Hawaiian and local literature: poetry, mele, short stories, novels, and plays. This rich body of literature, which poet, critic, and colleague Richard Hamasaki once described as vast "mountains in the sea," is the inheritance of our Hawaiian students, who increasingly stand upon its broad shoulders with pride and confidence.[5] And with the exciting translation work that is being done with the Hawaiian-language newspapers, more and more moʻolelo are published every year.[6]

Few would argue against the benefits of teaching moʻolelo at Kamehameha Schools. But what value do these moʻolelo possess for our private school students at Punahou or ʻIolani, Damien or St. Louis, who do not share a common Hawaiian ancestry? How might these stories benefit the diverse student populations that make up our public school system?

I believe that the insights and values embedded in traditional moʻolelo are not only valuable to the Hawaiian community, but for all of us who value Hawaiʻi. They provide us with a different model of being in these islands, a deeper understanding of this place that strengthens our capacity for ʻaloha ʻāina. It is no accident that many of these moʻolelo deal directly with issues of governance. They provide enduring insights into values and practices of sustainability and pono governance that allowed a people to thrive and flourish in Hawaiʻi for eighty-plus generations. Most of all, I believe that moʻolelo, nurtured and evolved in this place, can help us to expand our imaginations about what is possible, to begin to "decolonize our minds," as Ngũgĩ wa Thiong'o so elegantly put it.[7] They provide a paradigm that reaches beyond the narrow logic of global capitalism, beyond the folly of applying continental models of endless growth to our island ecosystem.[8] They are vital to the health of Hawai'i. Placed alongside the traditional Western and World canons, mo'olelo provide a balanced diet for our students. Why import 85 percent of our mo'olelo, when such fertile abundance grows here in this storied place?

FUTURE VISIONS

One of the greatest joys of my job as an English teacher is to read my students' stories. Through them, I can see the nascent fruits of a curriculum grounded in mo'olelo. Their modern-day mo'olelo offer me a glimpse into our collective future. More and more, I am finding stories like Mailani's. The daughter of an astronomer, Mailani Neal was a gifted sophomore from Kona whom I had the privilege of teaching in 2012. Her story, "Eyes of the Night Lights," which is reprinted following this essay, was the product of a short story assignment given after reading Emma Nakuina's version of "Kahalaopuna" and Gabriel Garcia Marquez's short story, "A Very Old Man with Enormous Wings."

Mailani's story not only conveys her passion for astronomy, but also demonstrates a deep sense of kuleana that comes with being a "keeper of the stars." This developed sense of kuleana is what I find truly amazing about Mailani's story: nowhere in my directions did I ask students to consider the responsibilities that accompany their dreams. And yet this came naturally for her. It is fundamental to the DNA of her story. Her protagonist, Nāmaka-onālamaokapō, whose name poetically connects her to the eyes of the Mauna Kea telescopes, looks to the source, seeking the wisdom of her grandfather, Kia'i. Through him, she accesses the wisdom of countless generations; for a year, she disciplines her mind, body, and spirit to prepare herself for the responsibilities she will inherit. And this from a fifteen-year-old!

Each time I read Mailani's story, and other stories like hers, I am filled with hope for our future. An aspiring astronomer, Mailani will one day stand at the cross-currents of science, economics, culture, and the environment, and will participate in the heated debates that accompany each new telescope proposed for Mauna Kea. She will be asked to weigh the competing arguments when the values of science and culture collide, to respond, to lead. In her mo'olelo, I see the foundations of knowledge that I saw lacking in my own friends. I see an imagination nourished by mo'olelo and other literary traditions, preparing itself for the challenges of Hawai'i's future. I see in her eyes, filled with the beauty of celestial night lights, an imagination in which sovereignty, in all its multiple meanings, is possible.

As educators working in Hawai'i's schools, we must assist all our students as they ascend their mountains and assume their kuleana as "star keepers." We must help them by providing a foundation of knowledge that will allow them to address the problems they will face here in Hawai'i. As English teachers, I believe we must make spaces in our curriculum for mo'olelo and other stories grounded in this place. We must support and nourish our students' imaginations until, as Mailani tells us, they are "faster, stronger, and wiser" than us.

And we must become students ourselves, joining them on this difficult journey.[9] Now six years into my teaching career, I have experienced the highs and lows of teaching, and continue to learn each day. I am filled with humility for our profession, and am constantly inspired by my brilliant colleagues who make teaching look easy, but whom I know push themselves each day with unwavering dedication and commitment. Most of all, I am inspired by my students—their perseverance, their passion, their incredible potential. There can be no shortcuts if we are to make Hawai'i's future what we dream it to be.

"It's time," Poli'ahu reminds us at the beginning of Mailani's story. Time for us, both teachers and students, to assume our kuleana as star keepers: to protect the fish, who are also the stars, to carry them skillfully so that they do not suffocate, to perpetuate this knowledge to the promising generations yet to come.

NOTES

1. Perhaps this educational connection has always been the case: armed with a graduate degree, I cannot help but think, half-humorously, of Louis Althusser's "Ideological State Apparatuses" when I recall "picking pineapples" during elementary school P.E.
2. In fairness, thirteen years have passed since my high school graduation, a lifetime in the educational field. My department chair recently shared with me a conversation she had with the English department chair at Punahou, who was very interested in the place-based and comparative approach we have been pursuing at Kamehameha.
3. David Malo's often-cited observation from 1837 reads as follows: "If a big wave comes in, large and unfamiliar fishes will come from the dark ocean, and when they see the small fishes of the shallows they will eat them up. The white man's ships have arrived with clever men from the big countries. They know our people are few in number and our country is small, they will devour us."
4. In addition, starting in the summer of 2010, members of our English department began working on the Standards Based Kula Hawai'i initiative, in which we were tasked with creating new benchmarks that aligned with the Working Exit Outcomes (WEO). This was part of a larger initiative in which Kamehameha Schools committed itself to the vision of becoming a "Kula Hawai'i"—a "Hawaiian school"—as opposed to a "school for Hawaiians." This experience was helpful for many of us in refining our views on the importance and value of teaching Hawaiian literature to our students.

5. For a more detailed catalogue of the historical topography of Hawaiian and local literature, see Richard Hamasaki's essay "Mountains in the Sea: The Emergence of Contemporary Hawaiian Poetry in English," *Readings in Pacific Literature*, ed. Paul Sharrard (Wollongong: U of Wollongong, 1993): 9–19.

6. According to Hawaiian language scholar Puakea Nogelmeier, of the one million typescript pages of text within these Hawaiian language newspapers, only 2 percent of that repository has been integrated into the English-speaking world. Many of the traditional moʻolelo published in English today have come from these Hawaiian-language sources. Today, community projects like ʻIke Kūʻokoʻa have enlisted thousands of volunteers (including all 2,000 of Kamehameha's high school students) to transcribe these pages into searchable typescript, making this rich body of knowledge increasingly accessible to scholars and the general public alike.

7. Ngũgĩ wa Thiong'o, *Decolonising the Mind: The Politics of Language in African Literature* (London: J. Currey, 1986).

8. For an example of the transformative power of moʻolelo in shaping our consciousness, read Dennis Kawaharada's collection of essays, *Storied Landscapes: Hawaiian Literature and Place* (Honolulu: Kalamakū, 1999). In it, Kawaharada, a local Japanese, explores through a powerful personal account how moʻolelo helped him to reimagine and deepen his connection to this place.

9. I find the words of Paulo Freire, Brazilian educator and philosopher, inspiring for the mutual learning that will be required of both teacher and student: "Through dialogue, the teacher-of-the-students and the students-of-the-teacher cease to exist and a new term emerges: teacher-student with student teachers. . . . They become jointly responsible for a process in which all grow." From *Pedagogy of the Oppressed* (New York: Continuum, 2000): 80.

RESOURCES FOR FURTHER INFORMATION AND INSPIRATION

1. S. N. Haleʻole, *Lāʻieikawai* (trans. Martha Warren Beckwith, ed. Dennis Kawaharada, Honolulu: Noio, 2006).

2. Hoʻoulumāhiehie, *The Epic Tale of Hiʻiakaikapoliopele* (trans. Puakea Nogelmeier, Honolulu: Awaiaulu, 2006).

3. Lilikalā Kameʻeleihiwa, trans. *A Legendary Tradition of Kamapuaʻa* (Honolulu: Bishop Museum, 1996).

4. Brandy Nālani McDougall, *The Salt-wind: Ka Makani Paʻakai* (Honolulu: Kuleana ʻŌiwi, 2008).

5. Rodney Morales, ed., *HoʻiHoʻi Hou: A Tribute to George Helm & Kimo Mitchell* (Honolulu: Bamboo Ridge, 1984).

EYES OF THE NIGHT LIGHTS

MAILANI NEAL

Originally written for Mr. Oishi's Eng10 class, Fall 2012, Kamehameha Schools at Kapālama

On the slopes of the **Mauna Kea summit**, the cold winds of Poliʻahu whispered in the ear of Kiaʻi, "It's time." Kiaʻi opened his eyes to the flawless surface of Lake Waiau casting the perfect projection of the night sky. Burdened by the command given, Kiaʻi rose and began to gather his ʻupena, fishing net, and waded into the glacial water towards the never-ending pattern of fish circling each other. He threw his net, encompassing and catching them perfectly, as he had done for many decades. Then, Kiaʻi quickly ran the several miles to Lake Hūnā. He ran so swiftly that the fish did not die from suffocation, and he released them into the lake to swim until the next night. These fish were no ordinary fish; they were the spirit of the stars.

Kiaʻi would perform this task to make sure the stars were in the sky every night. His real name was not Kiaʻi; his name had been forgotten when he accepted the role as star keeper and became Kiaʻi, which means "to guard." His family had been the star keepers for as long as time, and he was becoming old. Every day he felt his aging pains growing stronger and less endurable. His son, Alakaʻināiʻaikapō, had refused to accept the role as star keeper and left him without a protégé to take his place. He moved to Kona and became a farmer with a home and wife. Their first born was a girl, whom they named Nāmakaonālamaokapō, meaning Eyes of the Night Lights. When she was born, she would not stop crying until she saw the night sky filled with stars. Alakaʻināiʻaikapō knew this was a sign that she was meant to be a star keeper, but he refused to let her have that fate also. For all of her childhood and her late teenage years, he never allowed her out of the house at night, knowing that the stars would entice her away. But he could not hide away the entire night sky, for she longed to see the night and would often sneak peeks through the entryway.

The next night, Kiaʻi performed his task then meditated. Through the dream realm, he reached out to his son's mind and spoke to him, saying, "It

is time for a new Keeper. She is chosen by the stars. My son, you may have refused your fate, but you cannot refuse hers. Send her to me." Alakaʻināiʻaikapō
argued with him so angrily that he awoke with a start and ran to make sure Nāmakaonālamaokapō was still there. She was asleep safe and sound, but he did-
n't know that he was already too late. In her dreams, Kiaʻi had already reached
out to her and they were speaking. He explained to her his responsibility of
keeping the stars and how his son had refused the task. Nāmakaonālamaokapō
agreed to accept this responsibility; she had no desire to live in Kona.

She packed a small kapa bag with a few belongings and snuck off into the
night. Traveling for three days and nights, she crossed Hualālai, Mauna Loa,
and ascended the steep shoulders of Mauna Kea to reach Kiaʻi. She arrived
at Lake Waiau at sunrise, just in time to witness Kiaʻi performing his task of
gathering the fish.

After he returned from securing the fish in safety, Kiaʻi and Nāmakaonālamaokapō sat on the lakeshore. For hours they discussed the responsibility of keeping the stars and what she would have to do. Kiaʻi explained to her
the need for perfect balance in her physicality, emotions, mind, and spirit.
Nāmakaonālamaokapō accepted all of these challenges as her fate to be Keeper of the stars. He showed her the necklace he wore. It had a pendant made
of basaltic lava rock that glimmered so brightly that she was sure it was a star
too. Kiaʻi said to Nāmakaonālamaokapō, "When it is your time to be Keeper,
you shall wear this necklace."

For many months, Kiaʻi taught, trained, and challenged Nāmakaonālamaokapō. For physicality, she would run numerous miles to train her to run
fast enough that the fish wouldn't die of suffocation. He made her lift heavy
stones to increase her strength. Each day, her body adjusted more and more
to the altitude and climate of the Mauna Kea summit. For mentality and
emotions, he taught her meditation. For spirituality, he taught her the language of the stars and communication with the gods. And every day, his
health decreased.

For a year he trained Nāmakaonālamaokapō. Now she was faster, stronger, and wiser than Kiaʻi. She could perform the task of keeping the stars perfectly. She would talk with the stars effortlessly and listened obediently to the
conversations held with the gods.

That night, the moon was encircled by a rainbow, a sign of change and
ending. Kiaʻi knew it was his time; for weeks he had felt severely sick, but hid
it from Nāmakaonālamaokapō. While they both sat on the shore and silently
listened to the stars, an unusual warm breeze wrapped its tentacles around the
two as Poliʻahu whispered, "Kiaʻi, you are done." Kiaʻi and Nāmakaonālamaokapō opened their eyes. She could feel tears gathering on the brims of her

eyes while Kiaʻi placed the necklace around her neck, kissed her forehead, and said, "Granddaughter, if you shall ever need me, I will always be in the stars." Then he stood and again the warm breeze returned. Nāmakaonālamaokapō watched as the breeze carried Kiaʻi away as stardust shimmering in the light of the moon and stars.

THE WELO AND KULEANA OF MELE INTEGRITY

KAINANI KAHAUNAELE

KA WELO ʻOHANA

Wewelo ke aloha i ka ʻōnohi, ʻumeʻume mai hoʻi kau e kahi lei hoʻoheno[1]

While my mother, "Lady Ipo," embarked on her Hawaiian music career at a young age, little did I know the critical role Hawaiian music would play in my own life's work, kuleana, and passion. When it was time to start considering college and career possibilities, I wanted to work in the culinary field. A music career hadn't even crossed my mind. Nobody went to college to be a musician. A career meant work resulting from a college education.

I was born into a musical family and raised by my grandparents, Kanani and David Kahaunaele, great-grandmother Margaret Pānui, and a huge extended ʻohana in the Koʻolau and Haleleʻa districts of Kauaʻi. For many in my ʻohana, music in the entertainment and visitor industry served as their livelihood. For others, music was for pure enjoyment, stress relief, or spiritual communion.

In my grandparents' household, the family collection of albums was exclusively Hawaiian; the songs that were on the radio or sung at parties were in Hawaiian or were hapa haole. At our church in Kapaʻa, Ke Akua Mana, all the hymns and prayers were in Hawaiian. I learned to play ʻukulele at home and danced hula in the Hawaiian revue at the Coco Palms Hotel in Wailua. I was the youngest cast member in our three-generation family production. The prestigious Kapaʻa High Show Choir, under the direction of Renee Thronas, however, was my formal training ground in music, voice, stage, and performance.

When I entered college, I became part of a Hawaiian music ensemble that sang and danced our way across America, following a solar car race. It was where I experienced my first tour abroad performing exclusively Hawaiian music, and life on the road. We traveled cross-country, cramped up in a little van, from Texas to Minnesota. The landscape was flat with no textured mountain ranges; gas was a mere $0.99 per gallon; and there was no cerulean water feature in sight. I learned there was nothing glamorous about touring abroad. But it was indeed fun work.

Soon thereafter, I embarked on a life-changing summer cultural exchange program through the South Pacific. For the first time, I heard with my own ears the traditional music as sung by the natives, on their own lands of Sāmoa, Tonga, Fiji, and Aotearoa. I may have heard their songs in the Polynesian revues of Hawai'i, but that was no comparison. As we shared our Hawaiian music and hula, I couldn't help but take a deeper look into how we as Hawaiians represent ourselves through music, how Hawaiians are perceived through our music, the evolution of Hawaiian music, the responsibility we have as makers of Hawaiian music, and the relationship with our Pacific island 'ohana through language, culture, music, and dance.

On that trip, we didn't have a strong and coherent musical component, like our host cultures or like the other Hawaiian cultural groups who were there for the sole intention of sharing the music of Hawai'i. Traveling with such a sizable group of Hawaiian students and teachers from the community colleges statewide, we had pulled together our music and hula resources; this resulted in a diverse handful of dancers, musicians, and vocalists—including falsetto singers and chanters. Not everyone knew the same songs.

When our hosts sang, their powerful voices soared and harmonies filled the air with beauty and delight, touching my na'au. When it was time for us Hawaiians to sing and represent, our small makeshift band often sang with falsetto or gentle voices. Our Polynesian cousins weren't used to the sound. As I witnessed some of their reactions of surprise, giggles, and intrigue, I thought about how they—many of whom may have never greeted Hawaiians before—might perceive all Hawaiians solely through that one musical performance. And whereas Hawaiian music ensembles had generally evolved into small bands of a few select musicians responsible for representing the whole community group, it was obvious that for our hosts, the whole community participated in the "normal" practice of singing traditional music together, always in large groups.

Through this experience, I became critical of my Hawaiian music. For the first time, I wasn't performing for my community or tourists. Being visitors singing for our Polynesian cousins produced a very different vibe. I started to realize that I must present Hawaiian music with confidence, no matter the size or volume of the group, and take responsibility for every single word and image our songs depicted. I started to depart from the notion of "playing" music and entertaining, and instead to consciously sing with responsibility, accountability, and intention.

MŌHALA KA LEHUA

It was in a moʻolelo Hawaiʻi class with Kaʻimi Summers at Kauaʻi Community College that I had an epiphany. She introduced us to Hawaiian poetic devices found in stories and songs; I never knew we had our own poetic devices, like the ones I had learned when studying haole poetry. My high school teachers never explained Hawaiian songs as poetry, probably because they didn't know anything about Hawaiian music or culture.

I then moved to Hilo to attend the University of Hawaiʻi and further my studies in ʻōlelo Hawaiʻi. The Hawaiian songs I grew up hearing became an important launching pad for my language acquisition and understanding, and in turn, my growing understanding made familiar and new songs easier to follow, remember, internalize, and articulate. At UH Hilo, haku mele Larry Kimura became a kumu and mentor to me, and ʻAha Pūnana Leo's curriculum development and media arm provided me with a venue to create and apply the knowledge I was craving, learning, and putting to practical use.

My progression into creating mele began to flourish. I wanted to write mele as journal entries, as haʻawina, as tributes, and as a way to document our Hawaiʻi of today. For instance, my mele "Nani Pololū" was written in honor of kupuna Sonny Solomon, a kupa, or older person who knew all the intricacies of his land. A spontaneous holoholo adventure in the mid '90s led me to the Pololū Valley lookout in Kohala, where, amongst the flurry of malihini taking in the spectacular views, I saw one Hawaiian. We connected eye-to-eye, greeted each other, and became immediate friends by figuring out who we knew in common. He started to share with me place names and associated stories of Pololū valley, where he was from.

I didn't want to forget anything he taught me. My mind was turning as I returned home to the other side of the island. I knew that a mele would be a perfect way to document my time with him and make the mele my haʻawina of what I learned. It was also a tribute to a wise kupuna, father, and grandfather of my friends from the Makaliʻi voyaging canoe ʻohana.

ʻIke aku i ke kumu e kū hoʻokahi ana
Kahi hoʻokumu o Kamehameha ʻeā
ʻO ʻĀwini ka ʻāina nona ka lehua ʻeleʻele
He nani maoli nō ʻo Pololū[2]

Eventually, I was able to sing "Nani Pololū" to him surrounded by his ʻohana before he passed. Since then, this mele has become a proud symbol for their ʻohana. I sang this tribute at the graduation party of his great-granddaughter, and the entire ʻohana immediately stood up, made their way to the front, faced the audience and reminisced about Uncle Sonny. Everyone was over come with reverence and tears. Needless to say, I had to pull in all my strength to get through the mele because it was ultimately my kuleana to utter the images of this beloved patriarch and ʻāina that drove this poignant moment.

Our first musical group, Kahikina, was co-founded by Kīhei and Ron Nahale-a, and later included Kalaʻiokona Ontai and Sean Nāleimaile. Having consistent garage jam sessions eventually led to the official creation of our band, as we started gigging for community lūʻaus, weddings, parties, and other celebrations. Our bi-weekly gig at Cronies Bar and Grill in Hilo helped us further hone our skills and increase our repertoire; we eventually recorded a few songs and would hear them on the radio.

Knowing classic Hawaiian music and ʻōlelo Hawaiʻi was extremely important to each one of us. It armed and pushed us to create more mele as a means to continue to document our own history as Hawaiians and to become our own storytellers using the vehicle of music. My earliest compositions focused on my kulāiwi and natural elements of Kauaʻi and Hilo. Exploring vocabulary and metaphor was incredibly exciting, and it was but a tiny scratch on the surface of the depths of Hawaiian perspective.

As I learn more Hawaiian chants and songs, I better understand an important and meaningful way I can contribute to my lāhui as a haku mele—a composer. Haku mele is not something you can just pick up. It certainly requires understanding of our language at higher levels; experience and knowledge of our history, ʻāina, natural elements, and people; and ultimately a serious connection to our kulāiwi. My journey in haku mele is a work in progress: digging deep, making connections, dwelling in perspective, and selecting words and images.

HAKU MELE AS ACTIVISM

As I become more appreciative of my upbringing in the care of my kūpuna, I became further committed to learning about my ʻohana, especially their behaviors and perspectives. My kūpuna, seen and unseen, continue to guide me on this path of enlightenment to better serve our lāhui. From creating mele that make the kūpuna nod or tap their toes, to helping my college students remember Hawaiian sentence patterns, to inspiring hula people to create the visual to my audio, to helping preschool students have more fun in school through singing, to inspiring our youth to appreciate Hawaiian language and music—thereby continuing our mele legacy—I cannot help but embrace this kuleana, and serve.

This service and kuleana to my lāhui is my activism. Oftentimes, activism is negatively associated with radical, outspoken, and perhaps opinionated individuals. However, the root word of activism is "active." Active people are passionate, and passionate people embrace kuleana. There are many layers of comfort levels by which people participate in their activity or activism. My passions of learning, making Hawaiian-language music, cultivating the nation, and travel, have afforded me a profession in education and music with numerous opportunities to stay engaged in cultural practices that connect me to this land and our genealogy.

In all of my political activism surrounding Hawaiian struggles—including Hawaiian language revitalization and education, Native Hawaiian gathering rights, Native Hawaiian health, water rights, Hawaiian governments, and protecting our iwi kūpuna and sacred sites—mele have been and are an important component. Whether to invoke the spirits with the mele pale "Nā ʻAumākua"; to rally our fellow Hawaiians with "I Kū Mau Mau"; to ask for wisdom with "E Hō Mai"; to admonish the oppressor, educate the masses, lift our spirits, or celebrate victories, mele is a common denominator that inspires and supports activism and activists.

Hawaiian music has and shall be used as a tool of empowerment for our nation. Mele exponentially increase the value of our Hawaiʻi. Mele amplify our spirit, our minds, our potential, and our existence. In the "Kumulipo," we have learned of our origins. Our mele pule directly connect us to our gods and ʻohana spirits. We have learned how to honor through mele inoa and mele maʻi, how to heal through mele lāʻau kāhea, and hurt through mele ʻanāʻanā. "E Iho Ana" reveals omens and prophecy. "He ʻAi Na Kalani" shows what Kalākaua was fed, arming him to lead our lāhui. "Ka Wai A Kāne" teaches us the characterization of subtleties in nature. "Eia Hawaiʻi" shows us genealogy and the homelands of Kahiki. Mele show us how to behave. "Kaʻililauokekoa" takes us on a pursuit of a mate, and numerous classic mele hula overflow with examples of physical beauty and tantalizing images of good loving. Our haku mele poetic devices and techniques show us how to remember massive amounts of information. If there's anything any Hawaiian can add to their mana gauge, tool box, or mental rolodex, it is to know Hawaiian mele, for therein lie invaluable lessons and knowledge of our heritage. Learn Hawaiian mele about your area. Sing Hawaiian mele. Let Hawaiian mele inspire you to learn more about our Hawaiian consciousness. Oli. Mele. Hula. Haku.

MELE AS A CONNECTING FORCE

As the popularity of Hawaiian music grows at home and around the globe, my kuleana as a music-maker of Hawaiʻi includes hoʻokele, or the steering of our musical waʻa. Looking back to when I was a young dancer at a hotel show, I see how we provided audiences with a romanticized image of Hawai'i. Many of those songs only lived on that stage; they didn't rate to be sung at our family parties. Mele can be a genuine connecting force when there is integrity. In formal or informal performances, mele integrity permeates introduction of a mele, musicianship, and appearance. Oftentimes, even a humble kanikapila can better produce a higher-level of integrity and intention than a revue catered for tourists. When one has a good command of the language and a genuine understanding of a mele, chanted or sung, you or I can tell the vocalist is not merely reciting words, but delivering images as put forth by the composer. The performer invites you to engage.

In the documentation of my life experiences through haku mele, I believe some of those resulting mele have increased waiwai and connections between Hawaiians, locals, our Pacific cousins, malihini, and people who love Hawai'i and its music. One mele in particular, "E Mau Ē," was a humble tribute to Grand Master Navigator Pius "Papa" Mau Piailug in his homeland of Satawal, Micronesia. The mele was heard, acknowledged, enjoyed, and later sung and danced around the world in our wa'a community and abroad, increasing awareness, maintaining connection, and further honoring our traditions, origins, teachers, lands, oceans, and the auspicious 1999 E Mau voyage on the double-hulled canoe Makali'i, of Kawaihae, Hawai'i.

> *E Mau ē, ka ihu pani ho'okele wa'a*
> *Ho'ohanohano 'ia i kona 'āina hānau iho nō*
> *Makali'i, kahi wa'a no Hawai'i*
> *E holo ana no Maikonekia i ka moana nui ākea*[3]

Other mele, such as "Ka Hīnano O Puna" and "Lei Ho'oheno," have helped encourage courtship and perhaps even the further building of our nation. Hula has indeed brought plenty of attention to some of my compositions, breathing new life into each image. I am humbled to see and hear my mele being performed by others. While in Kaimū, Puna, Hawai'i, "Ka Hīnano O Puna" is sung and accompanied by the sweetest harmonies of Puna and Princess Keli'iho'omalu that blend perfectly like the orange, red, magenta, and purple skies of the evening.

> *'Ena'ena Puna i ke ahi a Pele*
> *'U'ina lā ka hua'ina i Pu'u 'Ō'ō*
> *Pu'ō ke ahi lapalapala i luna*
> *Pūnohunohu i ke ano ahiahi*[4]

The choreography by their sister Lei, cousin Pi'ilani, and numerous nieces, cousins, and friends depicts their deep connection to their 'āina and Pele energies. "Lei Hoʻoheno"—a mele about the loving relationship between mākua and keiki, and kūpuna and moʻopuna—has found much popularity at home and across the sea in Japan through the voice of Weldon Kekauoha. It has been truly heartwarming to see Hawaiian mothers expressing this aloha in hula.

We must maintain integrity in our mele Hawaiʻi: the language, as well as the phrasing and pronunciation. When we uphold this integrity, mele can connect us at its best, like a waʻa carrying us across the ocean. The ʻōlelo noʻeau "I ka ʻōlelo nō ke ola, i ka ʻōlelo nō ka make" and "ʻO ʻoe ka luaahi o kāu mele" are a great guiding star and a steering paddle to stay on course.

MELE AS PEDAGOGY

ʻEʻena Hāʻena i ka ʻehukai, i ka poʻina kai o Makua
Kū aʻe ka pali ʻaʻala lū ʻo Makana o ka ʻōahi[5]

In my role as a teacher of Hawaiian language, storied places, Hawaiian music, and haku mele at Ka Haka ʻUla o Keʻelikōlani, UH Hilo, mele have been an especially fun vehicle to engage the students in memorizing certain language patterns, learning about storied areas, and discussing what determines a mele to be Hawaiian. Kuleana comes with the territory: if they learn it they become responsible for it, whether they are from Hawaiʻi or not.

In my class, composition starts with recognizing and researching the numerous types of mele our kūpuna composed. We reflect on and look at the patterns in familiar Hawaiian tunes that surround us. Likewise, haku mele requires strengthening our observation of natural elements and using older mele as primary sources. We need to constantly create mele to define our times. It need not be reserved for the upper echelon of musicians, but we must learn from them to be able to create mele of quality and constant improvement.

Music is one of the most powerful tools to connect with young learners. Our public schools should not devalue our music. They should in fact learn how to infuse music as a tool of choice in all their content requirements. Culture- and place-based education through music can help engage and heal the nation.

This type of education, and our kuleana of music and ʻāina, have been exemplified in Project Kuleana. In 2013, a small group of talented friends and former bandmates produced two impressive music videos, "Kaulana Nā Pua" and "All Hawaiʻi Stands Together," featuring over a dozen of Hawaiian music's finest, including Palani Vaughan, Kekuhi Kealiʻikanakaʻole, the Brown ʻOhana of Hilo, and Kealiʻi Reichel performing and recording live in distinct locales across Hawaiʻi. My mother and I were fortunate to have been invited to participate in these first-class videos, which have since gone viral. The videos are evidence that mele are important, relevant, brilliant, and that mele can stand alone as haʻawina of history, language arts, fine arts, geography, current events, and more.

HAʻINA ʻIA MAI KA PUANA

Haʻina kou inoa e Kuʻulei, kuʻu lei hōkū o nā Hilo ʻekolu[6]

My future vision for Hawaiʻi is that all forms of Hawaiian music thrive, anchored in the language of the land and with plenty of room for innovation. I hear Hawaiians freely chanting, because we understand our mele and their functions. I see souls inspired to get to know our Hawaiian selves better. I see my ʻohana, community, and lāhui embracing our multiple kuleana and communicating in our mother tongue. In our own ways, we are all taking the baby steps necessary to grow our lāhui. Ola nō ke mele Hawaiʻi!

NOTES

1. Kainani Kahaunaele, "Lei Hoʻoheno," performed and recorded by Weldon Kekauoha, *Ka Lehua ʻUla* (ʻOhelo Records, 2007), CD. All lyrics quoted in this essay were written by the author.

2. Kainani Kahaunaele, "Nani Pololū," performed and recorded by Kahikina and Kainani Kahaunaele, Cronies Bar & Grill (Oki Leo Productions, 1999), CD.

3. Kainani Kahaunaele, "E Mau Ē," *Naʻu ʻOe* (ʻAha Pūnana Leo, 2003), CD.

4. Kainani Kahaunaele, "Ka Hīnano O Puna," *Naʻu ʻOe.*

5. Kainani Kahaunaele, "Only 2 U," *Naʻu ʻOe.*

6. Kainani Kahaunaele, "Hāʻenaala Sweeting," performed and recorded by Darryl Gonzales, *Into Existence* (Levine & Pendragon, 2013), CD.

RESOURCES FOR FURTHER INFORMATION AND INSPIRATION

1. Living Hawaiian Culture Resource, at http://www.kumukahi.org.

2. Hawaiian Online Library, at http://ulukau.org.

3. Nūpepa Blog and resources for Hawaiian-language newspapers, at http://nupepa-hawaii.com.

4. Project Kuleana website, at http://www.facebook.com/ProjectKULEANA.

5. ʻŌiwi TV website and online videos, at http://www.oiwi.tv.

KALIHI CALLS

DAWN MAHI

Let our children rest in a place
where thousands of stories
have been told.

With the ocean and sky no longer a refuge,
our loneliness eats up the walls,
clings like thick flesh to our hearts,
dragging us down.

Our community—
this constellation of unstrung stars,
lost in place.

THE BEGINNING

I feel a visceral connection with the mountains of our home. Their cracks and crevices like folds in my heart, razor knuckles reaching for heaven; seeking taut liberation from the ocean, drawing down the sky.

In the middle, we find our place between peaks and shoreline and beyond. During small-kid time, Hawai'i was everything. Our island kingdom was all around everywhere and there wasn't anything that wasn't this. My parallel flat planet, our infinite oasis.

When my family moved away, I didn't know what I didn't know. In geography class, a colonized map had been imprinted in my mind. Knowing, yet unknowing. With the death of my loving Hawaiian grandfather we were free to go. So my parents took us and they tried.

But I came back. Not only because of all the things that everyone loves, but because I was called. The mountains in all their verdant, invaded glory, sometimes ominous, shifty, possessed by gods and ancestors; the mountains came in my dreams and brought me home. And I am privileged to be home, in the place where my grandparents were born.

It took me a long time to return. Now that I've been back for six years, I work surrounded by mountains deep in a Koʻolau valley. This homecoming has been so important to me in many ways because of what I've learned working in Kalihi. Kalihi has crystallized for me the significance of ʻāina, home, and stories, and what can happen in their absence. Kalihi is a reminder and a message about the importance of claiming and reclaiming our narratives to create the kind of future we want our great-grandchildren to enjoy.

NEIGHBORS BEING NEIGHBORLY

Kalihi is a densely populated immigrant community where challenges such as our high cost of living, colonization, assimilation, and discrimination make it hard to succeed alone. At Kōkua Kalihi Valley Comprehensive Family Services, the community has worked towards "healing, reconciliation, and the alleviation of suffering in Kalihi Valley" for forty years. Yes, we have doctors and dentists, but also comprehensive elder programs, a youth bike shop, sewing program, a cultural café, a women's shelter, a credit union, a 99-acre nature preserve—and more.

The family-style motto of KKV—"neighbors being neighborly"—addresses Kalihi's challenges and strengths through building strong relationships that honor culture and foster health and harmony. One of the most important ways this happens is by telling stories. Our stories come from all over, because Kalihi is like a reflection of the liquid nation, the Pacific Ocean. Chinese, Japanese, Portuguese, Marshallese, Chuukese, Filipino, Sāmoan—and more. In Kalihi, aunties say: "Sāmoan medicine for Sāmoan illness, Western medicine for Western illness." The Chuukese aunties, they say: "Angang chek aramas, aramas chek angang," meaning "people are everything." We are everything. We know who we are because of each other, our cultures, our ʻāina, and our relationships.

This understanding influences everything we do. KKV started in donated trailers, led by a diverse handful of pastors and aunties going door to door, wanting to help their neighbors and build bridges across different cultures. Relationships. Not all of what we suffer from can be fixed with a prescription; we need the right medicine for the right illness. In that spirit, we seek to provide support for all of Kalihi's stories.

Being a small part of this work has meant so much to me, because the mission of KKV supports people where they are at and uplifts community strengths. I really believe in that. At KKV there is a host of aunties and uncles who look out for the community and take care of all of us. This happens through heartful listening and reciprocal sharing. The aunties and uncles hold our stories and weave them together; they describe how the breakdown in traditional systems and transition to economic-based relationships over generations has made us unwell. They seek to find a middle path: to succeed in this modern world, we need not only to work hard and get a good education, but also to respect traditions and pass down cultural values and heritage languages. Following their examples, as we work we learn to take care of each other, and ourselves. This creates a sense of family that is so important.

THE SCIENCE OF CONSTELLATIONS

Finally, western sciences are coming around to agree with our Kalihi kūpuna that in health, what makes us healthy is the strength of our relationships. How much stress are you experiencing? What's your support network? Are you connected to your culture? Who will teach you what is right and what is wrong, and show you that you are loved and important along the way? What stories do you have to tell? The strength of our networks—that constellation—will determine our future success, and help us navigate through rough waters. It will bring us home.

In the storytelling that we do at KKV, we seek to provide a physical and spiritual place where those who are away from their home can return—even while in Kalihi, which may be far from where their ancestors slept. Sharing becomes a way to make the community strong, generation to generation. As we connect to each other, we can celebrate our differences and our commonalities and address traumas, co-creating new stories together. We begin to see ourselves in each other and release our fears; we are not alone in our struggles.

Everyone needs to belong. However, the outside world would teach us that because we seem different we shouldn't get along, that if we don't have money we are not worthy. That same world artificially divides us, despite our common roots. All of this takes away our humanity. We fight for the crumbs of an economic pie when pie is not the recipe of our people. We evaluate and judge each other based on foreign inherited values; we blame each other for stealing resources, ignoring the sources of our conflicts. This perpetuates a negative system that reinforces the disparities in Kalihi, and everywhere in Hawai'i. How can we belong like this? Who will look for the strengths in our community if we don't do it ourselves?

in news media statistics and school
we have heard many stories
our failure has been foretold.

from the shadows
systems expectantly watch

stacking paperwork
like kindling
haphazardly
seeking our demise
burning the stars from the sky
with their indifference.

seemingly forsaken,
this refuge for so many

Kalihi calls
patiently awaiting our return.

NĀ KEIKI O KA ʻĀINA

Too many kids quickly learn to be ashamed of their cultures and of being from Kalihi. Two strikes! Where does that shame come from? Is it true that we suck, that we should feel shame just by being born? No way. To dismantle that, we have to look at the structure beneath what's happening around us, and see how it has isolated us and taught us to judge each other.

One day after a great tapioca harvest at KKV's nature preserve, a group of aunties taught us traditional recipes from Chuuk. With machete and picks, they cut fresh coconuts the way they did at home in their own islands, grinding the meat and squeezing fresh milk. I noticed that as they peeled, chopped, boiled, and prepared, a young grandson of three years watched with bright-eyed interest.

For that young one, it was a chance to see his aunties and grandma as experts, deftly wielding coconuts and knives to produce tasty, nourishing home food that they don't often get to enjoy. They laughed, talked, and shared; we all learned something new. How can our youth see and feel that pride all the time, knowing that their culture and community can provide physical, social, and spiritual sustenance? When we are able embrace our kuleana to sustain the ʻāina and each other, we perpetuate and validate something ancient and necessary deep within ourselves.

Those aunties are far from their beloved one hānau—their birthplace—and may never be able to return. The little boy might never visit there, may never see the home of his ancestors. Yet, on the ʻāina in Kalihi that day, they all felt home. That is true health.

Kalihi, which has such a rich and historied Hawaiian soul, has become an immigrant place, full of stories, but also silences. Why did our parents and grandparents move to Kalihi, or in the case of Native Hawaiians, move away?

What dreams did they have? What do they hope we will accomplish? Are there enough resources for us to be able to achieve their dreams? And what of our own dreams? We have to know that our own dreams have value. Our grandparents lament that we don't know the old stories, know our culture. Our values and understanding of success have changed over time. If we are going to break the horizon and seek another future different than what is foretold, we need reconciliation: where have we come from, what can the future be? Could we co-create a story for ourselves that has space for all of these things?

STORY SHARING

At KKV, we try to make spaces for stories to unfold in several ways. Story sharing and mapping aren't formulas with a known end. They are organic value systems to help each other find our place in the community through connecting to others. Validation. Often, stories manifest themselves around a table with tasty food where we explore community questions and issues, taking time to get to know each other as people. This can happen in the KKV lunchroom, during community meetings or events, or anywhere.

Through these processes we seek to slow down and listen deeply. We build story sharing into our activities as much as we can, following the lead of the original aunties who built relationships door-to-door. We hold support groups for caregivers, mommies, and people with chronic health issues. Hundreds of elders gather to dance together weekly for "senior exercise" at our Gulick and Kūhiō Park Terrace Elder Centers. We have weekly volunteer days on the land at Hoʻoulu ʻĀina Nature Preserve, where people can get their hands dirty and make friends. We bring a range of service providers together to figure out how to serve people better; we ask the community to help us do a better job by sharing their values and dreams. As community workers, we also share our own dreams and plans and make space to vision together.

This reciprocal community process is important because many of the most recent migrants to Kalihi come from places where small communities have a role for each member, including children. By fulfilling their role, individuals support the well-being of the whole and feel a sense of collective belonging and purpose. My friend from the Mortlock Islands told me that as a child, her job was to start the daily fire. When she could see the smoke from her aunties' cooking fires she could orient herself to the day, knew when it was time to begin. And in the ritual of helping to start that fire every morning, as a child she knew she was important.

What smoke do we have now that tells us we are a part of something larger than ourselves? Nowadays, with individual apartments and paychecks, we are flung to a nameless wind and must survive on our own. It can be so bewildering and isolating. When this same friend moved to Hawai'i to attend college at Honolulu Community College, she was terrified and everything was new. She had to learn on her own how to navigate. Being from one of the first Chuukese families to live in Kalihi Valley Homes, she was afraid and alone. However, she is from a clan of navigators including Papa Mau. Over time she found her place, and Kalihi keeps calling her back to help her people and all others who struggle to make a home in Hawai'i.

STORIES AS MAPS AND CONSTELLATIONS

The "mapping" part of this storytelling process takes our organic values and practices of human connections and puts them together in one place. Mapping also helps us to tell other stories, such as histories of the land, of our ancestors, and of other things like demographics, health data, political history, social forces, and research. It helps us constellate all these things in one place that can be shared and more fully understood, by seeing each singular story or data piece all together. By showing the deep interconnectedness between all these things we can illuminate cause-and-effect relationships that impact our lives, positively and negatively. Solely *exposing* stories of Kalihi is not our end goal. Through contextualizing these narratives and a deeper understanding of the relationships between them, we can better our community. Many organizations around the world have begun to do this story work, and seek to share the strengths of their community, or illuminate disparities to create change.

We started a new ad hoc group called "Kalihi Calls" that includes people who care about the community, from kūpuna to providers to students and professors. We take our inspiration from the peak Kilohana in the back of the valley, the ancestral home of Papahānaumoku and Wākea, earth mother and sky father. The hui has started to visit our own personal "sacred" places in the community, talking story and discussing Kalihi as a symbol of transformation. We want to invite anyone who cares about Kalihi or has a story to share to join our humble project.

Eventually we will create maps and a story database that can be shared on the internet. The maps would have many layers to show different parts of Kalihi's community, and history. These maps could be a way to experience Kalihi's past, present, and future with a click of a button.

But maybe that's moving too fast. When we began, one of our mentors, who is a great community peace leader, warned us of the dangers of mapping our community, making everything known, focusing on technology to suddenly expose our universe. Everything is so instant these days, she said, and our ancestors weren't instant people. What do you lose in the process of revealing everything?

Considering this advice, we are taking it slow. Now we find that we are gently rediscovering the sacred not just in Kalihi, but in ourselves. This happens through discussion, introspection, and pilgrimage, not just charting points on a map or maintaining a database. Our participating kūpuna have enjoyed guiding this process. In each other we find the path and stars; together we make our way.

'O KA HĀ O KA 'ĀINA KE OLA O KA PO'E

At KKV's 99-acre nature preserve, there are ancient walls deep in the 'ili of Māluawai. These pā pōhaku are evidence and hold energy for what once was —in Kalihi Valley, many hands once turned to the soil, and kalo grew abundantly in the uplands. The breath of the land truly was the life of the people. This is a different story than many stereotypes that abound today, depicting Kalihi people with hands open, grabbing for resources. The walls are a constant reminder of how much potential we have to grow and thrive, that we *are* worthy. They teach us that we are productive, and capable of growing food to feed so many people while also living a life of reciprocal nourishment and respect with the land. How is that not a model of a good life?

As staff and volunteers began to uncover and restore the walls, they realized that water used to flow there long ago and fed a large lo'i system. With each new wall, we reclaim our understanding of how the ancestors lived and worked in the valley, and we reclaim our own kuleana to perpetuate this story.

After years of restoration and clearing, the ko'ilipilipi rains of Kalihi inspired a small spring to emerge in the back of the valley, and water flowed by the walls once more. The spring only appears after a hard rain, but it feels like a hō'ailona—a sign of what is to come. If we all hold the vision and see the water, it will come. It will come because it was always there, waiting our return.

THE BEGINNING

Let our children rest in a place
where thousands of stories
have been told.

With the ocean and sky our forever refuge,
love expands the walls
of our hearts,
urging us on and on and on.

Our home—
this constellation of shining stars,
reminding us who we are.

Mark Twain once proclaimed that "Kalihi is the Valley of Enchantment come again," describing velvet green verdant mountain walls and a "vast green veil" of koa and kukui forests. Can you imagine a Kalihi like that? The community has changed so much since that time, and a lot of what he saw seems to be gone. However, even if the ground has been paved over, the ʻāina is still underneath; seeds lie dormant in the soil, biding their time. Our potential is here, and it is time now for a positive change. We must come together as a community if we want to achieve success and happiness, on our own terms. It's not that we will return to a romanticized idyll of our ancestors' past; however, we are the ones with the unique potential at this right time to create hybrid models of true health. We can excel while not forsaking our indigenous values and identities. We are stronger if we work together.

In the end the value of Hawaiʻi cannot be determined by one person alone. Here I can only share what it means to me, and that I want to sit and hear you share what it means to you. If we do that over and over again with many people, maybe then we'll know. Hawaiʻi has taught me that the most important thing that we do here is to take the time to value relationships, to hear and feel stories that are important. We keep traditions alive by passing them down, by telling those same stories over and over again until they become a part of who we are, until we become part of this land, timeless.

In my own way I can relate to the story of Kalihi. I have been lucky enough to be able to come back to Hawaiʻi, reconnect, and try to integrate all the stories I've experienced into who I am today. Seeing the pā pōhaku transform in Māluawai reminds me that I can transform too. Having left here so young, I tried to belong in a new place, didn't have enough resources, and felt disconnected from my source. Now when I look at the Koʻolau, I feel at home, and there's a sense of belonging and safety instead of fear. This inspires me to do what I can to help others feel the same.

However, this is just part of my story and the story of one small organization, KKV. What's yours?

RESOURCES FOR FURTHER INFORMATION AND INSPIRATION

1. The "Kalihi Calls" website, at http://www.kalihicalls.com.
2. "Exploring the History of Maunalua," at www.maunalua.net.
3. John McKnight and Peter Black, *The Abundant Community: Awakening the Power of Families and Neighborhoods* (San Francisco: Berrett-Koehler, 2010).
4. *Map Your World: A Global Network of Young People Making Real Change*, at www.mapyourworld.org.

I AM A FARMER

U'ILANI ARASATO

You should stop and listen,
the ʻāina is trying to speak.

Screaming for a voice to be heard over planning and development: can you hear it?

Building blocks stacked on rich soils from the works of our kūpuna before us, dirt-stained hands embedded into the creases of our ʻāina: can you feel it?

Overturned lifestyles and agreements between Aliʻi and Makaʻāinana as promised to work the land for generations to come, but you see, where is our land?

Farmers that fight for the right to produce food for you.

See, I am a farmer, holding strength and determination in my left hand, a pick and a pen in my right; while love, respect, and the willingness to work reside in my heart.

You see, I am a farmer.

Concrete mixes bury my boots as I stand here and fight, what about us?

See, 100 new jobs that they put in our visions even though they know we would never be able to reach them.

Potential drained bodies wait for answers as promises are being broken by people who don't even know my first name.

By people who don't bother to stick around to hear what I have to say.

Money-hungry monsters rip their claws of envy into our ʻāina, blindly leading us into a deep bucket with all the other ʻAʻama crabs trying to fight their way out.

With no guarantee of our future or a lifeline to help pull us out, what is the point?

They say this is my future, then why is it so dark?

Causing chaos upon chaos at intersecting roads that can never be re-routed.
Causing inconveniences to us while you convenience other people.
Spending money we don't have on things we don't need.

Why?

Do you say that the youth can't be farmers even as we picket outside your homes, screaming that we are here.

Learning like our kūpuna. We're trying.
Instilling values that we partake of in our everyday lives, handing us an education that we alone would never be able to afford.

See, I'm just trying to make it out like everyone else, but still.

With your signatures and forced handshakes you ignore our hard work, as we struggle, striving for a better tomorrow for our children and our children's children.

I hope that one day my children will be able to see all of this . . . but how?
When soon the 'Āina will be covered in concrete. See, this will never cease to exist.

But luckily, like my kūpuna, I know this . . .

When I plan for a year I'll plant Kalo.
When I plan for ten I'll plant Koa.
But if I'm planning for a hundred or more years then I'll teach my keiki how to Mālama 'āina, and in return the 'āina will take care of them.

So if you ever find time between your busy schedules, stop.
Try and listen because I promise that you can hear it as it is trying to speak
   to you.
So push aside your signatures and forced handshakes, and listen to me.

My name is U'ilani Hideko Kalawe O Kou Ola Ana Kokaua Pulama Arasato.
I am a Farmer.

Who Are You?

TELL THEM

KATHY JETNIL-KIJINER

I prepared the package
for my friends in the states

the dangling earrings
woven into half-moons black pearls glinting
like an eye in a storm of tight spirals

the baskets
sturdy
also woven
brown cowry shells shiny
intricate mandalas shaped
by calloused fingers

Inside the basket
I write this message:

Wear these earrings
to parties to your classes and meetings
to the grocery store, the corner store
and while riding the bus

Store jewelry, incense, copper coins
and curling letters like this one
in this basket

and when others ask you
where you got this
you tell them

they're from the Marshall Islands

show them where it is on a map
tell them we are a proud people
toasted dark brown as the carved ribs
of a tree stump
tell them we are descendants
of the finest navigators in the world
tell them our islands were dropped
from a basket
carried by a giant
tell them we are the hollow hulls
of canoes as fast as the wind
slicing through the pacific sea
we are wood shavings
and drying pandanus leaves
and sticky bwiros at kemems
tell them we are sweet harmonies
of grandmothers mothers aunties and sisters
songs late into night
tell them we are whispered prayers
the breath of God
a crown of fuchsia flowers encircling
aunty mary's white sea foam hair
tell them we are styrofoam cups of koolaid red
waiting patiently for the ilomij
we are papaya golden sunsets bleeding
into a glittering open sea
we are skies uncluttered
majestic in their sweeping landscape
we are the ocean
terrifying and regal in its power
tell them we are dusty rubber slippers
swiped
from concrete doorsteps
we are the ripped seams
and the broken door handles of taxis
we are sweaty hands shaking another sweaty hand in heat
tell them
we are days
and nights hotter
than anything you can imagine
tell them we are little girls with braids
cartwheeling beneath the rain

we are shards of broken beer bottles
burrowed beneath fine white sand
we are children flinging
like rubber bands
across a road clogged with chugging cars
tell them
we only have one road

and after all this

tell them about the water

how we have seen it rising
flooding across our cemeteries
gushing over our sea walls
and crashing against our homes

tell them what it's like
to see the entire ocean___level___with the land

tell them
we are afraid

tell them we don't know
of the politics
or the science
but tell them we see
what is in our own backyard

tell them that some of us
are old fishermen who believe that God
made us a promise

tell them some of us
are a little bit more skeptical of God

but most importantly
tell them
we don't want to leave
we've never wanted to leave

and that we
are nothing
without our islands.

KULEANA AND DEVELOPING HAWAI'I RESPONSIBLY

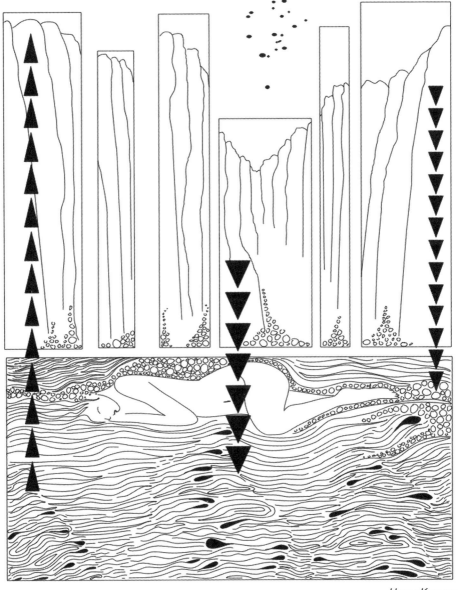

HALEY KAILIEHU

HONORING THE FAMILY OF KTA SUPER STORES

DEREK KURISU

I started working at Taniguchi Supermarket, founded in 1916 and known today as KTA Super Stores, when I was just sixteen years old. I am a third generation (sansei) Japanese, the second son of three boys and two girls, born and raised on the Hakalau sugar plantation on the Hāmākua coast of the Big Island. I am not a family member, but the Taniguchis treat me like family. I have been employed at KTA Super Stores for forty-five years. When I started, Taniguchi Supermarket had a store in Downtown Hilo, and in Kailua-Kona, at the King Kamehameha Hotel, and had just built the Pūʻāinakō Street store in Hilo. Today, there are also stores in Waimea, Keauhou, and Village Market in Waikoloa.

I first worked for the founder, Mr. Koichi Taniguchi, a petite, humble man who wore a three-quarter sleeve white shirt with khaki pants. He swept the entrance of the store daily, and walked about the store to greet and thank his customers, employees, and suppliers on a daily basis. He was often mistaken for the janitor. The humble way he carried himself inspired me to work even harder. While working part-time and attending school, I had the privilege of driving him home and between stores in his car. This gave me an opportunity to get to know this brilliant person. His sons—Yukiwo, Hidetoshi, and Tony—followed in his footsteps.

I am now working with the fourth generation of Taniguchis. There are very few articles or publications about KTA because the Taniguchi family didn't believe in publicizing anything about the family or KTA. The energy was spent performing and executing their duties and what they believed was right. This is why I am telling this story from my perspective and my involvement as an employee at KTA, starting as a "bag boy" at sixteen years old to becoming the Executive Vice-President of KTA today. This is a story about KTA as a successful local business, but also a story about Hawaiʻi families, and about respecting and honoring those who came before, about caring for those who are coming after.

CARRYING A 100-POUND BAG OF RICE

It is 2:15 p.m. The school bell rings at Hilo High School, ending another day of classes. It is also the beginning for me: a sixteen-year-old youngster's first day at a job that would eventually grow into a career. I was hired by KTA because my older brother was already employed there. It was as simple as that in those days. If you had a family member working that was a hard worker, the next sibling was almost automatically hired.

As I recall, one of the requirements to work as a "bag boy," called "courtesy clerk" today, was being able to carry a 100-pound bag of rice on your shoulders. In the Japanese tradition, rice was considered a sacred commodity, so we were taught to handle it with respect. I had wanted to work for Taniguchi Supermarket since I was fifteen, so my father encouraged me to start practicing at home carrying a 100-pound bag of rice. At that time, rice came in 100-pound bags; chicken, pig, rabbit, and horse feed weighed 50 to 80 pounds each. He told us we shouldn't use a wagon, and even if two bags were purchased, we needed to carry one bag on each shoulder. My training paid off! I got hired the following year. After a year of bagging groceries, I became a stock clerk.

Since I knew the owners and managers were constantly observing the part-time workers, and my friends in the sugar plantation also needed jobs, I worked hard to impress the owners. I wanted them to know that plantation students were hard workers with good work ethics. So, if the stock clerks carried one case of Vienna sausage, I carried three cases. When they walked, I ran. I arrived fifteen minutes before work and volunteered for any job regardless of how undesirable it was. I cleaned toilets, unloaded containers of rice, peeled rotten potatoes, whatever job the other workers didn't want to do. And yes, my friends got jobs at KTA. Perhaps this type of community-oriented thinking enabled me eventually to become the Executive Vice President of KTA.

A "FAMILY OF FAMILIES" AT HAKALAU

Growing up on Hakalau, a sugar plantation along the Hāmākua coast, fifteen miles from Hilo, we learned to respect our elders and treat everyone with dignity and respect. Since we were all poor, we looked at how individuals behaved and carried themselves, not what they possessed. Regardless of our race, age, religion, or character, we lived together as one big family, and saw the positive in everyone. The fishermen fished, the gardeners raised the vegetables, the hunters provided the meat, the mechanics fixed the car, the carpenters fixed the homes, the baseball players coached the kids' team, etc. etc. Everyone had strengths and used them to contribute to the plantation community.

Today, I think about all those who volunteered and sacrificed, like our scoutmaster, baseball and basketball coach, and aikido instructor, so we could have those experiences like the wealthier families. Those teachers somehow found the money to purchase uniforms, equipment, and food, and provided the transportation to the games. The retired seniors watched over the neighborhood so the entire plantation camp was our playground. There were people in the community who took the time to teach us how to swim, fish, live off the land, and even create our own entertainment. We were a family of families creating the force, energy, and strength of thousands of individuals working together.

While we were growing up, my grandmother, Shizue Kurisu, constantly reminded my brothers, sisters, and me not to get into trouble because it would tarnish our family name. This motivated me to stay out of trouble (or at least try not to get caught if I did something bad!). It also motivated me to do good to make my grandparents, parents, and family members proud! My grandmother passed away over thirty years ago, but I still follow her teachings. So today, wherever I go or whatever I do, I know I represent not only myself but everyone I'm associated with: KTA, my family, my friends, the people of Hawai'i, the plantation people, and all the organizations I'm associated with. This motivates me to work hard and try my best.

HUGE CHANGES, FROM SUGAR TO MOUNTAIN APPLES

As I worked my way up to becoming Vice President, I reported to Tony Taniguchi, the youngest of the Taniguchis and the company President, who passed away in 1989. Tony cared about people and always helped his employees, business associates, and community. I considered him to be my mentor and obligated myself to carry out his mission. At times, I couldn't fathom his style of leadership. I used to be a believer in the plantation mentality of obedience through fear of the boss. But Tony taught me a different approach than "my way or the highway." He hired a young, savvy, educated management team. Most of us didn't have degrees or prior leadership experience in business. I had an Agriculture degree and was amazed when he put me in charge of the entire perishable operation. He trusted us with million-dollar decisions. When mistakes were made, he did not reprimand us by demotion or letting us go. He forced us to be innovative, progressive, and different.

Several years before he passed away, he told me I needed to help the families when the sugar plantation closed. Growing up in an environment where sugar was our lifeline, I never ever believed this huge industry could disappear in my lifetime, and still wasn't convinced it was going to happen. A year after his death, though, the sugar mills started to close. One mill after another! Wow, now I had this obligation. I thought about it for weeks and decided that I should create a private label brand consisting of locally grown and manufactured products. The goals were to create jobs, revitalize the island economy, and fulfill my obligation to the sugar plantation families. We named this label the Mountain Apple Brand.

Mountain apple, or ʻōhiʻa ʻai, was one of the twenty-four "canoe plants" brought to Hawaiʻi by Polynesian voyagers over 1,500 years ago. Growing up, eating a sweet, juicy mountain apple was always a treat. We ate it tree-ripened because the fruit ripens at once, and the thin skin is easily bruised. These qualities make it not feasible to be commercially farmed, so owners of a tree usually give the fruit away and share it with others. When working on this project I felt the trees were disappearing, due to invasive species, disease, birds, and people not being concerned, and that the Mountain Apple Brand could help to educate people about the importance of preservation—not just the preservation of a natural species, but also the great-tasting recipes, traditions, and values of our ancestors, who made us who we are today. We need to use the greatness of the past to continue making our world a better place for future generations.

So the nightmare journey of building this idea started, and I spent many hours working with people, organizations, and businesses. With my agriculture degree and supermarket experience, I knew that most farmers failed not because of a lack of agricultural skills but because of a lack of marketing skills. Farmers or manufacturers often produce excess or inferior products, causing price decreases. So I decided the basic rule for Mountain Apple Brand would be to have one supplier per item. This would encourage a diversity of products within the farming community, rather than dog-eat-dog competition. If our beans farmer sold us beans for a dollar a pound and another farmer came to us to sell his beans for 50 cents a pound, the rule was we would still purchase beans from the original farmer at a dollar. I would then encourage the other farmer to grow another product we were importing from the mainland. With this philosophy, I helped our farmers and manufacturers develop higher quality products and improve production, enabling them to compete with the imports, even at a higher price. Today at KTA, about 95 percent of our leafy vegetables, 45 percent of our beef, 100 percent of our bananas and papayas, and 90 percent of our melons are local. We are the only island with dairies, and our private label milk is 100 percent locally produced and manufactured. Today, 20 years after the fall of the sugar industry, we have about 60 different partnerships and 220 products under the Mountain Apple Brand label.

Like in my childhood days in Hakalau, the strength of Mountain Apple Brand lies in people and businesses working together toward one goal and direction. All Mountain Apple Brand suppliers understand that they are part of a family of 60 other businesses. There's no greed, jealousy, or competition among suppliers. No matter how large or small the supplier, everyone is treated equally and is equally important. We work with our suppliers to insure they are profitable and the products are of the highest quality. We give preferential display location, help to reduce overstock, and price advantage on Mountain Apple Brand Products to maximize sales and profits.

To insure that local ethnic foods can still be consumed in the future, ethnic dishes—such as tsukemono, dried 'ōpelu, 28 different kinds of poke, Portuguese sweet bread and Portuguese sausage, blood sausage, wild boar sausage, mochi and manju, cascaron and bibinka—are all manufactured locally and sold under Mountain Apple Brand. We also have products to ease family meal preparation, such as laulau and kālua pork to microwave; marinated chicken, pork, and beef for hibachi, broiling, or pan frying; pancit, chop sui, stir fry vegetables, stewing vegetables, nishime vegetables; and marinades and seasoning.

Today, the success of the brand provides the opportunity for me to speak at conventions, private and public organizations, and schools, and Mountain Apple Brand products are used as teaching tools in my speeches. One example I would bring along is the Mountain Apple Brand PAVA, a drink made of locally grown papaya, guava, pineapple, and sugar. It was created by the College of Tropical Agriculture and Human Resources students (CTAHR) at the University of Hawai'i at Mānoa; manufactured in Hilo at the Meadow Gold Dairy Processing Plant, utilizing local water as well as labor; and the carton was designed by local artist Eddy Yamamoto. The product is 100 percent local and created to utilize surplus or off-grade papayas, which helps the farmers and industry. I use the PAVA story to teach about the importance of turning waste into value, about innovation, and the importance of supporting "local." Another example is the design on Mountain Apple Brand milk cartons. The carton contains 100 percent local milk and features the design of a cow in a beautiful Hawaiian pasture. Displaying the cartons together creates an impact of hundreds of cows in a large Hawaiian pasture. The milk cartons are used to show the power and impact of working together.

Through this project, we have realized the importance of supporting local agriculture, manufacturing, businesses, organizations, institutions, and communities to help keep money on our island. Local manufacturing creates value-added products with agricultural surplus and off-graded products. Local manufacturing creates jobs, and helps to export Hawai'i food items to the rest of the world. The success of the brand helps to promote buying local, and educates businesses and students about the importance of working together. Hopefully the philosophy behind Mountain Apple Brand creates a ripple effect, encouraging people and organizations to work together on common opportunities and similar beliefs. This helps to remove those walls and barriers so everyone can focus on what is good for the organization instead of themselves.

FOR GENERATIONS TO COME

KTA tries to do our part to provide the people of Hawai'i with all of their food and household needs. We also try our best to support our community to make our island a better place to live. We try to think outside of the box of a regular supermarket, and try to give back in other ways. For example, in the year 2000, I began to be disturbed by negative stories I saw spreading in our news media and ruining this beautiful place. I decided to create a television program, *Living in Paradise*, so people would be able to see all the great things happening on our island. For the past fourteen years, we have had an hour of programming for seniors as well as an hour-long family television program that airs every morning and evening on the Big Island, and on You-Tube via the KTA website. Currently, I'm digitizing the old programs so all of the positive people and events happening in our community can be shared for generations to come. In these ways, we continue to adapt and tell the stories of our island community. I hope to continue to share the lessons I learned growing up on the sugar plantation and working for KTA, treating people as family, and taking care of my community.

We live in the home of the Aloha Spirit, and I believe that businesses, organizations, our government, and people need to live with Aloha. We need to provide our youth with social skills and the values of the past in addition to the technical skills they are learning today. To learn to listen and keep an open mind to what people are saying. To respect the beliefs of others, providing those beliefs are for the good of humanity. I follow the philosophy of kaizen, where one must always strive to improve yourself, your area of responsibility, your community. Finally, I am a strong believer in respecting and learning from our elders. They worked hard and made many sacrifices. We need to learn their values and pass them on to future generations. Many of these values are found in the stories they tell.

ACKNOWLEDGMENTS

While working for KTA, I discovered that sales people selling products to KTA were of a different breed. Unlike average cut-throat businessmen, they worked together to insure the survival of their customers and fellow associates:

old timers helping the newcomers, sales people helping to entertain their associates' bosses during their inspection visitation. These special people worked as a group and not as individuals, spending more time together than with their families. Daily cocktail hour, monthly traveling to Kona and Maui, twice-a-week golf outings, twice-a-month fishing trips, daily card games and meals together made up the schedule of this tough group of people. It might seem glamorous, but it was a hard job. Although some of them are not here today, I will always remember them. They were all down-to-earth people who acknowledged and joked with even a part-time student helper like me.

Mr. Morimoto (Bonsan), Mr. Makino (Mac), Mr. Mashiyama (Mashi), Mr. Matsumoto (Masa), Mr. Kohashi (Saka), Mr. Horiuchi (Glen), Mr. Kondo (Bones), Mr. Maeda (Tiko), Mr. Kado (Fat), Mr. Hamane (Tada), Mr. Furuya (Porky), Mr. Oka (Bob), Mr. Yoshimoto (Roy), Mr. Sakamoto (Terry), Mr. Enoki (Tiger), Mr. Miyashiro (Curly), Mr. Machida (Mike), Mr. Kunishima (Poto), and the list goes on and on. To the others, too numerous to mention, my apologies. These were the salespeople who dedicated countless hours to our store. Many of them have retired but remained loyal customers. Some of them have physically left us but will remain in our memories. These sales people are the pioneers of the food business on the Big Island. Every year on the 2nd of January, I think of all of them. In the old days, every one of them, regardless of how much they celebrated New Years, would be there bright and early helping us with our store inventory. I thank them for helping to make KTA what it is today.

RESOURCES FOR FURTHER INFORMATION AND INSPIRATION

1. The KTA Super Stores website, at http://www.ktasuperstores.com.

2. The *Living in Paradise* TV show can be viewed on the KTA Stores YouTube channel, at http://www.youtube.com/user/KTAStores.

3. "Derek Kurisu: Championing Food Sustainability in Hawaii," *Long Story Short with Leslie Wilcox* (PBS Hawaii, 2012). This interview can be viewed online, at http://www.pbshawaii.org/ourproductions/longstory_guests/kurisu.htm.

4. Brad Watanabe, "Hawaii Snapshot—'The Enemy is From the Mainland,'" *Civil Beat* August 23, 2013, at http://www.civilbeat.com/articles/2013/08/23/19746-hawaii-snapshot-the-enemy-is-from-the-mainland.

LĀNA'I'S COMMUNITY WEALTH

CONSUELO AGARPAO GOUVEIA

GROWING UP INDEPENDENT AND INTERDEPENDENT ON LĀNA'I

Being born and raised on the island of Lana'i is unique in itself. In fact, I was one of the last babies to be born at the hospital there in 1978. They stopped delivering babies completely in 1979, instead sending moms to Maui. The community at that time was predominantly Japanese and Hawaiian, but I am full Filipino. But there wasn't one main group on the island of Lāna'i; we never thought of ourselves as different ethnic groups but more as one big 'ohana. The mom and pop shops were owned by Japanese families; Tūtū kāne and tūtū wāhine would be the ones in the community, working close by and watching out for us kids; and the Filipinos were the primary laborers in the pineapple fields. People in the community looked out for each other. When parents were working the fields, the other families helped to take care of the children. Different people's histories can be found around the island, from the Filipino Federation Camp on the north side of the island between Kaiolohia or Shipwreck Beach and Keomoku, the Hawaiian Fishing Village, to Kō'ele Ranch, which was owned by the Richardson family for generations. When you think of country living at its finest, Lāna'i was the place to be.

Although there were stores like International Food and Clothing, Pine Isle Market, and Richard's Shopping Center that imported things we needed from the neighbor islands, my 'ohana lived off the 'āina. We grew up as a hunting family. My dad was an avid hunter and 'opihi picker. He was also the town butcher, so he taught me how to cut meat the right way. We didn't fish a lot, but my mom loved to fish for halalū. So when halalū season would come, we would go and get bucketfuls. That would sustain us until the next season. I never knew then what my dad and mom were setting me up for when they taught me how to hunt, how to slaughter pig, how to skin deer and bury their horns in the ground to preserve them, how to fish, and how to pick 'opihi. Our entire backyard was a garden, and we had two chicken coops—

one for our egg-laying chickens and one for the fighting chickens. We also raised goats and rabbits. We basically learned how to live off of the land. I recall that the only things that came from the store were milk and bread. Everything else came from the 'āina. Growing up this way made me appreciate the hard work my parents put in to make sure we lived the good life, and set us up to be independent, sustainable adults.

When we were younger my brother and I would always complain, "We're poor!" We thought we lived poor. My parents made sure that we reused what we could, and if we didn't need to we would not buy new things at the beginning of the school year. If mom could make the pants a little longer, the shirt a little looser, or the dress a little bigger, she would. Things like that made me think we were poor. Now that I'm older, I see that we lived rich. We were rich when we were growing up, even though we never had things like cable TV or cordless phones. Believe it or not, we had one of those stuck-to-the-wall rotary phones, up until it died when I was in intermediate school. If I wanted to watch MTV or any other station that wasn't provided by the rabbit ears on the television, I had to go to my friend's house. Then again even though they had TV, they grew up the same way we did—*Lanai-an.*

It's amazing how much the Hawaiian culture impacted how we lived. Lāna'i, at that time, was like an 'ohana, very family-oriented. We were raised by a community. Everybody knew who you were, who your parents were, who you took hula from. I started taking hula with Auntie Elaine Ka'opuiki when I was four. I wasn't really into it; I was a tomboy who just wanted to be outside. I might go to one class, but then I would miss the next one. Auntie Elaine would see me at Taka's Sweet Shop and scold me: "eh, we get hula! Get up there!" I later tried dancing with Auntie Lehua Matsuoka and Auntie Rita Moon (who were students of Auntie Elaine) off and on, and although I kept going back at their registration times I never completed a year.

So, my introduction to Hawaiian culture came first from the Lāna'i kūpuna: the Ka'opuikis, the Kaho'ohalahalas, and the Richardsons, who were stewards of Kō'ele Ranch. We spent a good chunk of our childhood up at the ranch, because they welcomed all the keiki of the island up to the ranch. We would go up there and ride horse and talk story with Tūtū Rebecca Richardson and Tūtū Earnest Richardson, who told us of the rich history that Lāna'i had to offer.

Then, when I went to school, I had Auntie Martha Haia Evans as my teacher. She was the first teacher I knew who took the Hawaiian culture and embedded it into the school system. Her curriculum was built around Hawaiian culture. In 5th grade, we focused on Makahiki, the celebration of Lono and of the harvest. In 6th grade, we studied the history of Hawai'i Island. We took a close look at Kamehameha I, how he conquered the islands and how he built alliances and befriended other aliʻi of various islands. As the culmination of our learning, we spent a week on Hawaiʻi Island, and there we took the path of Lono, going around the whole island. We visited all the wahi pana that we had talked about in class, starting in Hilo and ending in Waimea.

Auntie Martha is still my inspiration, and she made me the teacher I am today. She was really strict in the beginning. No smile the first couple days. And she always seemed to know what we were doing. Even though there were thirty kids in the class, and she would be facing the board, she would say, "Consuelo, stop chewing gum." I would be like, "How did she know I was chewing gum? Does she have eyes in the back of her head?" I model my teaching after her. She was the first one who made school *worth* it. She took the Hawaiian way of teaching up a notch. For example, she introduced me to the concept of mālama ʻāina. She didn't just tell us; she showed us that if we just take care of the land it will take care of us. Even though that's what my parents were teaching my brother and I all along, Auntie Martha put it in a way where I finally understood *why* we lived off the land and why we were "rich." Auntie Martha taught us how to cultivate the land. We planted dryland kalo beds in front of our classroom. She cultivated a love of the ʻukulele and of singing. We even planted some pineapple, because it was slowly being phased out on the island. By the time I was in the eighth grade, the Dole plantation had completely shut down.

PINEAPPLE AND POST-PLANTATION LIFE

The plantation had shaped many aspects of life on the island. Under the pineapple plantation, there was a community-wide alarm system that would go off. Every night at 8 o'clock there would be a whistle that would go off, which would tell the workers to go to sleep. At 5 am, another whistle would wake up all the workers to tell them, "you better get to the base yard, before you miss the truck to take you out into the field for work!" While I was growing up in the 1980s, this was all still in effect. Ask anyone who lived on the island during the plantation years; they will remember the 5 am and 8 pm whistles.

The plantation was the main job source, and everybody worked there. When you were a freshman in high school, that's where you went during summer—you go work on the plantation. All that gear to work in the hot sun.

My dad worked with them for over thirty years. To this day, he still knows what the plot number is for each field. They would mark the fields with numbered stakes on the end. When we would go to different parts of the island, I would ask my dad, "Dad, what marker is that?" And he would know! I would run and go look, and he would be right.

"How did you know that?" I would ask him.

He would say, "Well, you know, it's laid out in a grid."

He worked across the whole island. From Pālāwai basin to Olopua Woods, he knew every single one. And all the truck divers knew that: all the plots, the different sections, and what kind of pineapple grew in them. That was part of the culture. We were expected to know it by the time we got to working age.

Within that culture, once I got to sixth grade, I started to see some of my classmates failing in school. As I saw them getting held back a grade, I began to wonder, "what's wrong with our education system?" I thought to myself that this shouldn't be happening. Since it's such a small community and the teacher most times is your best friend's mom, kids should be getting the help they need. It wasn't that the teachers weren't working hard. At that time, the custodians worked at night, not in the daytime. My mom was a room cleaner and she would see that there were a lot of teachers still there, until after dark, until 8 pm at night. So, what was going on that kids were failing?

As I got older, I began babysitting, and I started to see that parents were having to give their kids to babysitters so that they could go work two or three jobs just to survive. When the pineapple plantation shut down, the hotels came up. So, people either worked for the hotels or the grocery stores. There were three main grocery stores, locally owned. And if you didn't work for them, then you worked for what we called "the corporation"—Castle & Cooke. It started to become a hard life. The city started to cater to the new industry, and so the mom and pop stores like Taka's Sweet Shop, Akamai Trading, and Emura's Jewelry started to shut down one by one.

Eventually these stores closed or got taken over. The only one of the three remaining mom-and-pop stores, formerly run by the Tamashiro family, was taken over by the Lānaʻi Company, Castle & Cooke. It's hard to sustain that kind of business over there, with the transportation costs and taxes. Everything came by barge or plane, and you *paid* for that! Milk prices rose to $8 a gallon! In order to keep the store up and running, and because our subsistence means of living was slowly changing, the Tamashiros had to sell their store and the corporation took over.

For many years Lānaʻi was largely controlled by one man, David H. Murdoch, and his company. He was chief executive officer of Lānaʻi Company, which controlled the two hotels: Mānele Bay Hotel, overlooking Hulopoʻe Bay, and The Lodge at Kōʻele, situated on the former ranch lands of Kōʻele. I can recall many town meetings about the impending building of the hotels. Comfortable with the plantation style of living, our community had a hard time accepting that the time had come to make changes. I remember being in school, and the teachers would bring up the question, "If you could ask Murdoch to build something for this island, what would it be?" It was sad to hear people say that they wanted a huge mall in the middle of Pālāwai Basin, to bring in the hotels and essentially make Lānaʻi "better."

I was confused during this transition period. I wondered, how is Mr. Murdoch making it better when we already live the best life? How is he making it better by cutting into the ground and destroying the land? How is he making it better by offering to move the Richardsons off the ranch land they had stewarded for years, making them live instead on a small parcel of land off to the side of the hotel? I had difficulties trying to come to terms with strangers roaming the safe streets of Dole Park. Growing up, we always knew who were kamaʻāina and who were malihini.

The community finally came to terms with the changes that were happening with the phasing out of the pineapple industry. I felt better when Murdoch consulted with historians before making plans to build. He did leave some special aspects of Kōʻele Ranch intact. What he did right was to make sure he listened to the community. By the time I got to high school, the hotels were in full swing and two-thirds of the island residents were employed by Lānaʻi Company.

NEW FUTURES FOR LĀNAʻI

In my short lifetime, I have seen Lānaʻi go through many shifts, largely due to the changing economy. When the major shift from plantation to tourism happened, people voiced their concerns. Lānaʻi is now seeing another shift as we try to live in this ever-changing world of ours. I feel that during these changes, people have not been able to freely voice their opinions. With the need for finding a more sustainable way to provide energy, Lānaʻi has been pegged to erect a wind farm on the Kaʻa district of the island. This site holds a rich history that has recently been documented by the Lānaʻi Cultural Center. I am not afraid to say that I am opposed to the wind farm, as it will not service the island of Lānaʻi but provide service to the island of Oʻahu. If the energy stayed on the island, like the photovoltaic energy being generated at Lā Ola in Pālāwai Basin, I probably would not be so opposed to it. It will only be an eyesore for the island. If one just reads up on the long-term impact that industrial wind farms have had around the world, it has not been positive. If you were to poll Lānaʻi residents, you would find a split as to whether or not the wind farm is something the community wants.

In 2012, Murdoch's shares of Lānaʻi Company, under Castle & Cooke, were sold to Larry Ellison, the billionaire CEO of Oracle Corporation. The sale was behind closed doors, and the new owner was not revealed until the sale was complete. Unlike Murdoch, Ellison did not hold any community meetings or public appearances before acquiring ownership. Despite this, I have high hopes for what Ellison will do based on what he has already begun to do on Lānaʻi. He has closed the doors on the name Lānaʻi Company; his new company and team go under the name Pūlama Lānaʻi, a name that signifies a Lānaʻi that cherishes and cares for our valuable resources. According to its website, Pūlama Lānaʻi wants the residents of Lānaʻi to help shape its future and make itself a sustainable enterprise. According to its Facebook page, it is committed to attaining a new vision for Lānaʻi as a sustainable enterprise that meets resident needs for locally-grown agriculture, affordable energy, housing, education, healthcare and hospice care, cultural preservation, conservation, water resources, and economic growth.[1] I have not heard of Ellison actually holding the meetings, but I do know that Pūlama Lānaʻi has put on many community events, and a lot of the communication comes through the Chief Operations Officer, Kurt Matsumoto, who was born and raised on Lānaʻi. Although much of the communication comes through Kurt, he does still have time to make appearances to address the community.

I have hope that Lānaʻi will start to heal through the preservation of its history, the rebuilding of Maunalei Gulch as a working loʻi, the rebuilding of the fishponds out on the north side of the island, and with the new company in place. Ellison has employed a team with a wealth of knowledge about Hawaiʻi's unique culture and landscape. It is time that Lānaʻi transforms itself, looking back towards and valuing how it used to be. People need to return to our ancestors, help the land heal, and provide for those who mālama. I find this new shift a positive one, as the drive for this change is sustainability. The community will once again stand strong and assure that Ellison keeps Lānaʻi's uniqueness for generations to come.

NOTE

1. See the Pūlama Lānaʻi company website, at http://www.pulamalanai.com.

SOURCES FOR FURTHER INFORMATION AND INSPIRATION

1. Friends of Lānaʻi website, at http://friendsoflanai.org.
2. Lānaʻi Wind website, at http://lanaiwind.com.
3. Lānaʻi Culture Heritage Center website, at http://www.lanaichc.org/lanai-history/lanai_history.htm.
4. Oral histories of Lānaʻi Ranch, at the University of Hawaiʻi at Mānoa Center for Oral History website, at http://www.oralhistory.hawaii.edu/pages/community/lanai.html.
5. Jeanne Cooper, "More revelations, concerns about Larry Ellison's plans for Lanaʻi," *San Francisco Gate,* July 23, 2013, online at http://blog.sfgate.com/hawaii/2013/07/23/more-revelations-concerns-about-larry-ellisons-plans-for-lanai.

URBANISM AS ISLAND LIVING

SEAN CONNELLY

1) Authority

I am from Oʻahu. Growing up, all I knew about watersheds was that the stream near my house in Kāneʻohe was a tunnel that went to the sewage plant. At my Filipino Grandma's house in Kalihi, the stream was down the hill at the end of the street, but too dirty to swim in so I never went. When I'd go around Honolulu, I remember thinking how ugly the buildings were. I would think, if only someone would design better buildings, maybe we could better protect Oʻahu's natural beauty. So I decided to study architecture and urban design in college. I explored everything that interested me, like fractals, ecology, political economy, decolonization, sustainability. I learned aesthetics alone wasn't going to make Hawaiʻi a better place. I questioned what "better" even meant. I dreamed of more than a "war on ugliness." That buildings, like schools, didn't just need to be beautiful, but should also grow food, generate energy, and harvest rainwater for their surrounding neighborhoods.

An important influence was learning about traditional Hawaiian resource management, and how Hawaiians invented the ahupuaʻa to grow more food in a smaller area of land to support growing populations. That traditionally, Kāneʻohe had more than just a fertile bay. It also had a beach, because the land was organized to ensure access to resources from mountain to ocean. As I learned more about the watershed and its streams—natural, channelized, or hidden away—I realized how little a presence they had in the places I lived growing up. Even though I lived in Kāneʻohe for most of my life, it wasn't until recently that I actually got to see where the stream meets the bay—one of the most important parts of the watershed—because the shoreline today is mostly privately owned. It began to feel like I didn't even know my home, anymore. . . .

* * * * *

2) Identify a problem

Urbanism, or the way of living in urban areas, is like a foul word in Hawaiʻi. In many ways, it represents everything we hate about this place—traffic, sprawl, overcrowding. Historically, urbanization, or the growth and development of urban areas, has caused many of our problems. Our dependence on import-ed toxic energy and industrialized food resources, the contamination of our streams and beaches, and overall environmental degradation can be linked in some way to the process of Hawai'i becoming an urban place. Waikīkī, Salt Lake, Enchanted Lake, and now Ho'opili, Koa Ridge, and Kaka'ako, exem-plify Hawai'i's conflicted relationship with urbanism. O'ahu, once the most fertile of the islands, is now among the most polluted, congested, import-de-pendent metropolises in the United States.

Yet, with 91.6 percent of Hawai'i's total population currently living in an urban area—98.4 percent on O'ahu, 58.5 percent on Hawai'i Island, 81.3 per-cent on Kauai, 87.5 percent on Maui—urbanism is an unavoidable part of our future.[1] Whether we like it or not, "island living" is a predominantly urban con-dition. How can we protect our already jeopardized environment and unique island lifestyle in an urbanized world? The urgency of this conditon is astound-ing considering that [before western contact over two centuries ago, Hawaiians once supported almost the same population—sustainably—on the islands.[2]]

What if we redefine urbanism as island living? A form of ecological ur-banism, as a way of life that is rooted in Hawai'i's history, culture, and ecol-ogy? An urbanism that reaches beyond the imagery of palm trees, pineapples. suburban homes, and condo towers, and [restores watersheds—the forests, streams, and beaches that capture and filter all of our freshwater]—as the foundation of our politics, economics, and built-environment (the buildings and infrastructure that make up the places we live, work, play, grow food, and obtain other resources).   *3) THESIS*

To summarize [a future vision for an urban island living] Hawai'i is a place where healthy neighborhoods raise resilient communities on clean, renewable energies and locally-grown organic foods and materials, with less congestion and lots of open space. A place where our robust economy supports innova-tive local businesses and artists, and provides fulfilling jobs for everyone, with opportunities to invent new kinds of jobs for those who choose to pursue them. Where political districts reflect the hydrology of the watershed. A place where everyone has access to well-funded public schools that generate elec-tricity, harvest rainwater, grow food, and host weekly farmers markets, and all of the activities are also integrated in students' curriculum. Where every-one has access to quality housing options for multigenerational families, with rooftop and community gardens. A place with less traffic, and safer, more comfortable streets for bicyclists and pedestrians. A place where streams have been reclaimed and restored as publically accessible nature resources. A place where watersheds, sacred places, and other natural resources are protected, re-stored, and flourishing with native wildlife and Hawaiian culture. This vision relates to a larger problem of survival: how to provide enough food, clothing,

cont. →

and shelter for a growing population to live healthy, abundant lives, while still protecting the environment.

But so what? While it is easy to speak generally about a broad vision, it is difficult to choose the details of what that vision could or should actually look like, and how to make it reality. Some believe the solution is to return to a completely rural way of living, with plantation-style homes scattered among agricultural fields. Others think we need to completely urbanize, and live in shiny towers to preserve open space. The best solution most likely rests somewhere in the middle of these extremes. This debate is frustrating. How do we design our buildings, streets, neighborhoods, and infrastructure in a way to remake urbanism as island living? Thankfully, we have a starting point with traditional Hawaiian resource management—the collective knowledge of how to live on an island, how people coexist with their watersheds.

TRADITIONAL HAWAIIAN URBANISM

HISTORY

The conventional western perception of traditional Hawaiian society as agricultural and rural goes back to 1778. When Captain Cook arrived in Hawai'i, he did not fully understand what he saw: "The houses are scattered about, without any order, either with respect to their distances from each other, or their position in any particular direction."[3]

Although the houses he saw were scattered, they were far from disorderly. Since the pre-capitalist Hawaiian economy relied upon reciprocity and gift giving in an environment that provided everything needed within a close proximity, the dwellings did not need to organize around markets in the same centralized settlement patterns as villages in Europe. Hawaiians consciously dispersed their kauhale among a field of food and other material resources, according to access, adjacency, and alignment with these resources.

What if traditional Hawaiian resource management was reframed as traditional Hawaiian urbanism? Traditionally, Hawaiians were an urban civilization. This is a powerful perspective shift that creates new possibilities for what it can mean to be urban in Hawai'i. By "urbanism," I don't mean the images of what we consider urban today: buildings, streets, power lines, congestion. I mean a way of life organized around a physical infrastructure engineered to distribute resources, a political structure that manages it, and a concentrated population generating and consuming resources within a density of mixed land-uses that correspond to economic functions. Hawaiians had all of these aspects of an urban system. Their urbanism just looked different because it was unique to the ecology of an island, not a continent.[4]

To offer a reinterpretation: traditional Hawaiian urbanism emerged in response to environmental crisis, and the challenge of providing enough food, clothing, and shelter for people to live healthy, abundant, and thriving lives

ahupua'a → urbanism

without completely destroying the environments that supply the materials and resources needed. Twelve to fifteen hundred years ago, when the first peoples arrived to Hawai'i, they burned the forests and brushlands to clear land for agriculture.[5] Over time, the slash-and-burn technique could no longer support the demands of the growing population, as the consumption of natural resources exceeded the environment's capacity to replenish itself. Ecosystems began to collapse and many species became endangered or went extinct.[6] However, around 1100 AD, things began to shift. A new way of island living capable of supporting the growing population in proportion to the carrying capacities of each watershed began to develop. By 1200 AD, roughly around the reign of Mā'ilikūkahi, the chief who is said to have established the dominance of the ahupua'a system, evidence of slash-and-burn vanished, not reappearing again until after western contact. During these hundred years of transition, Hawaiians co-evolved with the land, searching for the insight to live intelligently and compassionately on Earth's most isolated, fragile environment. Hawaiians began to urbanize.[7]

[The catalyst for traditional urbanization was the innovation of a large-scale infrastructure that distributed freshwater to lo'i kalo and loko i'a (taro patches and fish ponds) via a network of 'auwai (irrigation ditches).[8]]This system was engineered to plug into the hydrology of the watershed, and designed to assist the natural flow of water, reinforcing the relationships between forests that attract and capture the rains, the streams and wetlands that filter it, and the shorelines that eventually receive it. This system was so effective, it intensified the cultivation of food by 100 times the previous amount.[9] Over time, this system became ingrained in the natural hydrology, and transformed the watershed itself into an advanced technology—a tool to intensify the production of food and other resources. The system was so advanced, specific names were given to the unique winds and rains of each area, allowing Hawaiians to relate culturally to the technical inputs and outputs of their watersheds.

To manage this technology, land was organized into[a hierarchy of political land-use districts that linked government and economy to the unique geology and ecology of each watershed,]taking into account resources like elevation, water flow, weather, wildlife, and other spiritual phenomena. The most well known of these land-use districts was the ahupua'a.[10] Areas with more freshwater were made smaller because more leaders were needed to manage the distribution of water, while areas with less water were made larger to provide enough land for dry-land farming, which requires land to lay fallow between crops. This ensured equal access to the range of resources available from mountain to ocean. The ahupua'a, in many ways, was the Hawaiian version of a city or town. Hawaiians thus lived among the places where they grew food and obtained resources, sharing surplus resources with other ahupua'a.

waiwai~ wealth   PAST- govt. + econ → watershed

wai~ water   Now -

social / econ   politics
process \ urbanism — shipping)
(X watershed)

FRAGMENTATION OF THE WATERSHED

Over the past two centuries, the relationship between urbanism and the watershed has changed drastically. Traditionally, urbanism was organized around a unified process that related the infrastructure and political economy back to water, designed to maintain access to the watershed as a continuous system of resources from mountain to ocean. Urbanism in Hawai'i today, however, is organized around fragmented economic, political, and social processes that destroy the connection between mountain and ocean, causing an overall decline of the watershed as a healthy productive system. This change reflects the fact that we no longer directly depend on our watersheds for food. We ship almost everything in. The current fragmentation of the watershed can easily be observed, graphically, in relation to our infrastructure, zoning, and political districts.[11]

STREAM CHANNELIZATION

The reengineering of meandering rocky streambeds into flat, straight, concrete channels disrupts the natural hydrology of the watershed and its ability to filter and absorb fresh rainwater, and produce food (see Figure 1). Without rain, the flat surface of the channel spreads water into a thin veneer, becoming too hot in the sun to sustain wildlife. When there is rain, the flat surface causes a dangerous surge of water that carries harmful effluents—fertilizers, pesticides, oil, and other pollutants from nearby urban and agriculture areas—into the ocean.

SINGLE-USE LAND-USE DISTRICTS

The size and functions of contemporary land-use districts are based on arbitrary economic functions rather than the vegetation, rainfall, weather patterns, and soil types of each watershed. In 1961, all the land in Hawai'i was classified into one of three districts: urban, agricultural, and conservation (in 1963, a rural district was added). At the time, this was considered very innovative because Hawai'i was among the first governments in the nation to implement a statewide zoning measure in efforts to limit development and protect the environment. Despite these intentions, aspects of this zoning framework actually contribute to the destruction of our watersheds. Typically, only mountain areas are zoned for conservation while the rest of the land areas are zoned for urban and agriculture developments. This absence of conservation areas along streams makes it impossible to maintain the stream as the most important ecological link between mountain and ocean. In urban areas, the overdevelopment of the stream area with houses, shopping centers, and gas stations prevents access to the stream as a public natural resource, undermining cultural connections between the public and the watershed. The

Figure 1. This image shows a USGS aerial photo of Mōʻiliʻili overlaid with the traditional ʻauwai system, in black. The solid patches to the left indicate ponds, while the thick band to the right is the original stream, which is now channelized (dashed line)

physical separation of urban and agriculture zones separates where people live and grow food, eroding cultural relationships with ʻāina. These negative effects are exacerbated by the disconnection between land-use and land tenure; the ownership of agriculture lands are unevenly distributed between large corporate entities and local people (see Figure 2).

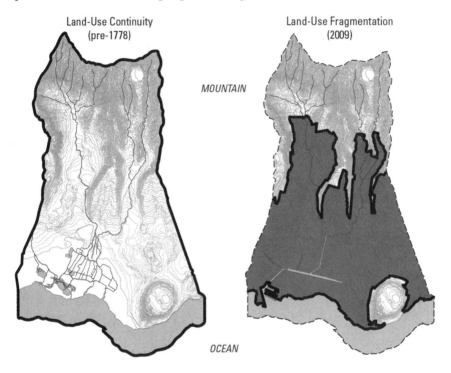

Figure 2. This image of the Waikīkī watershed shows its current fragmentation (right) caused by the zoning of the urban land-use district (grey) between the mountain and ocean, compared to the traditional treatment of the watershed as a continuous area (left).

POPULATION-BASED POLITICAL DISTRICTS

Today the size and boundaries of Hawaiʻi's political districts are based on population demographics rather than the geological features and ecological capacities of each watershed. This disconnects leadership and their constituents from the capacities of their respected watersheds. Typically, the different jurisdictions of government—City Council, State Senate, House of Representatives—do not align, creating unnecessary complications and inefficiencies in the political system. In highly populated areas, like Waikīkī, it becomes difficult to manage a single watershed as a cooperative unit, while in less populated areas, too many watersheds are lumped into a single political district that may lack adequate political support to properly manage the resources (see Figure 3).

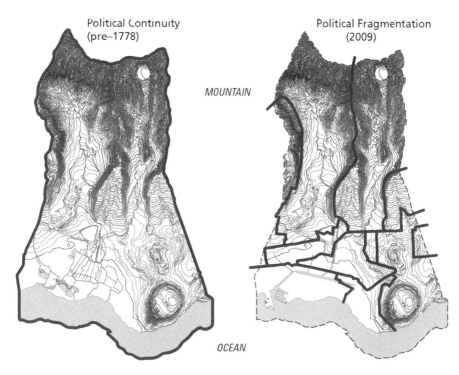

Figure 3. This image of the Waikīkī watershed shows its current fragmentation caused by the division of many political districts between city and state, compared to the traditional treatment of the watershed as a continuous unit.

RECLAIMING HAWAIIAN URBANISM[12]

The fragmentation of the watershed is a major, but often overlooked, contributing factor to our current environmental crisis. This essay is not meant to solve this crisis, but rather to highlight several connecting points that get us thinking about urbanism from a more Hawaiʻi-grounded perspective. How will changing our perceptions of urbanism help our community rebuild relationships to land, water, ecologies, and histories that sustain us? What will the visions mentioned at the beginning of this essay actually look like in relation to our watershed? These are important questions because urbanism in Hawaiʻi is rapidly changing, again, in ways that impact almost everything about our lives—from the design of our homes, streets, and neighborhoods, to the kinds of relationships we have with our friends, family, and environments. The positive aspects of this change are that people are talking about renewable energy, recycling more, installing solar panels and solar water heating on their rooftops, cycling, composting, restoring streams, and supporting more local farmers and local businesses. On the other hand, agriculture lands are being developed for housing. Billions are about to be spent on rail. Building heights are being raised to twice the current limit. We need to find a way to fit all this scattered progressive activity together as a coherent and refined theory for urbanism in Hawai'i, designed to reclaim our island watershed as a more necessary part of our politics, economy, and everyday life. Urbanism, when done correctly, will help us create a built-environment that maintains the overall continuity of the watershed, just as Hawaiians were able to achieve.

What kind of physical changes to our current built-environment would be necessary to make Hawai'i more sustainable over the next hundred years? Some general starting points:

• *Public reclamation of the properties along the stream edge over the course of several generations.*

The urbanized land along streams should, over time, be returned to the watershed as a publically accessible resource, maintained as something of a public land trust. These spaces would serve as ecological corridors to maintain the health of the watershed, adapt to fluctuations in water cycles (i.e., flooding), provide recreational and educational access to the stream, mountains, and ocean, and reintroduce space for traditional food and cultural production. Committing to the idea of the stream as a foundational organizing element of Hawai'i's built environment, I believe, is enough to catalyze a completely different conception of urbanism in Hawai'i (see Figure 4).

• *Reinterpret city blocks to generate, process, reuse, and manage shared resources, with building heights and densities that correspond to the natural geology and proximity to the stream, forests, and shoreline.*

Require city blocks to have access to common farming areas, which would promote integrated urban and agriculture land uses within every neighborhood. Rooftop areas can be used for aquaponics food production, clean alternative energy, or water harvesting. The focus on the city block as a productive resource unit would make it integral to the function of the economy in more ways than generating a property tax.

• *Create interdependent economic relationships between the different areas of each watershed.*

For example, create systems where houses in the valley would harvest rainwater, and houses along the shore would generate electricity. This would create an additional economic flow of resources (in addition to water) that would make the continuity of the watershed more relevant to the local economy. Schools, markets, libraries, and other civic structures could help to facilitate the exchange of these resources. For example, the energy or water generated by the various dwellings and city blocks would be collected at their nearest school or market, which would distribute those resources to other parts of the watershed, or island, as necessary (see Figure 5).

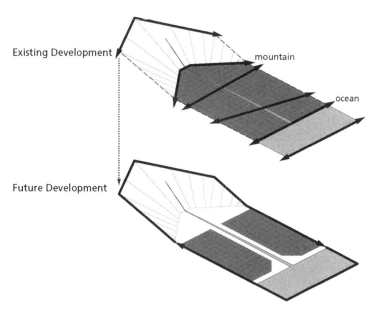

Figure 4. This diagram of the watershed conceptually outlines the current fragmented conditions (top), and a future scenario for development that would enforce a maximum development footprint within each watershed, while the stream is maintained as a publicly accessible resource (bottom).

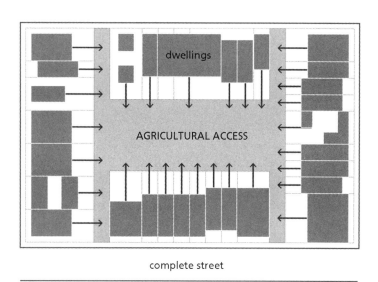

Figure 5. This diagram of a city block shows a conceptual arrangement of zero-lot line dwellings organized around a commonly accessible agricultural common.

These are only a few of the many possible starting points for a framework for a future Hawaiian urbanism. All this would require major top-down policy changes and public debate, lots of money and time, and slow changes over generations. Reclaiming Hawaiian urbanism is a powerful way to localize our economy and reestablish a government, land-use system, education system, water and energy system, and food and resource system whose core processes are aligned with the ecology of the watershed. The places we live are the physical and emotional records of the political, economic, and cultural processes that shape our lives. The only way to change positively these processes and take ownership over them is to change positively the ways we understand and implement urbanism.

NOTES

1. Globally, 50 percent of the world lives in an urban area, with an estimated increase to 70 percent by 2050. The urban demographic in Hawaiʻi reached the 50 percent mark between 1920 and 1930. Department of Business, Economic Development & Tourism, "Table 1.02—Characteristics of the Population: 1831 to 2010," *2011 State of Hawaii Data Book* (Web, 2011), http://files.hawaii.gov/dbedt/economic/databook/db2011/section01.pdf

2. Lilikalā Kameʻeleihiwa, "Traditional Hawaiian Metaphors," *Native Lands and Foreign Desires: Pahea lā e Pono ai?* (Honolulu: Bishop Museum, 1992).

3. E. S. Craighill Handy and Elizabeth Green Handy, *Native Planters: Their Life, Lore, and Environment* (Honolulu: Bishop Museum, 1972): 482. I have not yet learned to read Hawaiian, so the most influential texts I draw upon in this research are often English-language texts. The most important resource for me over the past several years for Hawaiʻi has been talking story with Hawaiians. Other great people I've talked to have often been active in sustainability, urbanism, and art, or are people who are just frustrated with the current state of environmental degradation in Hawaiʻi.

4. Urban settlement patterns are classically acknowledged to feature a population density centralized around markets. Because Hawaiian settlement patterns do not exhibit the same centralization around a market, they were written off as a non-urban system. However, I disagree, especially now that the western perception of what constitutes a city or urban area has changed over the past decade, particularly in reference to decentralized or informal approaches to urbanism.

5. Soil samples dating back to 800 AD contain high levels of charcoal particulates, suggesting periods of slash-and-burn agriculture and wildfire. See John L. Culliney, *Islands in a Far Sea: The Fate of Nature in Hawaiʻi* (Honolulu: U of Hawaiʻi P, 2006).

6. This kind of theory about societies is forwarded by scholars like Jared Diamond, *Collapse: How Societies Choose to Fail or Succeed* (New York: Penguin Books, 2005).

7. The earliest evidence of ʻauwai and loʻi development so far has been dated back to around 1100 AD. See John Culliney, *Islands in a Far Sea.*

8. According to some sources, cities and agriculture developed simultaneously; agricultural processes are created by urbanization, and urbanization by agricultural. Therefore,

they cannot be separated, or thought of as separate, as our current urban-agricultural dichotomy makes us believe. Rather, they are integrated and part of the same congruent system. See Jane Jacobs, *The Economy of Cities,* in the Resources for this essay.

9. Marion Kelly, "Dynamics of Production Intensification in Pre-contact Hawai'i," *What's New? A Closer Look at the Process of Innovation,* eds. Sander Van der Leeuw and Robin Torrence (London: Unwin Hyman, 1989): 82–106.

10. Larger divisions included 'okana and moku, which were managed by ali'i. Within the ahupua'a, land was further divided into 'ili, which were managed by families over generations. While many scholars refer to this as a feudal system, it was not. Families were free to settle in other ahupua'a. While the boundaries varied according to season, the 'ili remained steady, providing a system that was flexible, yet still grounding for the people who lived within that system. See David Malo, *Hawaiian Antiquities (Mo'olelo Hawai'i)* (Honolulu: Bishop Museum, 1951).

11. A graphic analysis comparing traditional and contemporary maps, constructed from geographic information and other data made available to the public online, is a valuable way to express the spatial dynamics of this problem. I chose to look at Waikīkī for both anthropological and personal reasons. It's the most urbanized area, being among the first to be transformed by industrial agriculture, then tourism. I also spent a lot of time in the area, growing up in the Kapahulu area until I was around four, spending endless summers surfing and bodyboarding, and then studying here.

12. This note is just to acknowledge respectfully that I am not genealogically Hawaiian, but that my worldview on urbanism is founded in the knowledge of Hawaiian resource management, and shaped by the specificities that make Hawai'i's environment unique.

RESOURCES FOR FURTHER INFORMATION AND INSPIRATION

1. This essay is based on my research, which I have made publically available online at http://www.hawaii-futures.com. If you have more questions or comments, please contact me through the contact page there..

2. A critical text that shares the history of land use in Hawai'i is by George Cooper and Gavan Daws, *Land and Power in Hawaii: The Democratic Years* (Honolulu: Benchmark Books, 1985). Since I grew up in Hawai'i and did not leave the state until I was eighteen, when I read non-Hawai'i texts, the only way for me to understand them is to rework their messages into a Hawai'i context. This has been a very compelling and enlightening process. Several resources that have been influential for me in this regard, in addition to those referenced in the essay, include:

> Manuel De Landa, *A Thousand Years of Nonlinear History* (New York: Zone Books, 2000).
>
> William Mitchell, *Cities of Bits: Space, Place, and the Infobahn* (Boston: MIT P, 1996).
>
> Benoit B. Mandelbrot, *The Fractal Geometry of Nature* (San Francisco: W. H. Freeman, 1977).
>
> Jane Jacobs, *The Death and Life of Great American Cities* (New York: Random House, 1961).

A PERSPECTIVE ON ENERGY
POLICIES IN HAWAI'I

MAKENA COFFMAN

I moved home to Hawai'i in 2002 with an undergraduate degree in international relations and an ambition to work in policy. I began as a researcher for 3Point Consulting and was assigned to be a recorder in the widely publicized clash over new power lines through Mānoa or Pālolo. Among other environmental concerns, both communities were upset about the impact to view planes as well as the role that the power lines would play in facilitating more development in Honolulu. This experience introduced me to the intricacies of energy planning, ranging from the technical issues of power reliability to community concerns about locating infrastructure. The experience reinforced my decision to pursue a PhD in economics and eventually planning as a career. The knowledge and tools of economics combined with the planner's engagement with stakeholders, ranging from policy-makers to community members, is how I work to turn ideas into action.

One of the more formative experiences of my early career was serving on the State of Hawai'i Greenhouse Gas Emissions Reduction Task Force [Act 234, 2007]. We were charged with identifying a work plan to reduce Hawai'i's greenhouse gas (GHG) emissions to 1990 levels by the year 2020. While the Task Force struggled to come to consensus, the process of inquiry helped to inform my research agenda in two main ways. The first finding, that the electric sector substantially increased its emissions as a result of introducing a coal-burning unit, motivates me to think about both environmental and economic outcomes in crafting policy. The second finding, that ground transportation is the fastest growing contributor to GHG emissions, piqued my interest in transportation planning, and specifically, initiatives to reduce vehicle miles. In this essay, I share some of the challenges and opportunities that Hawai'i faces in pursuing renewable energy and GHG emissions reductions.

* * * * *

It is tempting to frame Hawai'i's energy challenges as unique—to paint Hawai'i as a place unto itself that requires Hawai'i-grown solutions. It is certainly true that Hawaiʻi faces disproportionately high electricity prices and its island geography creates challenges in harnessing energy sources. But in broad terms, Hawaiʻi's experiences are like the rest of the world. We share a desire to wean ourselves from fossil fuels and mitigate human-induced climate change. And we face difficult challenges in deploying renewable energy technologies in cost-effective and large-scale ways. We must learn from others' experiences, and our lessons are globally relevant.

RISING ELECTRICITY COSTS

The defining characteristic of Hawaiʻi's energy system is its extraordinary cost. We meet roughly 75 percent of electricity needs by burning oil. This means that when oil prices rise, both our transportation and electricity costs increase. In contrast, the US is generally more dependent on coal and more recently natural gas. Hawaiʻi residents pay electricity rates about three times the national average (see Figure 1), and the gap is widening.

Sudden increases in oil prices result in periods of slower growth and even recession.[1] Rising and volatile oil prices lead to uncertainty that may delay capital investments,[2] and cause bouts of inflation that lower purchasing power.[3] Although the high cost of oil is an economic burden, it also provides an incentive for large-scale deployment of alternative technologies.

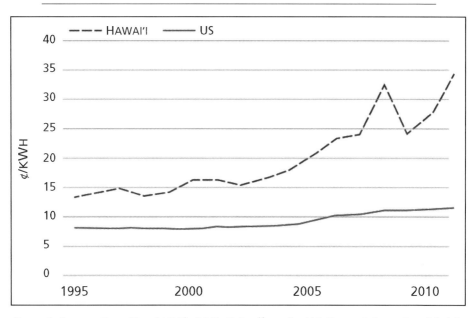

Figure 1. Average Hawaiʻi and US Electricity Rates (from the U.S. Energy Information Administration [EIA], Electricity. U.S. Department of Energy, 2013).

HAWAIʻI CLEAN ENERGY INITIATIVE

The US Department of Energy and the State of Hawaiʻi recognize this opportunity, and in 2008 launched a collaborative effort to achieve "a 70 percent clean energy economy within a generation." The motivation is that Hawaiʻi's high electricity rates make renewable energy technologies here more cost-effective than elsewhere in the country. The Hawaiʻi Clean Energy Initiative (HCEI) has acted as a catalyst to bring diverse stakeholders into conversation.

HCEI is intended as guidance for both electricity and transportation; however, its main effect so far has been codification into statute through a Renewable Portfolio Standard (RPS) for the electricity sector. RPS is one of the most popular policy mechanisms that states and nations use to ensure a minimum amount of electricity generation from renewable sources. Thirty states have adopted an RPS, and Hawaiʻi's RPS mandates 40 percent of electricity sales be from renewable sources by 2030. Mid-term goals are 10 percent in 2010, 15 percent in 2015, and 25 percent in 2020. This together with a goal of 30 percent energy efficiency by 2030 are intended to reflect the HCEI target. To date, the RPS goals have been met through an aggressive combination of purchase power agreements and subsidies. The graph below (Figure 2) demonstrates the impact of RPS beginning in 2010.

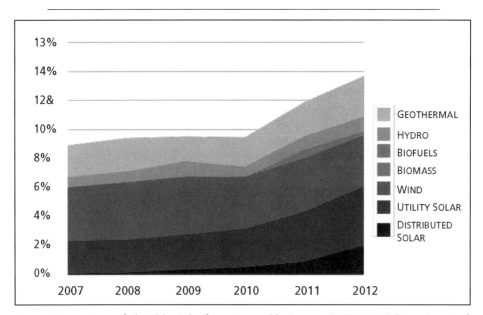

Figure 2. Percentage of Electricity Sales from Renewable Sources, 2007 to 2012 (Department of Business Economic Development and Tourism [DBEDT], "Hawaiʻi Energy Facts and Figures, June 2013," 2013).

While the electric utilities seem poised to reach the 2015 goal, the 2020 goal requires a leap in the current trajectory of renewable energy technology capacity. In the last three years, Hawai'i has added a tremendous amount of renewable energy. But much of the low-hanging fruit is now gone. Moving forward requires making difficult decisions regarding long-term land use and impacts to the tax/ratepayer.

The use of renewable energy technologies often requires moving production to the resource—to where the wind blows and the sun shines. With energy no longer being produced solely in industrially zoned areas, the possibility for conflicts with local communities increases. Moreover, the use of renewable energy technologies is particularly challenging in an island setting. Land is relatively limited, and the majority of residents live in urban O'ahu, while alternative energy resources are dispersed throughout the islands. These problems vary depending on the primary source—wind, solar, geothermal, or biomass—of the renewable energy. I discuss these as the major commercially available sources in Hawai'i.

The proposal to install up to 400 megawatts (MW) of wind generation on the islands of Moloka'i and Lāna'i and bring the power to O'ahu via an undersea electricity cable has been hotly debated for many years. The project faces major bottlenecks in the form of landowner interests and community concerns about committing the lands long-term to wind farms and their effect on local habitats and accessibility. People are also concerned about the autonomy of each island. Several on-island wind projects have been built; for example, there are now approximately 100 MW of wind energy capacity on O'ahu.

In contrast, the flexibility of siting solar photovoltaic (PV) on residential and commercial rooftops is one of its major attractions. A combination of the declining cost of PV, rising electricity rates, and high levels of subsidization[4] has led to the rapid deployment of solar PV in Hawai'i. We now have some of the highest levels of intermittent energy penetration of any grid system in the world. However, solar PV sparks debate over the equitable use of subsidies and maintenance of grid infrastructure costs.

Geothermal energy is historically controversial, and further development will require thoughtful conversation. Though still tremendously contentious, the level of interest in geothermal seems to be increasing. There has been expansion of the current Puna geothermal plant and a variety of proposals to put a second plant in place that would meet much of the baseload needs of Hawai'i Island. Beyond that, it will take connecting Hawai'i Island with other islands to make geothermal a statewide resource.

Biofuels are attractive because they can be burned in existing generators and could be a means of revitalizing under-utilized agricultural land. But currently, biofuel is more expensive than oil. As of 2013, the Hawaiian Electric Company is under contract to import up to 7 million gallons of biodiesel annually to produce electricity. An additional twenty year contract for 10 million gallons of locally-produced biofuel annually was recently approved by the Public Utilities Commission.

The cost of producing energy by burning oil or through renewable sources varies widely. Technologies such as wind and solar PV are associated with a large up-front capital investment but zero costs for fuel. Because the sun does not shine all day, solar PV is discounted heavily in terms of actual power generation—an approximate 20 percent capacity factor. In contrast, wind energy is expected to be twice as efficient. Lower-cost battery technologies are becoming available, which may lead to substantial changes in the operational and cost characteristics of intermittent power generation. A switch to biofuel, on the other hand, requires less up-front capital but is expensive in terms of ongoing fuel costs. Geothermal on Hawai'i Island is a relatively inexpensive resource while providing a source of "firm" power (i.e., not variable like wind and sun)—though the capital investment of an undersea transmission cable is substantial.

I focus much of my research on understanding the best mix and impacts of renewable energy technologies. Considering appropriate support policies and roles of government is important because of the rapid technological development of renewable energy, coupled with a changing landscape of environmental goals, community impacts, and economic constraints. It is a complex problem that warrants careful and ongoing community dialogue.

GLOBAL CLIMATE CHANGE

A primary motivation for the pursuit of renewable energy is to mitigate human-induced climate change. Yet, the politics around climate change make policy difficult. The US rejection of the Kyoto Protocol, an international framework for reducing GHG emissions, dramatically slowed the international community's adoption of more aggressive standards. A number of countries, mainly in Europe, forged ahead and adopted GHG reduction plans based on large-scale deployment of renewable energy. In the US, the lack of federal leadership has resulted in active and engaged state-level policy.

HAWAI'I'S CLIMATE CHANGE SOLUTIONS ACT

Hawai'i is among nineteen states that have a binding target for reducing GHG emissions.[5] Act 234, signed into law in 2007, commits Hawai'i to reaching 1990 levels of GHG emissions by the year 2020 (excluding aviation-based emissions). Act 234 is much less in the media than HCEI but is nonetheless likely to be environmentally and economically impactful. As of October 2013, the State Department of Health has released rules and is awaiting their adoption.

Hawai'i's 1990 emissions were 23 MMTCO2E (million metric tons of carbon dioxide equivalent), as shown in Figure 3, and grew by 5 percent by the year 2007 (including aviation fuels). In this time, emissions from electric power generation increased by 29 percent and ground transportation by 38 percent.[6] The 2007 per capita emissions are 19 MMTCO2E, compared to the national average of 24.[7] Hawai'i's per capita GHG emissions are in line with many other US states, and far above most people on the planet.

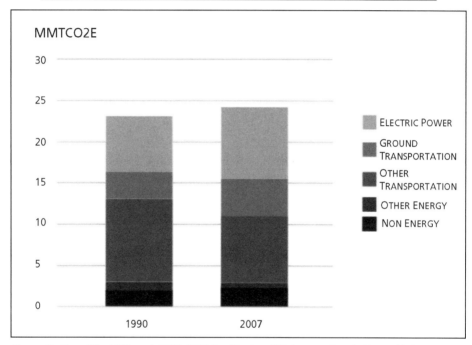

Figure 3. Hawai'i's 1990 and 2007 GHG Profile (see ICF International, "Hawai'i GHG Inventory").

From Figure 3 it is clear that Hawai'i's GHG emissions are primarily an energy problem—non-energy sources, such as changes to land cover, are small. It reflects that the electric sector increased its emissions substantially, in large part due to the introduction of a coal-burning unit on O'ahu in 1992. Coal was brought in to diversify fuel sources, without consideration of pollutants. Because it is one of the cheaper operating units, it serves as a base-load resource for O'ahu.

Hawaiʻi's GHG profile also reveals that ground transportation emissions are the fastest growing of any energy sector. Over 60 percent of petroleum use in Hawaiʻi is for transportation, and of that, 45 percent is for ground transportation. This makes ground transportation's use of petroleum similar to that of the electric sector.[8] Increasing energy and GHG emissions in ground transportation is a reflection of the increase in vehicle miles traveled (and generally larger vehicle sizes). Figure 4 shows total vehicle miles traveled in the State from 1985 to the present. It is easy to see periods of stagnation during recessions in the 1990s and around 2008.

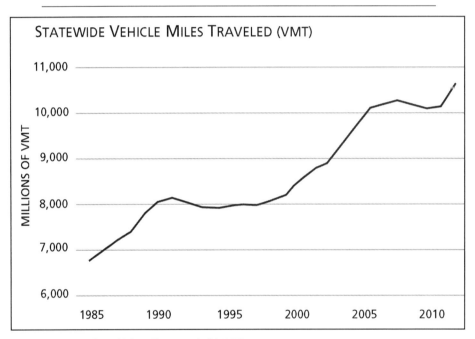

Figure 4. Statewide Vehicle Miles Traveled (VMT).

I sit on the State's HCEI Working Group for Transportation, and in time have come to appreciate the enormous complexity in changing transportation systems and policies. For example, there has been much emphasis on fuel-switching away from gasoline and towards electrification. While electric vehicles will almost certainly play a role in reducing vehicle emissions into the future, the slow adoption rates for new vehicles means that systemic change is also slow. Policies that would directly encourage faster turnover and efficiency of use, such as increasing the gasoline tax, are politically difficult and justifiably mired with concerns over their regressive nature.

FUEL STANDARD—A POLICY SUGGESTION

Hawai'i's position as a state that burns liquid fuel for both electricity generation and transportation begs for policy guidance in this area. Policy models for governing and prioritizing fuels are emerging. California has done tremendous work in adopting an alternative fuel standard that sets guidelines for lifecycle-based GHG emissions associated with liquid fuels (with a permitting mechanism). The US Environmental Protection Agency (EPA) is developing its Renewable Fuel Standard. There has been discussion within Congress of "partial credit" for fuels such as natural gas within a Clean Energy Standard framework at the federal level (though no such policy has been adopted).[9] The important point here is that *lifecycle* GHG emissions should be considered.

Lifecycle GHG emissions are all the emissions associated with a fuel/ technology during its entire lifespan, not just at the point of end use. For example, lifecycle analysis accounts for the burning of ethanol as well as the GHG emissions generated by the oil-burning that goes into operating machinery to plant and harvest corn to manufacture ethanol. Another example is the clearing of land (i.e., deforestation) for the purpose of growing biocrops. If only "out-of-stack" emissions are considered, the fuel may seem cleaner than it is in actuality.

There are currently no rules pursuing lifecycle GHG emissions reductions in Hawai'i. The result is that biofuels are treated as a net-zero GHG emission producer, when this is certainly not the case on a lifecycle basis. The absence of this consideration within GHG emissions reduction rule-making will give the electric utilities tremendous incentive to switch to biofuels (or even natural gas), rather than pursue more low-carbon alternatives. In addition, it doesn't serve to distinguish between types of bio- and fossil fuels, where the spectrum of GHG impacts is large. This omission gives me pause as to whether the rules as currently crafted will meet the spirit of Act 234, which urges the minimization of "leakage" (i.e., substituting GHG emissions in one place for another).

Moreover, the current GHG emissions rules focus solely on the electric sector and neglect ground transportation entirely. A policy along the lines of a "fuel standard" could not only provide more guidance to the electric sector but also be a first step in creating a framework for fuel-switching within transportation. It should complement the to-date HCEI-related policies (like RPS) and help achieve HCEI goals for transportation.

SYNTHESIZING EFFORTS

The pursuit of alternative energy and GHG emissions reductions in Hawai'i is occurring in parallel. While largely acting to achieve similar goals, there are ways in which the two main objectives of pursuing cleaner and lower-cost energy clearly diverge. Examples include the use of polluting but cheap coal as well as relatively clean but expensive biofuels. Bringing the multiple objectives more closely in line is important; as interacting policies are, at best, duplicitous, and at worst, add unnecessary cost burdens to Hawai'i's residents to achieve similar environmental outcomes.[10]

In addition, we have reached a turning point in the US politics around global warming. President Obama has made climate change mitigation a centerpiece of his second term. In *Massachusetts v. EPA,* the US Supreme Court ruled that GHG emissions are a threat to human health, and opened the way for the EPA to regulate emissions through the Clean Air Act. The President has given clear directives to use this avenue to reduce both stationary and mobile sources of GHG emissions.

As federal policies emerge, the roles of states likely will change. Broadstroke approaches, such as a carbon tax or quota, are likely better administered at the national level. However, the continued leadership of state governments is important. This is particularly true for transportation, where top-down approaches are best coupled with proactive development of alternatives. For example, Honolulu continually ranks at the top of the list for congestion, and its bus system is by many accounts operating at capacity. For a city with such moderate weather, it has an abysmal absence of bike lanes. The results of the 2012 mayoral election on O'ahu imply a majority of public support for the Honolulu rail transit project. From an energy perspective, ensuring high levels of ridership and connectivity to alternative modes of transportation is crucial to making it energy-positive. Plans like the *O'ahu Bike Plan* are ready for implementation. *Bicycle sharing*, which used to seem a more abstract concept, is in practice in cities across the globe, and plans are being made for Honolulu. Planners can have tremendous impact in pursuing low-carbon transportation options and supportive land uses. It is an innovating field—where energy and GHG emissions considerations are being woven into a profession more historically concerned with mobility and reducing congestion.

The challenges that Hawai'i and the world face in the pursuit of renewable energy and GHG emissions reduction are many—though the urgency of climate change and the opportunities for improving communities make them worth contemplating. We need the will to implement the numerous solutions at the global, national, and local levels. Ultimately, this takes a highly engaged citizenry—from conserving energy, advocating for local bike routes, providing input in locating energy infrastructure, to voting for leaders. Decisions related to land use, distribution of resources, lifestyle, and community impacts must be made—with planning processes involving full information and inclusive decision-making.

NOTES

AUTHOR'S NOTE: I thank Carl Bonham and Asia Yeary for their helpful comments, and Sherilyn Wee for her excellent research assistance.

1. J. Hamilton, "Oil and the macroeconomy since World War II," *Journal of Political Economy* 91 (1983): 228–48. See also R. Rasche and J. Tatom, "Energy price shocks, aggregate supply and monetary policy: The theory and the international evidence," *Carnegie-Rochester Conference Series on Public Policy* 14.1 (1981): 9–93; M. Darby, "The Price of Oil and World Inflation and Recession," *American Economic Review* 72.4 (1982): 738–51; J. Burbidge and A. Harrison, "Testing for the effects of oil-price rises using vector autoregressions," *International Economic Review* 25 (1984): 459–84; P. Perron, "The great crash, the oil price shock, and the unit root hypothesis," *Econometrica* 57.6 (1989): 1361–1401; and M. Olson, "The Productivity Slowdown, the Oil Shocks, and the Real Cycle," *Journal of Economic Perspectives* 2.4 (1998): 43–69.

2. B. S. Bernanke, "Non-Monetary Effects of the Financial Crisis in the Propagation of the Great Depression," *American Economic Review* 73.3 (1983): 257–76.

3. R. Barsky and L. Killian, "Do We Really Know that Oil Caused the Great Stagflation? A Monetary Alternative," *NBER Macroeconomics Annual 2001* (ed. B. S. Bernanke and K. Rogoff, Cambridge: MIT P, 2002). See also R. Barsky and L. Killian, "Oil and the Macroeconomy Since the 1970s," *Journal of Economic Perspectives* 18.4 (2004): 115–34.

4. As of 2013, there is a 30 percent federal tax credit and 35 percent state tax credit (where a 5kw system is capped at $5,000) for the up-front cost of solar PV systems. In addition, there is a "net metering agreement" that allows households and businesses to sell energy back to the electric utility, effectively at retail rates, such that the consumer is "net zero" within a year's time. There is also a feed-in-tariff rate set for larger producers.

5. GHG emissions reduction strategies clearly affect energy sectors, but also offer a broader policy context that can, for example, affect land use and forestation, agriculture, and the handling of municipal waste.

6. ICF International, "Hawai'i GHG Inventory: 1990 and 2007," prepared for the Department of Business, Economic Development, and Tourism, December 31, 2008, at http://energy.hawaii.gov/wp-content/uploads/2011/10/ghg-inventory-20081.pdf

7. US Environmental Protection Agency (EPA), "Inventory of US GHG Emissions and Sinks: 1990–2007," April 15, 2009, at http://www.epa.gov/climatechange/Downloads/ghgemissions/GHG2007entire_report-508.pdf. See also the US Census Bureau, "2007 Population Estimates," at http://www.census.gov/popest/data/historical/2000s/vintage_2007/index.html.

8. See "Hawai'i Energy Facts & Figures, June 2013," Department of Business, Economic Development and Tourism, at http://energy.hawaii.gov/wp-content/uploads/2011/10/FF_June2013_R2.pdf.

9. US Senate Committee on Energy and Natural Resources, "The Clean Energy Standard Act of 2012," at http://www.energy.senate.gov/public/index.cfm/files/serve?File_id=e9c14b4a-2b2f-4602-bbc9-bfe68ac5069a.

10. C. Fisher and L. Preonas, "Combining Policies for Renewable Energy: Is the Whole Less Than the Sum of Its Parts?", *International Review of Environmental and Resource Economics* 4 (2010): 51–92.

RESOURCES FOR FURTHER INFORMATION AND INSPIRATION

1. M. Coffman, J. Griffin, and P. Bernstein, "An Assessment of Greenhouse Gas Emissions-Weighted Clean Energy Standards," *Energy Policy* 45 (2012): 122–32.

2. M. Coffman, "Oil Price Shocks and Hawai'i's Economy: An Analysis of the Oil-Price Macroeconomy Relationship," *Annals of Regional Science* 44.3 (2010): 599–620.

3. IPCC, "Climate Change 2007: Synthesis Report," *Contribution of Working Groups I, II and III to the Fourth Assessment Report of the Intergovernmental Panel on Climate Change* (ed. R. K. Pachauri and A. Reisinger, IPCC, Geneva, Switzerland, 2007), online at http://www.ipcc.ch/pdf/assessment-report/ar4/syr/ar4_syr_frontmatter.pdf.

4. IPCC, "Summary for Policymakers," *Climate Change 2007: Mitigation. Contribution of Working Group III to the Fourth Assessment Report to the Intergovernmental Panel on Climate Change* (ed. B. Metz, O. R. Davidson, P. R. Bosch, R. Dave, L. A. Meyer; Cambridge: Cambridge UP, 2007).

5. C. Campbell and J. Laherrere, "The End of Cheap Oil," *Scientific American* 279 (March 1998): 78–84.

A WAY WITH WASTE

HUNTER HEAIVILIN

It is a hot summer day in the late 2000s. I am sweating in my air-condition-less truck, windows up in a futile attempt to keep the dust and smell at bay, waiting in a line of vehicles at the Waimānalo Gulch Sanitary Landfill. I have come prepared to do my civic duty and deposit some bulky materials from a long-forgotten home improvement project. In front of me, a semi-truck bucks forward as we all advance a pace towards the burial place of the detritus of Oʻahu's population.

As my stomach grumbles about hunger, an arm appears out of the truck ahead of me holding the remnants of a plate lunch: styrofoam clamshell and utensils encapsulated in a plastic bag, closed with a bow redolent of holidays past. The arm extends and drops the bag to the ground. I'm initially struck by such brash littering, indignant that someone would do such a thing, as if the "Keep America Beautiful" campaigns (ironically funded by the likes of Philip Morris and Coca-Cola) had never managed to reach our shores across the Pacific. But there is no public outcry. No other drivers leave their vehicles to claim this misdeed. And suddenly the hypocrisy of the situation strikes me: I am here to do just the same thing, to dump my own debris, and drive home without a second thought.

Waves of understanding roll upon me like the quivers of heat beyond my dashboard: all garbage is litter; we have just found ways to sanctify our waste, to make pollution tolerable, to couch it in "responsibility," and even veil it in supposedly noble stewardship. But ultimately there is no "away," no place beyond where our actions have no impact. We are inextricably wed to our lifestyles and their repercussions. I drive home with an empty truck bed, but a full mind, determined to do something, anything, to lessen my impact and to walk more lightly through this life and on this land.

A few years later I find myself standing in front of a roomful of tired-eyed middle schoolers, recounting this tale and asking them: "What is waste?" The usual answers emerge: "junk," "trash," "stuff we don't want," "things we can't use." To which I offer a now rote response: "What is waste in nature?" The room falls silent until the answers come tentatively forward: "leaves?", "bird poop?", "branches?", and finally "nothing . . . ?" I can't help but crack a smile as heads cock and turn to look at the precocious speaker. I reply, "Yes! Nothing is wasted; in natural systems the waste of one becomes the food of another."

This is my gambit towards reconceiving waste: building the understanding that waste, more than anything else, is a mindset. The goal for the day is to get the kids interested enough in waste to have them help me perform an onsite audit of the trash their school had produced the day prior. Mid-audit, their intrigue peaks as they watch me find a whole discarded banana and proceed to carefully peel and consume it. With that transgressive act, any remnant tired eyes grow wide, as "waste equals food" goes from being a concept to a reality.

WASTE IS A MINDSET

Etymologically, "waste" derives from the same root as "vast," connoting emptiness and desolation. Only a cursory exploration of this connection brings to mind the landscapes we leave in the wake of our processing: the stumps where forests stood, the mines where mountains ranged, and ultimately the windswept desert landfills. The items we cast aside represent not the progress of our day but more so the hubris that we can continue to live on the overextended credit of our natural resources, hoping the debt never comes due.

Waste, through designation, is an act and an expression of a mindset, whereas *resources* are what are really being lost by such action. When we recast our understanding of waste as misappropriated resources, we are faced with a design problem: How do our islands, nearly wholly reliant upon imports,[1] manage the overwhelming amount of resources shipped to our shores? Are these problems or opportunities? Whether or not we wanted them shipped here in the first place, we must find a way to deal with the onslaught of resources. In 2011, Hawaiʻi generated an average of 7.12 pounds of waste per person per day.[2] In 2008 we earned the dubious honor of producing far more waste per person than any other state,[3] and that within a nation that produces more garbage than most.[4]

THE TRIBUTARIES OF THE WASTE STREAM

The first step towards tackling this issue is source separation—by pairing like with like, we begin to isolate the tributaries of the waste stream and gain a better understanding of what our waste consists of. In my work with schools, we use four primary categories: reusable, compostable, recyclable, and refusable. Reusables are the items that, while not necessarily as convenient or cheap, can be used again and again—like Ziploc bags, jars, and other durable goods. Compostables are all the organic materials that we can process onsite—like food waste, green waste, and, for the daring, manure. Recyclables are the items the City and County of Honolulu or similar willing entities will accept—cardboard, newsprint, bottles, cans, and so on. "Refusables," a neologism coined by a student at Washington Elementary, are all other refuse, mostly consisting of various plastics.

Each county has been making strides towards source separation. Most Oʻahu-ans and many on Maui now have a brigade of colored bins outside our homes, each collecting a different type of material. On other islands, which produce considerably less waste, personal hauling remains the norm. Each island now offers various means of waste diversion, from "green waste only" dumps to metal recycling centers. Overall, this is a boon for the recapture of resources, since the home and business are the headwaters of the waste stream. Overall, diverting the waste stream into rills of organics, recyclables, and so on makes the resources much more manageable and reduces the remnant amounts that are landfilled.

But is making sure to toss our green bottles into the blue bin sufficient? Can we really recycle our way to sustainability? The simple feel-good act of putting things in the right bin or using biodegradable plastics often overshadows more in-depth exploration of our wasteful systems. We are optimizing the wrong things; these acts allow us to experience the drops of altruism and do-gooding without any real work to change our behaviors. Of course, styrofoam is not preferable to PLA bioplastics, not by a longshot. The key to remember, though, is that each purchase drives production and further resource use, no matter the materials used.

To better understand the implications of our actions, we can look to the waste hierarchy of "Reduce, Reuse, Recycle," often represented as a triangle or pyramid to portray the amount of energy each "R" requires. Reduction, or non-consumption, takes the least amount of energy, and thus finds itself atop the pyramid. Most of all it requires foresight and a tinge of planning to avoid materials destined for the modern midden heap. Reuse takes another step of consideration, begging the question of whether or not a given product was designed to be reused or whether we are prepared to invest the time to contrive secondary and tertiary uses. Recycling is ordinally placed last, occupying the largest area at the bottom of the pyramid, to symbolize the intensive energy required for reprocessing. As of 2013, there are no recycling facilities for most products within the state, meaning that each item shipped in is also shipped out. This is true of nearly all plastics, glass, and paper.

Once the waste we actually discard leaves our homes, where does the stream flow? As of 2013, Oʻahu's municipal waste is collected through curbside

haulings and deposits at transfer stations and convenience centers, and to-
taled over 1.6 million tons during 2012. Much of Oʻahu's waste, with the
exception of construction and demolition materials, then goes onward to H-
Power, the waste-to-energy incineration plant, which significantly reduces
the volume of waste and also yields electricity. A new boiler has been built,
expanding the capacity of H-Power, which will allow for even more of our
waste to be converted into ash (destined for the landfill) and power. The City
and County of Honolulu's Department of Environmental Services, the entity tasked with waste management, waxes brightly about the H-Power plant
expansion and the "renewable energy" that is produced.[5]

"Renewable" is a misnomer in the case of energy produced through waste
incineration. Lauding H-Power energy as helping to reduce Hawaiʻi's reliance upon imported oil is an example of "greenwashing." Energy produced
from H-Power is nearly wholly reliant upon exogenous resources instead of
local ones. H-Power is fed mostly by resources manufactured and shipped
here through oil use, and does nothing to reduce our reliance on those resources. The net fossil fuel use for energy production drops through H-Power, but the reliance persists. Additionally, though currently all EPA standards
for air quality are being met, it should be noted that combustion (and the
aforementioned oil use) yields gasses which enter the atmosphere and contribute to anthropogenic climate change. We may be burning less oil overall,
but we are still burning it.

Most crucial to note, though, are the contracts that bind the City and
County of Honolulu to quotas of waste generation. The contracts to provide waste to H-Power eliminate any incentive on the part of the City to em-
phasize waste reduction as an overall solution. This situation contrasts most
starkly with that of Hawaiʻi County, which has a adopted a Zero Waste Goal,
falling much more closely in line with the law (HRS §342G-2) dictating
the priority of source reduction over recycling, landfilling, and incineration.
Hawaiʻi Island has created reuse centers at many dumps which accept and
then resell items that would have otherwise been landfilled; comparatively,
transfer stations on Oʻahu are placarded to keep even the most keen gleaner
from harvesting. On Hawaiʻi Island, each waste deposit point has become an
additional opportunity for resource capture and income. Not a bad idea for
Oʻahu, where due to funding constraints, many community recycling deposit
points have been removed.

A PERSONAL JOURNEY TO NO WASTE

In 2008, with the knowledge of this daunting flow tide of waste, I resolved
to ebb my contributions and to navigate towards the goal of producing no

waste within five years. Year One I committed to only doing environmental-ly-oriented work (and have never looked back). In Year Two, I set myself to composting all of my food waste (a trait now innate). Year Three I graduated to processing all of my human waste through composting (staring down my toilet while perched on a bucket[6]). Year Four was focused on paring down remaining waste, mostly through growing or gleaning much more of my own food. Since I'd found that most of my waste stream consisted of grocery items, I sought to decrease consumption by upping production. Year Five never came to be, but continues to haunt me as a specter of youthful enthu-siasm accosted by reality. By the end of my five years I realized that nothing short of dropping out of society, if even that, would bring me to my goal. We are as bound to the production systems we rely upon as they are to us. In the course of those years, though, I found myself lighter, happier, better fed, and less entangled with the systems that I didn't agree with. I became hopelessly addicted to horticulture, to local food, to sidling up as closely as possible to the material supply lines upon which I am dependent. I came to understand that it is our designations that define what is wasted and what is not; that it is our actions, or lack thereof, that can manage and transform waste into resources.

Personally and collectively, we can reduce our waste through vigilance and concerted actions. A technique I've found useful is to collect an inter-ested hui and agree to store individually all of one's waste for a week. At the end of the week, perform an audit to see what remains, and who has the least. This slight competitive aspect heightens our awareness of what is tossed, and rewards reflection and creativity. I've done this with friends on other islands, in petty races to produce the least that ended up yielding in-novative ways to compost, recycle more, consume less. The land is the ulti-mate victor in this game, with less pressure put on our landscapes to absorb the byproducts of progress.

The simplest act to be made at a personal level is to compost. Diverting compostable waste out of the waste stream helps increase the efficiency of H-Power's incinerators while working to close the nutrient cycle of food pro-duction and agriculture. The water held in our foods makes up most of the weight associated with hauling and is notoriously hard to burn. Composting helps to divert part of our waste stream into landscapes, not landfills. A word of caution, though: composting has also been shown to lead directly to other subversive acts, like gardening, condoned looting of neighbors' green waste bins for grass clippings and mulches, and in serious cases, even farming.

There are numerous conscientious community organizations like The Green House in Pauoa Valley, Kokua Hawaii Foundation, Kanu Hawaii, Ku-pu's R.I.S.E. program, and Re-Use Hawai'i, all of which have programming working to address waste at scales ranging from back porch to policy. Most of my work (with the Kokua Foundation and The Green House) has centered around schools that, despite high food service plate counts, are often not subject to the food waste diversion standards that some hotels and restaurants are. Working or volunteering with your neighborhood school to divert and compost organic wastes will not only reduce the amounts being taken to landfills but can garner nutritive compost for educational gardening programs. Many school administrators are open to such work, and when done in concert, this work can be a leveraging tool that can reduce the hauling costs to individual schools by reworking waste contracts at the complex level. By reducing or eliminating the organic content entering dumpsters, unwanted scents wane, meaning that hauling can occur less frequently. Better yet, we could keep the hauling contracts, jobs, and rates as they are, but redefine the work by having the companies pick up and sell recyclables (currently not institutionally accomplished by the DOE), on the days now relieved of waste hauling.

WEALTH AND WASTE

My experience working in other island communities, from Haiti to Vanuatu, has driven home the realization that more "wealth" equates to more waste. As income increases, so does one's impact. To close the loop on our resources, a new vision of wealth is just as crucial as a new understanding of waste. Wealth, just like waste, determines our operating procedures, our pathway through this life, and the footprints we leave. How we express wealth and waste defines who we are and our possible futures.

When our concept of wealth can only be expressed through increased material consumption, then increased waste is an inevitable outcome of being wealthy. If we instead define our wealth by the health of the social and ecological systems we rely upon, then waste has no place. "Waiwai" does just that, and the word alone is a reminder that our well-being is wed to the health of the land and water. By taking waiwai as our understanding of wealth, the decrease of waste then becomes a means of increasing our collective wealth.

To confront our waste is to confront our sovereignty. Focus and critique of the larger systems we currently rely on lead us to explore solutions to decrease our dependence and enhance our self-reliance. Changing our means of production is paramount to changing our waste stream; just as in watershed management, we need to work upstream, where each action has a greater downstream effect. The transition from individual consumers to communities of producers is one that will take us simultaneously closer to our pasts and to a future that considers our actions beyond just the years we have on this earth.

Consumption and production are often polarized to opulence and subsistence, as if our only two modes of being are to have a high thread count or to be threadbare. Cultivating communities that are independent for our needs and interdependent for our wants is the middle path towards thriving environments, which house healthy societies served by viable economies. We need to chart a path away from models of globalized codependency on distant production systems that have us all exporting value and receiving waste in return. I imagine a future where communities are connected to their resource base, where biotic and abiotic materials are valued, and where the cost of waste is more directly felt by all. In such a community or culture, where all are consciously wed and interacting with the systems upon which they rely, a new word may be needed. Neither the stratified pyramid of opulence nor the flattened back of horizontal subsistence typifies such an existence. *Supersistence*—the local production of what is needed with sufficient surplus for trade—may serve as a better term, and a guiding star, for a future without waste lands.

NOTES

1. Take a look at the room around you as you read this; what, of the items you are surrounded by, was not flown or shipped here? With the exception of kamaʻāina, strikingly little.

2. Author calculation based on 2011 US Census data and the State Department of Health Annual Report on Solid Waste Management to the Legislature. You can read the report online at http://co.doh.hawaii.gov/sites/LegRpt/2012/Reports/1/Final%202012%2OS WM%20LEG%20Rpt.pdf.

3. 2.89 tons per capita per year in 2008, more than double that year's total generation average for the US of 1.28 tons per capita per year. The data is from Rob van Haaren et al., "The State of Garbage in America," *Biocycle* (Oct. 2010), available at http://www. biocycle.net/images/art/1010/bc101016_s.pdf.

4. 4.40 lbs per capita per day in the US during 2011. Data is from the US Environmental Protection Agency, "Municipal Solid Waste," June 2013, available at http://www.epa. gov/epawaste/nonhaz/municipal/index.htm.

5. City and County of Honolulu Department of Environmental Services, "H-Power Recognized by Engineering Organization," April 24, 2012 Press Release, available at http://www.opala.org/solid_waste/pdfs/ASME%20Names%20H-POWER%20Top% 20Facility_120424.pdf.

6. Joseph Jenkins's *The Humanure Handbook* (Grove City, PA: Joseph Jenkins, 2005) is an insightful and hilarious how-to on safely processing human manure.

RESOURCES FOR FURTHER INFORMATION AND INSPIRATION

1. Composting classes are regularly offered by The Green House in Pauoa Valley. Also go ask your local organic farmer to get another in-depth and Hawai'i-pertinent how-to.

2. *Worms Eat My Garbage* (Kalamazoo: Flower P, 2003) by Mary Appelhoff is a great introductory book to dealing with kitchen waste through vermicomposting. Worms are a great means of composting inside for the landless highriser.

3. *The Story of Stuff* and related videos, online at www.storyofstuff.org.

4. William McDonough and Michael Braungart's *Cradle to Cradle* (New York: North Point P, 2002).

5. Gunter Pauli's Zero-Emissions Research Institute and his book *Upsizing: The Road to Zero Emissions, More Jobs, More Income, and No Pollution* (Austin: Greenleaf, 2000), address the broader processes of connecting production systems to reduce waste.

THINGS YOU MISSED
(OR, THE DOG-EARS, REVISITED)

DONOVAN KŪHIŌ COLLEPS

the time i went out past the breaks at hau bush four days after you died it rained and pleny pua were jumping out of the water coming towards me reminding me when we saw this once together and you told me it's because a shark is somewhere near by.

> *My mother also had a pet shark out near the entrance to Pearl Harbor. . . . Some of the catch always went to Kaʻahupūhau, her shark, which she raised from when it was small until it reached over 25 feet in length.*
> *Change We Must*, Nana Veary

our family god is the shark you told me.

I was silent
on my fiberglass belly
not knowing
where rain ended
or ocean began.

> *Because our body seems so convincingly to exist, our "I" seems to exist and "you" seem to exist, and the entire illusory, dualistic world we never stop projecting around us looks ultimately solid and real. When we die this whole compound construction falls dramatically to pieces.*
> *The Tibetan Book of Living and Dying*, Sogyal Rinpoche

the time right after the mortuary guys wheeled you from your room past the file cabinet and out of the house in that black bag and nana was still talking story with you a giant moth with white circles on its wings slammed into the living room window and t.j. screamed and said something something moths something your spirit.

you would've laughed.

the time i returned to las vegas for a friend's wedding to the spot under the freemont street experience where we met years ago years after not seeing each other and we hugged under the electronic f-14s zooming over us in red white and blue formations and i left my friends at the strip and caught a taxi to stand there again to remember the worried look on your face when you saw the struggle in mine.

Crazy shit I saw on the train/bus to Vegas:

> **in the middle   –one piano   of a field**

> **—a giant Clorox manufacturing plant
> with smoke stacks like a church organ**

**—one torn red felt couch
somewhere in Barstow(?)
with one marbled kitten sleeping on it**

> **—the bus driver stopped at a diner in the desert
> and this family kept staring at me, licking
> ice cream cones. (even the baby
> had a cowboy hat)**

the time i found myself circling the house checking for tears in any of the screens because i found the drawer of bent nails that you had me pull out because you said i did it all wrong and that everything i do should be done well even if it's as small as hammering a nail into wood because this house needs to be repaired when it's broken so that the family always has a place to live.

i found a few tears in nana's bedroom screen and fixed it for her.

the time i found the first orange growing from the tree that i bought for you on your last birthday when i dragged it into the house in its green plastic pot and got dirt everywhere and said hauʻoli lā hānau papa and you looked at me like i chose this gift wisely while ma yelled because of the trail of dirt through the house.

the time i started eating meat again after living in san francisco for so long because i heard joseph campbell on the radio say that life eats life and it reminded me of you and how you forced me to learn how to kill clean and cook our chickens when they were fully grown and how you knew that i needed to learn how to deal with that.

> *The goal of life is to make your heartbeat match the beat of the universe, to match your nature with Nature.*
>
> *The Power of Myth*, Joseph Campbell

the time i opened the tool shed and smelled you in the grease crumbs on my fingertips.

RECLAIMING OUR STORIES OF STRUGGLE

CADE WATANABE

"You only live once!" That was among the many sayings Grandpa liked to share.

Grandpa was known for many things. Khaki pants with homemade sewn patches along the knees, a worn-out belt that slowly made way for a simple rope cord, blue-pocketed long-sleeve shirts and hats. Ice cream, musky after-shave, and Coke, always sipped with a straw. He was a very proud man, and like so many in his generation, he seemed to have experienced too much for one person in one lifetime. His greatest talent was using his warmth and genuine sense of care to wrangle folks in. He was never short of stories, and if you gave him the chance, hours would pass before you knew it. A story or two, maybe three, or often many more than that. And he didn't discriminate. It happened to all of us, and Grandpa was always around.

My beloved Grandpa passed away a year ago. He certainly lived a productive and long life, and what seemed clear from his many stories was that life was worth living only if you could share a little of your story with others.

There were stories of winning his eighth-grade oratory competition, of fishing adventures and ʻōkolehao drinks, of going to school with nothing but rakkyo (Japanese sweet pickled onion) and rice, and of hard work and "buss ass." For me, Grandpa's stories revealed my family's journey from one side of Hawaiʻi Island to another. I learned that the origin of my family's name was intimately connected to Grandpa's own involvement with organized labor. His stories spoke of a Hawaiʻi that valued relationships forged through struggle: the heart and soul of Hawaiʻi's labor movement. In more recent times, this has become a lost movement, desperately holding on to the legacy and expectations of the past instead of possessing the courage to tell the true story of our working families today.

Grandpa was never ashamed of who he was or what he had to endure to help keep his family afloat. He never shied away from what he represented. He was a plantation worker, and his stories were full of self-worth, a sense of place, value, and pride. That is my Hawaiʻi. A Hawaiʻi where workers take pride in their work so that their stories, our values, can be shared in ways that inspire and motivate us to overcome the imposed scripts that leave us begging and "pointing the finger," rather than uniting and organizing for a Hawai'i that meets our needs. We only do live once. Sadly, the Hawai'i we're living in now is not reflective of who we are or what we represent.

STUMBLING INTO A MOVEMENT

At the age of twenty-three, I began work with UNITE HERE Local 5—one of Hawai'i's largest labor unions, and today arguably among the State's most powerful. With a statewide membership of 10,000 hotel, health care, and food service workers, Local 5 has been the standard-bearer for wages, benefits, and a decent quality of life for seventy-five years.

But the challenges we face today are immense. In the seven years that I've worked at Local 5, drastic cuts in hotel and health care jobs have all but crippled our economy and eroded an important part of our State's tax base. We've lost 1,600 Local 5 members, but it's not just the Union or workers who have lost, the community has as well. More than $89 million every year are not being paid out in wages and benefits because of the loss of Local 5 jobs alone, and that amounts to over $10 million each year lost in State and City taxes—money that goes to pay our teachers, policeman, fire fighters, and government workers, including our politicians.

It doesn't take a trained economist to understand that some things just don't add up. Booming tourism and health care profits, yet less and less for Hawai'i's people. That's not the Hawai'i my Grandpa fought hard to build, and cherished in his stories.

I entered Hawai'i's labor movement with very little to offer. Like so many young people out of college, I wanted to do something good with my life. I wanted to make my family proud and make a difference in my community. Yet, news of my settling in on my first real job was greeted by a sincere sense of awe and some disbelief. It may sound cliché, but the script written out for me—local, educated, fourth-generation Japanese male, from a small town and plantation values—didn't necessarily translate into "union organizer." Play by the rules, go by your script, do good, and don't bring about unwanted attention to the family, mostly translated into some 9-to-5 job or engineer. "Union organizer" wasn't one of the options my high school counselor talked about. Even my family members who were part of the labor union were confused.

Only when I started working for the Union did my Grandpa's own history with labor organizing slowly reveal itself. At the age of fifteen, my Grandpa became the sole breadwinner in his family. He had no other choice but to work full-time to help provide for his five siblings after his stepfather nearly died in an industrial accident while digging irrigation ditches along the rugged and hilly terrain of the Hāmākua Coast. In 1946, at twenty-two, my Grandpa joined more than 20,000 other unionized sugar workers to stage perhaps Hawai'i's most significant and impressive mass demonstration of people power: the Great Hawaiian Sugar Strike. For seventy-nine days, under the leadership of their union, the ILWU, sugar workers walked off the job, and their families joined in—nearly 80,000 people in all—organized across ethnic lines in pursuit of better pay and benefits that would eventually make the Big Five "pay," and bring about widespread social and political change throughout Hawai'i.

By the age of twenty-three, my Grandpa had already accumulated years of experience as a union activist, brought on by his own personal quest to seek justice for his stepfather, whose last name he took on because of the man he was to my Grandpa. Unlike my Grandpa, I had no compelling story of struggle, disappointment, and anger that would have driven me to seek out the union.

Yet I found purpose in my work at Local 5. My own life experiences up until that point, and the lessons learned from my Grandpa's own stories, now began to make more sense. I may not have been a plantation worker, but like my Grandpa, I was eager to feel valued and empowered.

I quickly learned that the feeling of empowerment that I was desperately seeking was one experienced in connecting with others. Our individual stories matter and help situate who we are, but they live and can transform our realities when we're willing to share and connect with others. My work with the Union has greatly influenced my own perspective on what it means to do good in the community. Making a difference is an honorable goal to pursue, but I have also learned that if you want to transform the community you so dearly care about, then you have to attach yourself to an organized base of power that can sustain, validate, and capture one's hard work and contribution.

AiKea: AN EXPERIMENT IN PEOPLE POWER

In 2012, my Union took a meaningful leap toward rethinking its own purpose and value in addressing the crisis facing our community. After years of organizing experimentation and alongside nearly ninety community leaders, Local 5 helped launch a new movement that, at its core, puts forth a comprehensive vision for a Hawai'i that meets our needs as working people—a Hawai'i where 80,000 people could take to the streets and exercise people power on a mass scale once again. We call our movement "AiKea," the local

Pidgin pronunciation for the English words "I care." A simple phrase to reflect a movement filled with the hope, determination, and pride needed to protect the people and ʻāina with aloha. AiKea seeks to recapture the value of our stories as workers through direct conversations, relationship-building, and organizing to reclaim power for our families.

Although AiKea is just over a year old, we've already knocked on over 42,000 doors, had over 12,000 direct conversations, and identified over 7,000 AiKea supporters in districts that cover nearly a third of the island of Oʻahu. In 2012, we helped elect two new City Councilors and one State Representative who are committed to representing our interests as working people.

More importantly, AiKea has been able to garner the attention of other key elected and community leaders, and in 2013 helped to lead a campaign that included students, Native Hawaiian and environmental activists, concerned residents, and workers to repeal Act 55, which created the Public Land Development Corporation (PLDC). The PLDC was a State-run corporation that would have allowed just five appointed people the power to fast track development on our public lands, like that our State harbors, parks, and public schools sit on, while removing adequate public input from the process. In so many ways the PLDC was yet another short-sighted solution brought forth by representatives who had the interests of banks and developers in mind, not ours. As was the case in the 1946 Great Hawaiian Sugar Strike, the ruling elite refused to confront our reality. But we own this town, and our victory over the PLDC showed us that people power could stop our State government from moving on an initiative that would have left all of us behind.

AiKea has begun to unleash the true potential of the Union's value to our community. It teaches us to value the stories of our members in a way that will allow workers to serve as the foundation for our growing movement. As a Union, we fight for good jobs because we care about the kind of education our kids receive. We fight for decent health care, and at the same time we fight to protect our precious agricultural land because we care about the kind of food our kids eat. We stand up for the right to organize into the Union, and at the same time we fight for more public input and transparency in government because our kids need to see that our voices—as workers—matter. Today, AiKea is a growing movement of organizations like Local 5 and other key leaders from various faith, civic, and community groups, in addition to educators and students who care about the future of our Hawaiʻi.

THE LEGACY I SEEK

Most of my childhood was spent in the plantation camp of Haina, just down the hill from the town of Honokaʻa on the Hāmākua Coast of the Island of

Hawai'i. On the day of last harvest, when Hamakua Sugar closed for good in 1994, all of us, even those in school, came down to the main street for a final goodbye and thank you. And on that day, so many of us also felt a unique sense of pride. Not just for our town, but for our neighbors and family members—like my Grandpa who built his life, and what would become my Hawai'i. Now I realize that what we were most proud of had everything to do with the strength of a community held tightly together by a common set of economic circumstances, and of a foundational struggle that lived on through the stories of workers, their connection to the sugar fields, and the dreams they shared of building a better Hawai'i.

Sometimes I still don't know where I want to be or what I want to do, but at least now I can begin to recognize the value of my own work. I want a powerful Hawai'i, and that power rests in large part in the stories we share. My Hawai'i is one that values the basis of our struggle as working people, and recognizes that our push for change is also about reconnecting with that feeling deep down in our gut of being wronged.

On any given day, workers are fighting back to reclaim their power. These stories of struggle and for justice in the workplace need to transcend the confines of the four walls of our hotels. The story of a housekeeper that leads her coworkers in taking over her department's morning meeting in order to collectively demand more linens and trash liners is one full of self-worth, value, and pride. It can also be one that inspires others, including young people, to get engaged in efforts that lead to building the labor movement.

AiKea has helped to create a space where we can reclaim our own stories and connect with others through sharing them. AiKea is a movement that allows both a housekeeper and a young artist to tell their stories, share their experiences—albeit drastically different on the surface—and collectively seek out that mutual need of being valued and empowered in ways that can transform the Hawai'i they both call home.

In their own way, each can proudly declare, "I am AiKea."

Grace is a mother, an immigrant, and up at 4:30 a.m. each morning, just enough time to pack a favorite meal, get dressed, and climb on the express bus from 'Ewa Beach to Waikīkī. She arrives at least an hour before the start of her shift to partake in a potluck-style breakfast alongside her coworkers, eating her fill, knowing that she'll have no time for lunch on her own. After a backbreaking day of lifting dozens of mattresses, changing scores of pillow cases, and completing nearly forty other cleaning tasks for each of the fifteen rooms assigned to her, she finally gets some rest on the two-hour bus ride home. It's already been a twelve-hour day, and she barely has enough strength to grasp the handles of the pot that holds her family's dinner. As she finds time to relax, her trembling hands make it difficult for her to maintain the steadiness needed to apply nail polish to her bruised fingers, the result of tucking in so many sheets, corner after corner. And as she prepares for bed, she musters just enough strength to squeeze what little toothpaste she can as she stares intently into the mirror, brushing her teeth.

Lauren is a young artist, a descendant of immigrants, and daughter of working-class parents. She studied sociology and theatre at the University of Hawai'i, and the relationships she built with workers as an organizer have transformed her perspective about the value of her own story. She writes:

Vanity is insanity,
Yet I confront the mirror daily.
Reflecting on each curve, feature, and outline,
I take inventory of the experiences that shaped me.
Years spent believing:
My home,
My heritage,
My story,
Weren't good enough
For society's hard-to-please eyes.
Staring a little longer, the mirror reveals another truth.

I see the world with honest eyes.
A descendent of immigrants,
Of hard work and struggle,
A fight burns from within.
A deep down desire to search for truths
In a world shaped by lies.
A history clouded in violent oppression,
Perpetuated by systems of power built on false privilege.

Connected to my story,
I am more than enough!

I want a Hawai'i where young people not only develop a passion for making a difference, but a Hawai'i that will be ready for change on a mass scale. We have to think big, almost recklessly. We have to fight to tell stories that reveal truths about the intimate origins of our collective struggle. We have to value our stories and our power so we believe that we can take back power from the banks and developers, and that we can elect *our* people to elected office. Our stories need to motivate us to organize and build power in ways that can transform our community, not just change it.

Organizing and building a movement is so very personal. As young people, we want to make sense of our experiences and situate our own stories. We need to be proud of who we are and take pride in our work. The labor movement is not just about fighting for unionized workers and their rights or about securing good wages and benefits. It is about the fulfillment and immediate satisfaction of exploring our own innate limits and potential. It is about acknowledging our self-worth and sharing just a bit. AiKea may not "save" the labor movement, but at least it makes labor fulfill its true potential in unlocking opportunities for people like me.

I need a radical movement
To liberate and evolve humanity,
Just as much as it needs me!
My home,
My story,
I suffer for humanity.
My thoughts, courage, and passion
Dependent on those willing to take risks.
Providers, fighters, and healers
Acting out of our shared oppression,
Awakened by a powerful truth,
Together we have already won.
I need the movement,
The way it needs me.[1]

I am prepared for a better Hawai'i. I'm pissed off and I'm going to do something valuable about it. I'm a worker, I struggle, but I'm damn proud of it, and more than willing to share.

NOTES

1.   As an organizer, I am blessed. I have had the privilege of working with many talented and inspirational leaders whose stories have driven me to become a better steward of my own. The poem here was written by Ms. Lauren Ballesteros, a young artist whom I first met in 2009. After participating in a two-day student leadership workshop, Lauren went on to become an organizing intern while completing her senior year at the University of Hawai'i, and was later hired as a Local 5 community/political organizer in 2010. I am truly grateful to Lauren for allowing me to use her story as part of this essay. Today, Lauren lives in El Monte, California, and continues to nurture her passion of engaging communities through the transformative power of storytelling, as an actor and playwright involved in community theater.

RESOURCES FOR FURTHER INFORMATION AND INSPIRATION

1. You can learn more about "The AiKea Movement" on our website, at http://www. AiKeaHawaii.org.
2. Ben Sadoski and Ivan Hou, "The Goose That Laid the Golden Time Bombs: How Hawaii's Changed Hotel Industry Threatens our Futures," Local 5, April 2013.
3. "UNITE HERE Local 5" website, at http://www.unitehere5.org.
4. "The State of Poverty in Hawaii & How to Restore our Legacy of Fairness," Hawaii Appleseed Center for Law and Economic Justice, April 2012, available at http://hiap pleseed.org/sites/default/files/State%20of%20Poverty%20FINAL.pdf.
5. "Center for Labor Education and Research" website, at http://www.clear.uhwo.hawaii. edu.

THE URBAN ISLAND PENDULUM

PRIME

REDEFINING HAWAI'I'S "URBAN YOUTH"

Kids can smell bullshit. They feel like they're being lied to every single day. When they're a part of what we're doing with our organization, 808 Urban, the struggles are real. They can see it. And they get frustrated. "Now you know how the kūpuna felt when they were fighting for this place," I tell them. It's like a pendulum. On one side you have progress and development, and on the other you have tradition and culture. But ultimately, I don't think fighting is the answer. Creativity is.

808 Urban is a collective of community cultural workers: artists, organizers, and volunteers committed to improving the quality of life for our communities through arts programming. We believe that through mentoring youth in the urban arts, based upon a platform of cultural and political education, grassroots community organizing, entrepreneurial skill sets, and community murals, we play a vital role in shaping Hawai'i's up-and-coming leaders. We're smashing the negative associations you get when you think of "urban youth": "at risk," "criminal property damage," "gang affiliated," "drug abuse."

The idea of "urban" today has everything to do with *how* a place is developed. Say there is this land and there used to be a hale there. The hale used to be where everyone would sit down on the porch, play Hawaiian music, kanikapila, invite anybody come sit down. That was "the urban setting." Now, we have freakish high rises tweaked out in every single way possible. The urban youth of today are all about upgrading iPhones, staying current with the latest technology, the apps. If you ask them what our lives were like prior to all that, they cannot tell you; they don't even care to tell you.

Initially, the youth that I have worked with have this false idea, that in life you have to murder the city and get arrested to say you have "street cred." They want that big-city respect and they are going to get it no matter what! Their source? The internet. Gone are the days of doing things face-to-face, in true ALOHA fashion. You can now hide behind screen names and never feel accountable to any drama that you take part in. With the average attention span of today's youth literally shrinking by the minute, it is imperative that we look to our kūpuna for guidance, to understand their struggles and how they adapted to and overcame adversity to provide for us today. There's no quality today because there's no struggle. And so we have to identify with another struggle in order for them to get it.

A HISTORY OF HIP HOP WRITING

A lot of kids today are really disconnected from the past. For example, they want to listen to music imported from the continent, talking about degrading our women, treating them like dogs. Spam Jeezy, Hollywood, Tinseltown. Nothing that has to do with this place. Other kids like to honor their Hawaiian culture, but usually through the more popular reggae music, and weed. Although these alternatives are cool, the local music scene often lacks a "call to action" in its lyrics.

The more I see these kids disconnected, the more I realize how disconnected I was. My dad was so patient. He didn't push me to be Hawaiian. He let me discover that on my own. Unfortunately, he passed away, and now I realize I missed an opportunity to sit down and dialogue with him about our culture.

For a lot of our families, sharing and talking about this was painful, so they never really talked to us about what really happened. And this is sad, because if they don't share it with us, I can't share it with my kids. What motivated me to learn more about my culture was trying to apply for Hawaiian Homelands in the '90s. My wife could prove her lineage. I only had one or two newspaper clippings that I could use. And since then, it's been a constant journey.

My grandparents grew up speaking the language, educated in their culture. My dad understood the culture and the language but was taught in English, because that's how everyone was pushing their children at the time. My generation was born and taught strictly in English, with little connection to culture. That's where hip-hop came in to fill that void for us, the "gap generation."

During the 1980s, hip hop took Hawai'i teens by storm. One of the foundations of Hip Hop is "writing," known as "graffiti" by the general public. Some of the early influences on Hawai'i included PHASE2, DOZE, DONDI, and SEEN from New York. In turn, we produced legends of our own: SLICK, KRUSH458, SKEZ520, KATCH1, QUEST, EAST3, NA-KAZ, BAM, and others. Some kept it real on the homeland while others went global with their art.

Growing up, I remember one song in particular by Grandmaster Flash and the Furious Five, called "The Message":

It's like a jungle sometimes
It makes me wonder how I keep from going under.
Broken glass everywhere
People pissing on the stairs
You know they just don't care.
I can't take the smell
I can't take the noise
Got no money to move out
I guess I got no choice.[1]

When these lyrics came up in these songs, I was like, boom. Holy crap, somebody's talking about my life. I could *feel* it; growing up in the housing projects, you had to pass by people in the stairs walking around, high on something. And you're scared. When I was about eight years old, everyone knew me as Little John in Chinatown. I was this little kid that used to go up and down, running all over the place. All the pimps and prostitutes would give me money, tell me to go get something for eat. They took good care of me and treated me like family. All the gambling houses and pool halls did the same. The night life was different though. I remember waking up in the middle of the night to some yelling and decided to investigate. I saw a group of sailors get their asses beat outside of Swing Club by some of the uncles that took care of me during the day. Over time, the violence and abuse stopped phasing me. Looking back on my life, I realize I didn't know any better. I thought that that's how every kid lived. Nothing Hawaiian about that.

Hip hop was a totally different culture, but the struggle was the same. Hip hop empowered us here to resist the system, to fight the power. It turned violence into creativity. B-boy battles instead of gang fights. Graffiti was our way of destroying the system that's not indigenous to us. I knew that my people were suffering, but hip hop alone didn't tell me how, why, or how many. It wasn't enough at the time. But it connected all of these things that I loved to do, and it was the only thing that I knew that touched all the senses.

But today, hip hop is turning into fanfare, vanity, gymnastics, circus moves that don't really tell a story. Because these kids pretty much turned all our blood, sweat, and tears into a circus act, it's forcing those of us from that early generation of hip hop to come back and correct the scene.

THE BIRTH OF 808 URBAN

It was 2005, my two oldest children were just entering middle school, and life was good for me. I owned my home, had great neighbors, a great job, and most importantly, a wonderful family. Memories of my life's past were all behind me now, or so I thought!

My two oldest came home from school one day with a small group of friends and asked me for permission to paint the garage. I consented, until the smell of aerosol began to seep through my garage door, prompting me to investigate. To my dismay, my garage was covered from top to bottom with tags! I was upset! Not about the tagging, but because it lacked *style*. My kids had no idea about their dad's involvement in the writing culture prior to their birth. On that day, an old spark was re-ignited within me.

In 2006, there was no program in Hawai'i for kids who did tagging. I approached the State, but they thought I was crazy, probably because of the negative ways graffiti was represented in the press. I said, screw it, I'm just gonna do it anyway. I built my own walls in my backyard. I was doing mortgages at that time in real estate. Usually you tithe a certain percentage to the church. I tithed to the kids. I bought food, barbecued for the kids, and invited the kids to come and ask questions from the "graffiti kūpuna." We called it a "bench," and imagined these workshops as a safe space for kids to learn and ask real questions: "What is it like to go bombing at night?" "How many times have you got arrested?" To us, it's silly, but to them, those were real questions. And I wouldn't judge. I would say, "whatever you guys do, that's what you guys do. Just don't do it here." And this helps them heal. For some of them, it kind of killed their curiosity too.

We went from four kids the first month to 187 kids in six months. By then, I couldn't fit everybody in my yard. They came from Kailua side, from Wai'anae side, all over. My yard became "the spot" for the kids. And we just kept growing. In 2008, we moved to Palama Settlement, with our Writer's Park right off the H1 Freeway. Now we have a space in Kaka'ako. A few years ago, I decided to call the kids out on this free program, "If I'm gonna commit to you kids, you kids gotta commit to me." And that's how we created the Junior Boards.

YOUTH BOARD *NOT* YOUTH BORED

This kid kept stalking me.

I couldn't shake him loose. He would say, "Uncle Prime, you gotta mentor me, I want to learn from you, I want to be your student." I would reply,

"I'm not taking any students. And you're too young. I can't be hanging around with idiot kids like you." Just to see if he would back off. But he got worse.

So I finally told him, "I'll mentor you, but first I need you to create this group for me, with these positions. Then let's sit down and talk." I thought I had got rid of him, but two weeks later, he had the group ready. That's how the Junior Board Initiative started.

The board is made up of different characters. You got the organizer: the person that loves art, but doesn't necessarily know how to do art or doesn't care to do it. The documenter/photographer: the person who loves documentation but really doesn't have any good stuff to document. The social media people: the ones who just can't keep their lives personal. They have to expose everything. They open up the world to the whole group.

The first test for the first Junior Youth Board was the mural we did at Highway Inn in Waipahu in 2011. They organized, hit the businesses and politicians, hit the community with the flyer they designed themselves. They even designed and printed their own team shirts. The mural took them about a week to paint. After school, they would come to the wall and paint until about 11 or 12 at night. And still do their homework and go to school the next day. That's how committed these kids were.

To figure out what to paint, we first sat down with the business. The owner had a specific idea, but it was too close to advertising. I suggested we talk about the history of Waipahu instead. So I asked the kids: what do you know about Waipahu? And I was surprised; they knew a lot about Waipahu's past. The word aloha seemed to be a common denominator in everyone's interpretations. So we did a series of sketches around aloha and Waipahu, and voted on the best concept. Then we kept building and building on that concept, to the point where, if you grew up in Waipahu, you would know exactly what everything stood for on that mural.

And everyone who had something to do with Waipahu came together for our kids. The granddaughter of the Arakawa family gave her blessing, and thanked us for honoring her grandfather. A kahu in Maui, who was a Waipahu alumnus, volunteered to do the blessing and flew himself down. Natural Vibrations performed at the unveiling. At the unveiling, we did stencil T-shirt workshops for the community, with designs that had to do with Waipahu, with tribal and Hawaiian art.

Community murals like that have such wide-reaching impacts. For example, the kids would always say, "someday, one day when I get older, I'll be able to do it." We're trained to go to school, get our degree, and then we can become somebody. But why can't we just be somebody *now* and learn along the way? This process empowered the kids to say, "I can do what the adults are doing. I don't have to wait until I'm that old."

We got some pushback at first from the neighboring businesses, especially when we told them we would shut down the parking structure. So working with those guys and trying to break them in to this whole idea of community was one of the challenges. But now they're asking, "Eh, when are we gonna do this again?"

And you would assume that because you're in "the ghetto," and you have all these residents and scary-looking dudes walking by, they would be the first to paint over that mural. But after the unveiling, the coconut wireless started going: "Eh, got these kids who went paint the wall." "Eh, it's good they're using their talents for something positive." Nobody touches it.

These Junior Youth Boards have created clusters of young leaders throughout O'ahu. High school students can come together after school and on the weekends to learn about all the components that make up visual storytelling. Each team is required to go out into its respective community to form partnerships with businesses, district representatives and other clubs/organizations in the area. The group gains experience in business, art, marketing, cultural education, and activism.

ART IS JUST THE VEHICLE

Art is just the vehicle. It has nothing to do with what we're really trying to do. That's what Spirit says: "You think your talent is in the art? It's not. It's in the kids. It's in the lives that you're gonna touch." My job is to use art to wake people up, whatever that means. We're painting stories, creating visual references that young people are attracted to. "Oh, I didn't know you could do this with spray paint." And that's the segue to what you really want: to help people remember their culture. Then they can anchor themselves. Our process teaches them to look back and really ask questions.

"Papa, what was it like growing up?" When I was growing up, my dad would always tell me "you know, boy, when I was your age, bread was only a nickel. And you could get all these groceries for a dime." I heard it so many times, I just got sick of it. But for him to get to tell that story to my kids—I hadn't seen that kind of spark in my dad's eyes for years. His health was going down. But he remembered everything like it was yesterday. To see him really engage and talk to the kids—that really felt right. We all need to engage.

With some of the incarcerated youth I work with, I tell the parents, please make time, once a week, to have dinner on that table, no technology. Just sit there and have a conversation. Even if you guys don't talk for the first two or three meals. Just practice that. And something so simple like this really helps. Some of these families tell me later, "hey, my son is finally opening up. And now we're eating dinner three times out of the week. So thank you. Thank you very much."

When I first started this program in 2006, there were a lot of people just damning us. Once we were at 'Ewa Beach doing our live painting. This one kid kept coming by us and watching. And then what looked like his grandfather came and took him away, told him, "Don't stay by these bad people. They're doing this really bad thing." A lot of the guys I was painting with got really pissed off, but I told them to just keep doing it. Those were the early struggles. Now, people say, "I love what you're doing in this area. I love to see the kids going out and doing these different things." And now my kids are starting to inspire other kids. Now they're getting their own letters and thank-yous.

Many of the kids that stick with me throughout the program grow into leaders who feel there's a greater purpose for their work. When I asked a few of our youth to offer their perspectives in this essay, they said:

> *"808 Urban has helped me define myself as a person and gave me the opportunity to do things I never thought I could. I went into this wanting to get better at art and put my art to good use, but through being here I realized that I have gained so much more. Art is just the tip of the iceberg. I learned to communicate better with others in and outside my family. My family is closer too. I am much more business-savvy, and also have a better understanding of community empowerment. That's just to name a few, but without 808 Urban, I honestly don't know where I would be."*
>
> —Jesse Velasquez, Waipahu Junior Board Director

> *"It sounds corny, but 808 Urban changed my life. Before, I hadn't thought being an 'artist' was even a possibility, and now there's nothing I am more passionate about."*
>
> —Emma Dold, Punahou Art Team Leader

And I'm really clear about who we're doing this for. When we started expanding our Junior Board Initiative to public and private schools, I would get challenged by people saying I should only serve "underprivileged neighborhoods." No, I work with at-risk youth. There's a difference. All of Hawai'i's youth are at risk. Private school kids, they're suffering too. They're troubled just like everyone else. Gangs, drugs, prostitution, all those things don't care what school you went to.

FUTURE VISIONS

1. Following the spiritual journey. We're starting to practice Hawaiian cultural and spiritual protocol. Before, we were just painting, but it was always along the lines of showcasing our identity as a sovereign people. We're doing the right thing, we just couldn't explain why. And now we're finding connections to the kūpuna, the ʻaumākua. And just by sharing this spiritual right with the kids, they're beginning to open up and finding their own spiritual connections.

2. Recreating spaces and archives. We want to build a facility strictly focused on art, photography, video, etc. We want to have the kids film and document the kūpuna who are still here, to record the face and the voice, not just the written word. At some point, we'd like to document in multiple languages, and build archives for the youth, organized by ahupuaʻa. We'd also like to see more educational and creative programs throughout the city that are grounded in culture. Imagine an overhauled public school system that translates the ahupuaʻa into modern times, and allows for different centers of knowledge and exchange. If a student prefers the ocean, send them to a makai school. Mauka schools might focus on agriculture and medicine. Constant collaboration between these schools would allow students to learn different disciplines. The youth would be recreating spaces and archives hand-in-hand, transforming what it means to be urban.

3. Think about the city changing. I saw Waikīkī go from a local playground in the '70s and '80s, to neo-Tokyo, to whatever it is today. Our urban spaces depend so heavily on the market. What's going to happen to Kakaʻako? Will locals be able to afford to live there? Or will it be filled with vacation units, sitting empty? In my opinion, we need to make sure the memories we leave our youth are memories that are unique to Hawaiʻi. And we need to learn to forgive the memories of an unjustice system, and leave them behind. The Massie murder, and more recently, the Deedy trial. By maintaining our "front porch" in the city, where folks from different places can come, sit down, talk story, or "just press," we can heal and rebuild together as a community.

* * * * *

People always ask, "so what kind of funding do you guys have?" Nothing. And that's how it is on the streets; we had to steal to make something happen. In 808 Urban, we're not stealing, but we're working with what we have. People have always come through to support us and make sure we can succeed. And if nobody wants to fund us, well then, shit, guess what, we haven't really been funded all this time anyway. So, we're just gonna keep eating mayonnaise and rice for a few more years.

NOTE

1. Grandmaster Flash and the Furious Five originally released "The Message" as a single on Sugar Hill Records in 1982.

RESOURCES FOR FURTHER INFORMATION AND INSPIRATION

1. 808 Urban's website, at http://808urban.org.
2. Pow! Wow! Hawai'i's website, at http://powwowhawaii.com.
3. The Estria Foundation's website, at http://www.estria.org.

SEDILIA

JILL YAMASAWA

Do you know the alma mater[1]
still plays the lyric of the dead?
"Loyal serve" severs
the melody. You see smiling
faces, stoic faces, when you march
down this hall.

Here we get plenny fighter jets and
helicopters. We get plenny red
shirts, red shoes, dyed hair,
bolo heads, MWH & WELA tattoos,
Piru Boyz 4 Life graffiti,
and JROTC uniforms.

From a Chinatown church basement
to Princess Ruth's castle
to other locations of insurance claim importance
to this place of sea, of marsh, of wetl&.
My last name, Yamasawa,
山沢, mountain stream, mountain marsh.
Sawa, 沢, small stream, small marsh,
from Hiroshima to Kewalo only to meet up
with an emptied stream,
an emptied marsh.

The heat comm&s us outside
under the giant canopies, our bunkers.
We are blind to all color except
the black & gold for Princeton,[2]
for the Monarchy.
McKinley in the center,

flagpole in the center,
& us on the side like *Korean Sushi*,
like the JROTC.
"Did you know *Lost*
shot McKinley in the back
-ground?³ What would Reverend
Maurice Beckwith think
if he saw us now?⁴
A half Buddhist teaching Christian children
how to order radicals &
inequalities on a number line?

My students pile on one another,
their arms & legs a heap of limbs.
At a distance, If you didn't know
them, they'd seem to such an observer,
only a collection
of bodies.

J, who's 6'4, 240, jumps on top.
There's a collective moan.
For a moment, I panic;
they don't have
the proper equipment:
no helmets,
no pads,
no protection, but
I allow them to play on.
They love it,
& it's only one day until the end
of school.

The ground feels shriveled
as if ready to become a desert.
We are drowning
in this terrible heat.
The students are restless for a change
of temperature. K moans,
"This is hell.
I want waterrr!
Can I please have waterrr?"

It's hot, *puff out the hot-air balloon now,*
it is about to burst, it is bursting
with something invisible.

S is at the bottom, holding
on to the football.
The pile grows larger,
but he won't let go.
It's what he's been taught;
it's what I've taught him,
I'm ashamed to say.

We mimic the leaves of a tree,
turn to the sun;
our veins full of Tang & Shasta from
Times & Safeway. This conversation
is like a freed tiger
only to end recaptured or dead.

To be a Vienna sausage,
I keep pulling out your teeth,
believing a new set will appear
(it's what I've been told)
& I think at some point
you'd like to know why.

Behind McKinley & to the left is
the U.S. Army Recruiting Center.
To the left, to the left, everything you own
in a box to the left.
'Cause the truth of the matter
is replacing you is so easy.

Repeat.

Behind McKinley & to the left is
the U.S. Marine Recruiting Center.
To the left, to the left, everything you own
in a box to the left.
'Cause the truth of the matter
is replacing you is so easy.

Repeat.

S yells, "McKinley was a racist,"
and pretends to aim the football for his head.

We are not on a conveyor belt.
There are too many words
like *onomatopoeia* & *chee-hoo*.
Like *esoteric* & *Tokelauan*.
It took me nine months
to find the Times they meant,
no, the one on Vineyard;
to memorize W liked seed,
A didn't eat chocolate,
B ate strawberries only when paired with sugar & Cool Whip,
K just like suck on lemons, &
J didn't care—he would eat anything.

The Ward Estate's groundskeeper chased
kolohe students exiting school through the broken
fence. His name shoots
in & out of my memory like a Blue Angel.
"Get outta hea you kids."
I imagine his voice, deep & calm
as open water.
We hear, & sometimes learn,
pressing so close. A foreign vessel
off the coast, inhabiting the reef
like evil in live, written in inequalities:
Kukui Gardens>Lanakila>MWH.
During lunch when a student
came to the locked
door, sobbing, Mrs. H turned him away.
"I don't allow students inside
during my free time."
She turned to me a moment later & said:
"The tall boy, the giant,
I forget his name,
he wanted to talk to you.
But I sent him away

cause I nccd
my peace."

Peace be with you.
And Peace be with you.
She didn't underst& then
& maybe I don't underst& either.

With the grit
of chocolate milk on
our tongues,
we savor
the last bit of watery poi.
It's not enough,
but it has to be.

NOTES

1. McKinley High School's alma mater: "Hail, McKinley, hail, / Hail, McKinley, hail, / Thy sons and daughters sing thy praise, / And loyal serve thee all their days. / Alma Mater, thee alone we love / And thy colors floating high above. / Hail, McKinley, hail, / All hail, all hail."
2. McKinley HS was considered a feeder school to Princeton in the '60s.
3. *Lost* shot a flashback scene with actress Michelle Rodrigues as a police officer in LA. The scene included driving down King Street, and McKinley HS was clearly visible in the background.
4. Fort Street English Day School (FSEDS) was started in 1865 by Reverend Maurice Beckwith in the basement of the Old Fort Street Church. FSEDS eventually became McKinley High School.

I AM OF OCEANIA

INNOCENTA SOUND-KIKKU

When my daughter was 12 years old, she came home one day from school, upset and confused. She couldn't stop thinking about what her substitute teacher had told her that day: *"It's because of you people—it makes me frustrated to come to teach."* My daughter came home, asking me "what did the teacher mean by 'you people'? Did she mean me as Chuukese? As Micronesian? Or me as someone from the Kalihi area?"

I felt so upset for my daughter, thinking how wrong it was for a teacher to say something like this. I know many other Micronesian kids face different kinds of discrimination daily in their schools and neighborhoods. They're not seen as beautiful, talented, smart, and sacred, but rather looked upon as "Nothing but Trouble." My daughter and I had a long talk that day about her experience, and what discrimination is.

It pained me to think about her carrying this kind of burden on her shoulders. I wanted to paint a different view from the negative things said about being Micronesian. I want my daughter to know she is beautiful, wonderful, and special, for she's a part of something much bigger than a tiny island in Micronesia. I want her to know she's part of a greater call, and that we learn from our sky, our ocean, our lands, and environments to keep us strong. My daughter is of value and a treasure, so I wrote this poem, "I am of Oceania," for her.

I am of Oceania
I am of the Islands
I am of my Ancestors
I am of my
Mother and my Father
the next Generation
of a beloved Nation
Who hopes for a
better tomorrow promised

To multiply and navigate the
earth as my Maker
calls me to steward
that of which He birthed me:
the Ocean
and Islands of the
Pacific Realm

This poem makes my daughter proud and unashamed of who she is. She began wearing her Chuukese skirts and dresses often out in public. I hope many of our kids growing up in Hawai'i or abroad will find interest and value in reconnecting to their Chuukese cultural values and identities. Maybe not in my time, but whenever that will be. I hope these kids will rise up and reclaim what they have lost. The true good nature of Chuukese men and women. And that they will be confident in the wisdom of their ancestors behind them, to create a better future for the next generation to come.

MOLOKAI STORIES, IDENTITY, AND KULEANA

MATT N. YAMASHITA

It's an honor to be able to say that I am the first professional filmmaker from the island of Molokai.[1] Over the past twelve years of my career I have independently produced over a hundred videos for a wide range of clients. From the windswept slopes of Kahoʻolawe to the open ocean aboard Hōkūleʻa, from building traditional stone structures in Kona to preserving native fisheries in Moʻomomi, from fighting back shoreline developments to promoting sustainable living practices, the content of my work has been a continuous journey of understanding and celebrating life in Hawaiʻi. It has also been a constant unfolding of better understanding myself, my connections to these islands, and the kuleana that life has given me.

My name is Matt Noboru Yamashita. I am thirty-five years old, and Molokai is, and always has been, my home. Today, I live in Kamiloloa, just east of Kaunakakai. I work in a small office that also serves as my video editing studio. This space was once my great-grandmother's sewing room, an extension of the quaint two-bedroom house that my grandmother's parents built in the early 1970s. Outside, my children play in the same dusty yard that I once played in as a child.

My family's roots in Hawaiʻi go back to the late 1800s, when my grandfather's parents arrived from Japan. Today, these great-grandparents are buried in Keʻei on the Big Island. This is where my great-grandfather escaped his contract as an immigrant laborer and got by as an entrepreneur and gambler. This was also where my grandfather, Henry, was born in 1908. His mother died when he was very young and life got difficult, so his father moved the family to Oʻahu. Self-motivated and intuitively intelligent, Grandpa gravitated to Honolulu as a young man and found work as an electrician.

The most pivotal moment of my grandfather's youth was a trip to Molokai in 1932 at the age of 24. Grandpa had been hired to wire Molokai's first electrical power plant. When he arrived on Molokai, there was only one light in Kaunakakai. He fell in love with the island and eventually became the manager of the Molokai Electric Company, bringing light and energy to the entire island. In his ninety-two years of life, he earned widespread respect as a businessman, fisherman, community leader, and friend to many.

My paternal grandmother is also an important part of this story. Grandma Marie was born in Hawai'i to Japanese and Filipino immigrant parents. She grew up in the booming Waikīkī of the 1920s and through the Great Depression years of the 1930s, graduated from the University of Hawai'i, and moved to Molokai during World War II to teach elementary school at the age of twenty-two. Grandma met Grandpa and got married on Molokai. For over thirty years, my grandmother dedicated herself to educating Molokai's youth as both a teacher and librarian. Now in her early nineties, she chooses to live on Molokai, on her own, in the house that she and Grandpa built.

I share the history of these two grandparents because they are my anchors to these islands. Growing up, their stories and their love for Molokai left a heavy impression on me. I credit them for planting the foundation of who I am firmly in this soil and giving my life direction.

Like my grandparents, I grew up wandering freely through the mix of Hawai'i's diversity. I was raised with my older brother in the cool, forested uplands of Kalae in an area known as Ka'uluwai. My mom, a hard-working haole woman from Southern California, raised us. A Hawaiian cowboy, whom I knew as Uncle Earl, lived with us through my formative years. We would also fly to O'ahu once a month to spend weekends with my father in the city.

I had really good friends growing up. Their families—whether Japanese, Filipino, Haole, or Hawaiian—were like my own. We grew up surfing, fishing, riding horses, skateboarding . . . but we also worked hard. And whether it was yard work, herding cattle, or cleaning Mom's restaurant, we worked together and enjoyed it. That was life on Molokai—rich and diverse, yet grounded in family and a rural lifestyle.

My first taste of video production came when our high school received equipment through a grant from the Office of Hawaiian Affairs. A handful of us were asked to figure out how to use the new S-VHS cameras and editing decks. We produced typical kid stuff at first, but our teacher encouraged us to explore more meaningful content. I remember a video we made called "Back to the Land," a documentary of a Hawaiian kupuna sharing about the old ways of life. I also did a piece on the Vietnam War and how it impacted Molokai. I was enthralled by the interviews and stories and by the idea that I was helping to share them with others. I then wrote and directed a video that won Grand Prize in a statewide video contest sponsored by the University of Hawai'i. No one could believe that a ragtag bunch of students from Molokai could win. But we did, and it gave me the confidence and drive to stick with video.

I graduated from Molokai High School in 1996 and went on to earn a degree in Film Production from Chapman University in Southern California. Stepping outside of Molokai was an opportunity to see and understand other parts of the world and to look within myself. My early adulthood became a time of soul-searching, and at every opportunity, I traveled to places like Montana, Mexico, and Costa Rica. I wrote a lot of poetry and produced videos that explored how urban life contrasted with the rural life I left behind. I enjoyed the experience of being away, but I always missed Molokai.

The last adventure of my early twenties was a three-month journey through New Zealand. I left my video camera at home and took only my surfboard and journal. About a month into the trip I found myself at the Bay of Spirits, the northernmost tip of Aotearoa, looking back towards Hawai'i. The sun was setting and the vast Pacific Ocean was churning out into the endless horizon. In that moment I knew where I belonged. I felt Molokai calling me home.

Returning to live on Molokai was like a rebirth. I had new eyes and perspective that allowed me to appreciate things that I did not notice or consciously value growing up. I had a new desire to better understand my connection to the island, her people, and Hawaiian culture. I immersed myself in outrigger canoe paddling, Hawaiian language, dancing hula, and I spent time listening to the stories of kūpuna.

Most importantly, with my degree in filmmaking, I had returned with something to give back. I came home with a powerful tool. Not that people didn't have video cameras or that no one had ever made films about Molokai, but no one actually *from* Molokai had ever really used video as a mechanism to effect change and promote understanding by telling Molokai's stories from the inside out.

A year after returning home, I was hired to manage a satellite office of the Akakū Maui Community TV public access station. In this capacity, I became an educator and helped put video cameras into our community's hands. It was an especially exciting time because of the shift to digital technology. Inexpensive video cameras and editing programs like iMovie were making video production accessible and easy for the average person. With these tools I taught people how to utilize public access TV and take Molokai stories to thousands of viewers across Maui County. But I also urged our producers to use media carefully and thoughtfully, so as not to reinforce accidentally the negative stereotypes that mainstream "off-island" media often placed on us. These negative perceptions came from the fact that Molokai has always had statistically higher rates of unemployment, poverty, and welfare, because of our long history of resisting development. The view that the outside world had of us, aside from being the marketable "Friendly Isle" and the "Hawai'i of 50 years ago," was that we were backward-thinking activists and government freeloaders. But this is an unfair and limiting perspective. The truth is that we are too often measured by urban, economic-driven metrics, and that our true strengths are entirely overlooked. The only way to change this, I realized, was to tell our own stories.

In my five years managing the Akakū Molokai Media Center I trained over five hundred youth and adults in video production. For a while, our community producers were airing as much content on public access TV as all of Maui's producers! This was incredibly exciting. My hope for the thoughtful use of media had been realized in the quality, uniqueness, and rich diversity of the programming that our producers were creating. They were covering public meetings, sports, and cultural events, documenting family histories and traditions, interviewing kūpuna, retelling ancient moʻolelo, and discussing controversial issues. They were doing it in English and Hawaiian languages! Of course, I cannot claim this success as mine alone. It came through the passion and brilliance of our people and via supportive partnerships with schools and other non-profit agencies that grasped the value of video production. Grants from trusts and private foundations were also critical in funding our programs.

Today, Molokai-produced videos are shown at public meetings, at graduations and funerals, at rallies and fundraisers, on the Internet, and broadcast on public access TV. Because of continued support for media-based programs, our community has successfully harnessed video as a tool for giving a voice to our people and reflecting our island in a positive light. We are effectively taking control of our image, so that it is no longer purely at the mercy of off-island media. Exposure to video production has also given confidence, direction, and opportunity to countless Molokai youth as they begin their path into adulthood.

While working at Akakū, I was also producing my own videos under my company name, Quazifilms Media. In 2003 I produced one of my first short documentaries about our community's protest of a major cruise ship company that wanted to make Molokai a port stop. The protest was led by Hui Hoʻopakele ʻĀina, under the leadership of Walter Ritte and Colette Machado. The group thoroughly researched the harmful effects that the cruise ship industry had on other small communities, and measured the potential negative impacts to Molokai's social, cultural, and natural resources. Hui Hoʻopakele ʻĀina members rallied the community and called on politicians. And they prayed for guidance and assistance.

On the morning that the cruise ship was scheduled to arrive, the group marched and protested down the length of the Kaunakakai wharf. On that particular morning the winds of Molokai were so fierce that the ship could not safely make its way into our harbor. Those of us who knew the ancient names of our island were deeply moved by what was taking place. *Molokai Pule Oʻo*—"island of ripened prayer"—was awakened by the prayers of her people, just as legends of old told. The powerful winds of *Molokai Nui a Hina*—"Great Child of the Goddess Hina"—were on our side. The cruise ship never came back.

And all of this was caught on video.

Another project I was working on around the same time was a documentary about a new canoe club, Kukui o Molokai, that was formed primarily by the Helm family. The team was comprised of young Molokai adults wanting to give back to the community. I documented the earliest beginnings of the group, through its growing pains to its climactic accomplishment of paddling around the entire island. The longest, most dangerous leg of the paddle was along Molokai's north shore, an inaccessible stretch of coastline isolated by notoriously rough seas and the world's highest sea cliffs. For months, we researched our course, planned, trained, and prayed. Our pule ripened, and Hina held back her winds. On the morning we launched our canoes from Hālawa Valley, the winds came to a halt and the ocean became so calm and flat that, like a mirror, it reflected the red rays of the rising sun on the towering sea cliffs above us. This type of weather only occurs on a handful of days each year. It was an amazingly beautiful experience.

And all of this was also caught on video!

These types of moments and stories have inspired me through the years. To have the magic of nature, mankind, and spirit reveal itself on camera, in intimate and timeless moments, instills in me a sense that I am doing work that is beyond myself. It is a reminder that I am merely a vehicle and conduit for stories that want to be shared.

Many filmmakers tend to pop in and out of worlds, rushing in with their cameras and capturing stories through foreign eyes. But shared connections and trust are important in Hawaiʻi. Therefore, I enjoy telling local stories of people and places that I know. Working this way often gives me deeper access to stories because people trust that I will understand the boundaries and the protocols: that I will see what I am supposed to see and show what I am supposed to show and that I will do it in a culturally appropriate way. This is both rewarding and challenging because it comes with kuleana. I am given access to rare and sometimes sacred moments, stories, people, and places with the unspoken understanding that I must tell the story correctly. My work serves as a bridge to carry these stories to others in an effort to foster greater understanding and connection, so that the embedded messages, knowledge, and values can be respected, understood, and perpetuated.

I have also realized that telling the story behind the story is critical. When I produce a video about Molokai it must include the broader context: the

Hawaiian story of how a thriving society sustained life on this island peacefully for hundreds of years. That larger story must also include the negative impact of Western culture and the fact that Molokai today has a population ten times smaller than in ancient times and is struggling to sustain itself. Yet, and this is the story I will spend the rest of my life trying to tell, the connection to ʻāina and ʻohana-based values—a sustainable way of life based on ancient knowledge—is still alive on Molokai. It hangs on by a thread and there is much damage that needs repair, but the potential to revive these values and incorporate them into our modern world keeps the promise alive. And if we can succeed in the microcosm that is our island, then maybe there is hope for the world.

As the content of my work has broadened and taken me beyond Molokai, I have come to realize that Hawaiʻi has a great wealth of stories that need to be passed on. Some of these stories are meant for video; some are meant to be told in hula, in song, in art, in books. Some stories are meant for the world, and some are meant only for particular families. Some leave us happy, others leave us sad, but all of them have the ability to inspire and educate and therefore add to our collective understanding of what Hawaii was, is, and can be.

And while I am not Hawaiian by way of ancestry, my kuleana is to tell Hawaiʻi's stories of today, the ones that take place in a modern world where ancient values are struggling to survive. It is an interesting position for me to be in because my very existence is a part of the change. My family arrived from foreign shores and brought with them foreign ways of life. But they did not come with the intention to alter or make worse the lives of those who already lived here. They came simply hoping for something better in their own lives. And they had children who were born into this place and that knew no other home. And Hawaiʻi would hānai these children because that's what these islands do: care for the keiki in the hope that they will grow up knowing and loving this ʻāina and her people. This is the kuleana I feel all Hawaiʻi-born children carry: the responsibility to understand the land and the sea, to know the names and the stories, to know what came before and how life was lived, to embrace the cultural values, and to give back, so that future generations can understand, find balance, and thrive.

At thirty-five years old I can't guess what the future holds for me or my career, but I am excited to see a network of likeminded passionate local filmmakers expanding in the islands. There is so much potential for what we can achieve together. And while I could probably make a lot more money if I moved to Oʻahu or the US continent for work, I don't even consider it. I love where I live. The rolling green pastures of Kalae set against brilliant blue skies; schools of fish hovering over a liquid blur of rainbow-colored coral along the shores of Manaʻe; the pounding surf and foamy seas rushing up onto the white sands of west Molokai; the lazy pace of dusty and hot Kaunakakai, people waving, hugging, stopping to talk story when they meet; the cool valleys and verdant lo'i kalo of North Molokai, with the muddy bodies of families working the land, singing ancient melodies, laughing. . . . This is the place that I am from and these are the things that I love. I am both honored and deeply grateful to have an opportunity to help tell their stories.

Mahalo.

NOTE

1. The author spells "Moloka'i" without the 'okina (Molokai) because this is the way that the kūpuna of the island taught him to pronounce it outside the context of song.

RESOURCES FOR FURTHER INFORMATION AND INSPIRATION

1. See Matt's YouTube channel, at http://www.youtube.com/user/molokaimatt.
2. 'Ōiwi TV's website, at http://www.oiwi.tv.
3. "The Eyes of the Land / Nā Maka o ka 'Āina" Hawaiian documentary and educational videos, at http://www.namaka.com.
4. The Academy for Creative Media website, at http://acm.hawaii.edu.

HOW WE CHOOSE OUR FOOD
AND HOW OUR FOOD CHOOSES US

ELISE LEIMOMI DELA CRUZ-TALBERT

[A growing body of research on eating behaviors and the industrial food system shows that our neighborhood, socioeconomic status, and ethnicity affects our diets.]Looking at the contexts in which people make food choices helps to explain the unequal distribution of diet-related diseases in Hawai'i. People often learn about health trends like the obesity and diabetes epidemics, hear that minorities and low-income populations have higher rates of these diseases, and don't see where they fit on the graphs. Still, Hawaiians and others, friends and family, say, "I eat what I want. Don't you think that people choose how they want to live?"

Yes. We have opportunities to choose what we eat. A coworker asking the office, "so what should we eat for lunch today?" has choices. A parent planning what to cook for dinner after work has choices. A child at school, looking down at the cafeteria lunch . . . well, children often can't be choosy. Imagine that you go with the flow of what your family and friends are eating, dine in your neighborhood, and gravitate towards the foods you see or hear about on television. How would you be eating? Depending on our mood, budget, schedule, location, nutrition needs, food that is "in season," and our control over the menu, we all have different "choices."

I was twenty-four when a friend convinced me to try to run a mile. I thought this should be easy enough since I could run miles in high school. But after a short burst forward, my foot didn't go as high as I expected. Breathing didn't calm my heart the way I remembered. I started wondering, "Whose body is this?" I had to stop running, and the *walk* home gave me time to start thinking about why my body wasn't listening to me. I thought about my broke and busy college phase, when I didn't make time to cook for myself or exercise enough, and ate to cope with stress. I thought about the illnesses in my family, my mom's cancers. I decided not to accept the unhealthy way I felt. I joined a gym, I started to choose more unprocessed foods, and I gradually lost weight.

At first, limiting many of the foods I grew up with—saimin, rice, canned meats, many things fried to perfection, "juice," and value meals—was the hardest. I made healthy choices more often as I began to prioritize health with my time and money and increasingly recognize healthy opportunities—like being able to find the right meal on a menu, enjoy the healthy foods that I grew up with, and share recipes that my family liked.

Reflecting on my own health challenges and the health of many others in my community fueled my work and research in food and public health. Despite the many joys food brings us, we face many signs that our *food systems*—the ways in which most food is grown, processed, transported, eaten, and disposed of—are affecting our health, social traditions, and the environment. Food can be complicated. How can we make it easier for everyone to have access to affordable, culturally appropriate, healthy foods? What are the impacts of traditional foods and food practices and eating local on community health? How can our diets support environmental sustainability? How can diverse members of our communities feel empowered to affect their food system? Tackling these questions from a public health perspective can help us better understand the intersection between food, health, culture, and natural resources, and help us find ways to make individual and systemic changes.

FEEDING THE BODY Avg. lifespan ↑, w/th 2005 study

Public health data shows that for the last hundred years, the average lifespan for a person living in the United States has consistently been increasing. Facets of modernization—medical advances, the widespread availability of food, science technologies, the globalization of knowledge and goods, and our easier lifestyles—have propelled lifespan up and up. Then in 2005, the *New England Journal of Medicine* published research that found that the current generation of American children may be the first that would not outlive their parents. This research combined data on population trends for mortality rates and body mass index or BMI (a clinically defined measure of weight status) to adjust life expectancies. Many educated people had assumed life expectancy would keep rising, especially with increasing investment in medical technologies. We did not account for an obesity epidemic—tied to increasing rates for type II diabetes, cardiovascular disease, and some cancers.

The best protection against obesity is for people to eat healthier and be more physically active; it should be that simple. But many of the same forces in modernization that pushed life expectancy up are now coming down on our health. The amount of calories people use has not increased much since the '80s, but the amount of calories consumed has. We shouldn't forget the damage of past famines, the days when people died from vitamin deficiencies such as iron (anemia) or vitamin C (scurvy), and medical progress on those fronts.[3] However, perhaps Americans have gotten used to cheap, convenient food, and getting vitamins out of a bottle. We need more programs that re-create relationships to food that provide personal and community foundations for health.

Nutrition is a concern for everyone; however, indigenous people, minorities, and low-income communities experience diet-related diseases at disproportional rates. In Hawai'i, for example, in 2010, 57.2 percent of the state adult population was overweight or obese compared to 75.5 percent, 90.9 percent, and 71.5 percent of Native Hawaiians, other Pacific Islanders, and Blacks, respectively.[4] In 2011, Japanese adults had the highest prevalence of diabetes among all the races, at 12.1 percent, double the Caucasian prevalence of 5.6 percent. Adults in the lowest income bracket had a diabetes prevalence of 11.8 percent, almost double the 6.5 percent rate of adults in the highest income bracket. The alarming facts around obesity in Hawai'i should have us asking what determines health and how do we really invest in it.

COLONIZATION OF A FOOD SYSTEM

Sustainable use of resources & care for land = healthy lifestyle

In contrast to recent health trends, pre-Western contact Hawaiians experienced good health. In 1778, at the time of first Western contact, there were an estimated 400,000–1,000,000 Native Hawaiians growing, hunting, and gathering enough food to eat and live well.[5] Their diet included the roots and shoots of complex carbohydrates such as taro and sweet potato, protein from fish, pork, and other seafood, gathered ferns and seaweed, and fruits such as banana and coconut.[6] The journals of Captain Cook's crew testify to a healthy population that was "above middle size, strong, muscular, well made; they walk very gracefully, run nimbly, and are capable of great fatigue."[7] Research on the era shows that Native Hawaiian knowledge of cultivation on land and the sea, sustainable management of natural resources, and a strong belief in mālama 'āina (care for the land), provided them with a healthy lifestyle.

Current health problems are more likely due to modern environmental and social factors than genetic dispositions or traditional attributes. Just one hundred years after Western contact, introduced infectious diseases led to a 90 percent population decline.[8] The population had dwindled to around 30,000 by the year 1900.[9] The Hawaiian population that survived found themselves minorities in their own kingdom and faced continual cultural assaults. For example, the 1848 Mahele enactment of the foreign concept of land privatization resulted in only 0.8 percent of the land going to 30 percent of maka'āinana (common Hawaiians),[10] and left many landless and unable to access resources previously used for food, medicine, or cultural practices. Later in 1893, a group

land privitization = – resources

of American businessmen orchestrated the illegal overthrow of the Hawaiian monarchy. [11] We need to look to history to understand how political power and land "ownership" have impacted food systems and community health.

Because of changes in political power, land access, and population demographics, Hawai'i transitioned from communal living, community-based food systems and a subsistence economy dictated through the ahupua'a system to a capitalist system that favored foreign interests in the islands and the beginning of the agribusiness of monocrops such as sugar and pineapple.[2] Like other indigenous populations displaced from land and assimilated, Native Hawaiians were forced into a different lifestyle and subsequently different food systems.

As Hawai'i moved away from local food production, imported and processed foods gained prominence in the local diet for all who live in Hawai'i. It's not surprising then that among middle-school-aged youth, over 40 percent have less than one serving of fruit or one serving of vegetables per day.[13] In the last couple of decades, traditional Hawaiian diets (THD) have been shown to improve the health of participants in several studies, but many participants reported difficulty continuing THD long-term due to limited supply and high costs.[14]

Despite these tribulations, some families and communities continue to carry on the knowledge and traditions of Hawaiian agriculture, protecting the 'ike (knowledge) for revitalizing food security in Hawai'i through a range of efforts. For example, there are wetland taro and fishpond restoration projects across the state. Charter schools are incorporating traditional Hawaiian agricultural knowledge into their curriculum. In 2012, the USDA partnered with Hawai'i Island's Kona Pacific Charter School to restore eight acres of land to traditional cultivation methods. And individual activists are bringing public attention to various threats to traditional food practices. These examples encourage us to examine critical questions about indigenous knowledge, food, and health. How do social norms that accompany traditional food practices affect community health? What resources and inputs are necessary to support traditional food systems?

IF WE AREN'T GROWING FOOD, WHAT ARE WE GROWING?

Eighty-five to ninety percent of food we consume in Hawai'i is imported,[15] due in part to lower farming costs in other places, national and international trade partnerships that favor imports, and changing food preferences. Our participation in the global industrial food system increases our consumption of foods that are highly processed, that have a high carbon footprint for transportation, and that have been grown using non-traditional farming methods. Hawai'i agriculture seems to be experiencing a renaissance recently, with more public attention towards supporting local farmers. Local food production could improve community control over our food, increase economic opportunities for farmers, and protect Hawai'i against events that might disrupt imports. However, costs and competing interests over natural resources such as water and land are often cited as barriers to local food production.[16]

The diversion of water from streams across the islands impacts agriculture, especially the taro farmers whose water gets diverted from their 'auwai (irrigation ditches created to sustain wetland taro fields). Further research is needed to identify water needs for agriculture and other uses, and to identify best practices for allocating public water supplies. The Commission on Water Resources within the State of Hawai'i Department of Land and Natural Resources sums up the water issue well on its website: "Hawai'i's growing population has resulted in greater competition for water resources between municipal, military, agricultural, private, environmental, and traditional water demands."[17]

Similar forces threaten agriculture lands. Between 2002 and 2007, land used for agriculture in the state decreased by 13.8 percent,[18] and more prime agriculture lands are slated to be developed for other purposes.[19] Arguments to protect agricultural zone land for food security have been weakened by 1) a lack of quantitative data on how much land is required for Hawai'i to achieve food self-sufficiency, 2) an overestimation of how much agricultural land is available, since only a fraction of land designated as agricultural is actually prime land for farming,[20] and 3) fractured responsibility for land-use planning between major Hawai'i land owners. The current lack of data-driven decisions may have long-term impacts on Hawai'i's potential agricultural productivity. Our industrial food system continues to raise global concerns—including animal cruelty, pesticide use, seed patenting, GMOs, global trade agreements, community food shortages (exacerbated by climate change and global supply demands), and farm labor rights. Creating cheap food at any cost has especially impacted rural communities and ecosystems, farm workers, and low-income populations. At the core of all these concerns, communities are feeling a loss of control over land, water, and their food systems. With more information, we can educate each other to be mindful of our food choices—to purchase food that will fund the farmers, farming practices, and businesses that we want to support, or to eat homegrown and support the land beneath our feet.

FOOD POLICY COUNCILS AS A STEP TOWARD SYSTEM CHANGE

We can work towards systemic changes that create environments where individuals, especially children, have an easier time choosing foods that protect their health, culture, and sustainability. Food Policy Councils (FPCs) have been popping up across the world to organize communities around transforming local food systems. FPCs show that a focus on system changes can benefit society in various ways. For example, countries that support diversified farming and traditional food systems through agriculture policies show lower rates of obesity.[21] An FPC could help Hawai'i address interrelated problems:[22]

• Hawai'i imports about 85 to 90 percent of its food.

• From 2002 to 2007, the State of Hawai'i saw a 13.8 percent decrease in land used for farming.

• 16.6 percent of Hawai'i households experienced food insecurities.

• Among adults 25 to 34 years old, 64.8 percent of the state population is considered overweight or obese.

• 28.5 percent of students K–12 are overweight or obese.

• Among high school students, only 14.7 percent eat three or more servings of vegetables per day, and only 16.8 percent eat three or more servings of fruit per day.

HOW CAN WE BEGIN TO ENGAGE A RESPONSIVE FOOD POLICY COUNCIL?

Years ago, I worked on a project with the goal of increasing fruit and vegetable (F&V) intake in a target community in Hawai'i that experiences high rates of diet-related diseases. We conducted an assessment of the types, quality, and prices of foods sold in the community. We pulled together measures on diabetes, obesity, F&V intake, physical exercise, and socioeconomic status for the community. With this information, we called organizations—such as community health centers, youth groups, and schools—and civic and political leaders to talk about what we found. We collected their thoughts on their community's well-being, neighborhood resources for eating healthy, and challenges; and the community was given this guide to its resources. Community members cited issues that were outside the public health purview. Together, we uncovered the ways that food access, culture, and sustainability were affecting their diets and health. It took time to gain the community's trust and get their guidance in shaping the intervention. Then they were eager to seek out money and expertise—especially to expand programs that were already established in their neighborhoods. I learned so much from this project and others like it, and at the end of this essay, I offer some starting questions and suggestions for others interested in working on FPCs.

A healthy food system requires a healthy environment and a society that values all people. We can't understand and reform our food system without involving leaders who intimately know the strengths and challenges of food processes—from farm-to-table, to working conditions of farmers and food service people, to waste—and who want to put community well-being before profit or politics. Effecting community level change requires that FPCs involve and develop leaders from communities that are most negatively impacted by the current food system. In Hawai'i, that includes small farm owners, laborers, low-income communities, medically underserved inner city and rural residents, and the indigenous people of Hawai'i. Genuine empowerment is achieved when these individuals have the ability to advocate for justice across issues, as their own spokespersons, as often as possible, to be their own heroes, in this struggle for food justice.

SOME SUGGESTED PROTOCOL TOWARDS STARTING A FOOD POLICY COUNCIL

• First, look for organizations that already exist that may be doing work that you should support with your valuable energy.

• Convene a diverse group of collaborators who are interested in food system issues. Some communities may already be aware of food issues in their home environment, while some may need to see data to understand why they should get involved with your efforts.

• Reflect on your organization, early and often, to see what perspectives are missing from the conversations. Marginalized populations are often less likely to be reached out to, to be heard, and to expect their efforts to make a difference. Reach out to people or organizations who are missing and ask what they would like to see in your organization in order to participate.

• FPCs play many different roles—community education and organizing, research, policy writing, policy advocacy, creating programs and activities, etc. Learn about these different roles with your constituents to identify what your group has the skills and desire to do.

• Above all, FPCs should establish themselves as facilitators. They should facilitate different stakeholders in the food system to share information, challenges, and opportunities together. They should facilitate people from the community who may feel angry, scared, frustrated about their food, land, and livelihoods to express and document their stories, while looking for answers or solutions.

EXAMPLE HAWAI'I FOOD SYSTEM QUESTIONS FOR AN FPC TO ADDRESS:

1) Who are the entities in Hawai'i involved in the following: food production, food processing, food distribution, food retail/restaurants, food waste, nutrition education, emergency food, agricultural education, and writing food policy?

2) What are the major contributors (for example: location, pricing, media consumption, ethnicity) to food purchasing behaviors of Hawai'i residents? To food consumption behaviors? Where do people get their food?

3) How many acres of agricultural land would be required for Hawai'i to achieve food security and food self-sustainability? How many acres of prime ag land are suitable for diversified farming on each island? What are the long term effects of different farming techniques on soil, water, and ecological systems?

4) What is Hawai'i importing that can be locally grown? What are examples of community-based food systems and how can they be strengthened?

TARGETS FOR HAWAI'I FPC ACTIVITIES OR PROGRAMS

• Retail access

• School meals and snacks

• Worksite cafeterias

• Community-based food production

• Public hunting, gathering, fishing rights

• Home gardens

NOTES

1. Stuart Jay Olshansky et al., "A Potential Decline in Life Expectancy in the United States in the 21st century," *New England Journal of Medicine* 352 (March 17, 2005): 1138–45.
2. David M. Cutler, Edward L. Glaeser, and Jesse M. Shapiro, *Why Have Americans Become More Obese?* (No. w9446, National Bureau of Economic Research, 2003).
3. Jeffrey R. Backstrand, "The History and Future of Food Fortification in the United States: A Public Health Perspective," *Nutrition Reviews* 60.1 (2002): 15–26.
4. Hawai'i Health Data Warehouse, "Behavior Risk Factor Surveillance System (BRFSS) Reports," 2010, at <http://www.hhdw.org/cms/index.php?page=brfss-reports.

5. David Stannard, *Before the Horror: The Population in Hawaii before the Eve of Western Demographic Statistics of Hawaii 1778–1965* (Honolulu: U of Hawai'i P, 1989).

6. Terry T. Shintani et al., "Obesity and cardiovascular risk intervention through the ad libitum feeding of traditional Hawaiian diet," *American Journal of Clinical Nutrition* 53.6 (1991): 1647S–1651S.

7. Qtd. (394) in Claire K. Hughes, "Overview: Uli'eo Koa-Warrior Preparedness," *Pacific Health Dialog* 8.2 (2001): 393–400.

8. See Stannard, *Before the Horror.*

9. Bradley E. Hope and Janette Harbottle Hope, "Native Hawaiian Health in Hawaii: Historical Highlights," *California Journal of Health Promotion,* Special Issue: Hawaii 1 (2003): 1–9. See also Ka Uhane Lokahi, *1998 Native Hawaiian Health and Wellness Summit and Island 'Aha* (Honolulu: Papa Ola Lokahi, 1998).

10. See Hope and Harbottle Hope, "Native Hawaiian Health in Hawaii."

11. See Kekuni Blaisdell, "The Health Status of Kanaka Maoli (indigenous Hawaiians)," *Asian American Pacific Island Journal of Health* 1993.1: 116–60.

12. See Hope and Harbottle Hope, "Native Hawaiian Health in Hawaii." See also Christina Page, Lionel Bony, and Laura Schewel, "Island of Hawaii Whole System Project Phase I Report" (Rocky Mountain Institute, 2007), at http://www.kohalacenter.org/pdf/hi_wsp_2.pdf.

13. See Hawai'i Health Data Warehouse, "BRFSS Report."

14. See Ruth Fujita et al., "The Traditional Hawaiian Diet: A Review of the Literature," in the Resources for this essay.

15. See State of Hawai'i Office of Planning, Department of Business, Economic Development, and Tourism, "Increased Food Security and Food Self-Sufficiency Strategy," in the Resources for this essay.

16. See State of Hawai'i Office of Planning, "Increased Food Security."

17. State of Hawai'i Department of Land and Natural Resources, *Commission on Water Resource Management,* 1997, at http://www.state.hi.us/dlnr/cwrm/

18. The breakdown per island includes a decrease of land used for farming on Hawai'i Island by 16.7 percent, O'ahu by 14.6 percent, Kaua'i by 0.2 percent, and Maui by 12.1 percent. The Healthy Communities Network and Hawai'i Department of Health, "Land Used for Farming," *Hawaii Health Matters,* 2007, at http://www.hawaiihealthmatters.org/modules.php?op=modload&name=NS-Indicator&file=indicator&iid=7233669.

19. Miwa Tamanaha, "Land Use Commissioners Approve Development on O'ahu Prime Ag Lands," *Kahea: The Hawaiian-Environmental Alliance,* September 30, 2010, at http://kahea.org/blog/land-use-commissioners-approve-development-on-oahu-prime-ag-lands.

20. Adrienne Iwamoto Suarez, "Avoiding the Next Hokuli'a: The Debate over Hawai'i's Agricultural Subdivisions," *University of Hawai'i Law Review* 27 (2004): 441.

21. See Cutler, Glaeser, and Shapiro, *Why Have Americans Become More Obese?*

22. Data collected from Hawai'i Health Data Warehouse, "BRFSS Report," and The Healthy Communities Network and Hawai'i Department of Health, *Hawaii Health Matters.*

RESOURCES FOR FURTHER INFORMATION AND INSPIRATION

1. State of Hawai'i Office of Planning, Department of Business, Economic Development, and Tourism, "Increased Food Security and Food Self-Sufficiency Strategy" (2012), at http://files.hawaii.gov/dbedt/op/spb/INCREASED_FOOD_SECURITY_ AND_FOOD_SELF_SUFFICIENCY_STRATEGY.pdf.

2. Ruth Fujita, Kathryn L. Braun, and Claire K. Hughes, "The Traditional Hawaiian Diet: A Review of the Literature," *Pacific Health Dialog* 11.2 (2004): 250–59.

3. Institute for Agriculture and Trade Policy, "Principles of Food Justice" (Washington, D.C., 2012), at http://www.iatp.org/files/2013_02_08_FoodJusticePrinciples_v2_0. pdf.

4. Lahela Han, Emillia Noordhoek, Harmonee Williams, and Malia Akutagawa, "Sustainable Molokai: Agriculture Needs Assessment," *Sustainable Molokai.org,* 2012, at http:// sustainablemolokai.org/wp-content/uploads/2012/06/MKK.Agriculture.Needs_. Assmt_.SMI_.PUBLIC.051512.pdf.

FISHPONDS, FOOD, AND THE FUTURE IN OUR PAST

HI'ILEI KAWELO

Our nonprofit, Paepae o He'eia, has been around since 2001. We have a vision and mission you can find on our website.[1] But we like to let the place speak for itself. This pond is massive: 88 acres of water space, completely surrounded by a wall that is 7,000 linear feet long, about 1.3 miles. Our kūpuna built this pond in about two years time. It's estimated that He'eia Fishpond is about 800 years old and fed a community of about 2,000 people. The low estimate is that this pond was able to produce 200 lbs of fish per acre, per year. The higher estimate is 500 lbs of fish per acre per year.

Photograph by Manuel Mejia of The Nature Conservancy, Hawai'i (appears by permission of the photographer).

Paepae o He'eia is answering a challenge that our kūpuna presented us. In the past twelve years, we have been able to complete 3,000 feet of the 7,000 foot linear wall. What we've been doing is working to <u>restore</u> the pond for continued use. In essence, we are not just restoring the pond itself, we are revitalizing fishpond practitioners. A lot of times, people come down here and automatically ask, "Oh, where's your fish?" I always try to explain to them that this is part of the process. Right now, we don't have a lot of fish to sell; we have a lot of smaller fish. But we are training practitioners, and this in itself is a process.

In order to commit to a mahi i'a lifestyle, we have to shift our mindset. Fishpond work is dictated by the tide, which in turn is controlled by the moon. When we think about work or professions these days, it's all about the sun; the workday begins with the rising of the sun and ends when the sun sets. For fishpond hana, it's all about the tide. What the tide is doing dictates what we can do. Is it low, allowing us to cut mangrove, reset the foundational niho stones, or rebuild the wall? Or is it high, not allowing us to work on the wall but rather to transport material out onto the wall in preparation for wall work. Recently we've been committing to practice <u>building the wall at night.</u> During the winter months, our low tides are at night, while in the summer, low tides occur in the light of day. Building wall at night allows us to get a lot more work done in a given year. Prior to building wall at night, we were able to restore about 150 ft of wall in a year. With this shift, we are now are able to restore 300–350 feet of wall per year. Like I said, it's all about the process of shifting our minds and our hana.

Wall work isn't the only work at the fishpond. On any given day, you can often find the pond bustling with learners of all ages. The present-day iteration of the fishpond practitioner is one that takes on the challenge of education. <u>Education is a must</u>—to change the mindset of all residents of Hawai'i first and then to extend globally beyond our shores. People are like fish. Yes, they need the bare essentials in order to survive, but with a little bit of nurturing, they will hopefully not only survive, but grow. We are looking to grow a nation of island-minded fishpond advocates, ones who will support our efforts and other sustainability efforts throughout the state. Support means recognizing that fishponds are not just relics of the past, but, in their potential to feed a community, they are very much functional and relevant today.

Just like the fish in the pond, we are still in the infancy stages of self-determination. [You cannot be a sovereign people if you cannot feed yourself.] Those of us who do fishpond work are not very vocal, but we try to lead by example. Sort of a soft-spoken kind of activism, I guess. I never took to politics or what we normally view as "activism," because that is typically seen as negative. Fishpond restoration is based upon a very positive outlook, and that's what I like about it. Remember the movie *Field of Dreams*: "If you build it, they will come?" That is sort of what we're trying to do here. Silent activism is present here at Heʻeia fishpond. It's our little bit, our contribution to a very large moʻokūʻauhau of this place.

We don't usually talk about fishpond work as activism, but without speaking it in words, each and every one of us is doing what we do because we are passionate about making use of something that our ancestors engineered 800 years ago for its functionality. We believe that fishponds continue to have relevance and value for us today and into the future. We feel so strongly about the ingenuity of our ancestors, and what they've left for us, that we are willing to do whatever it takes to make it work. And it *will* work; he mana ko ka ʻōlelo. Our voice comes from restoring the function of fishponds, which is to cultivate fish protein. That is our contribution to the sovereignty movement and to Hawaiʻi.

People always ask, "why you gonna go back in time?" Or they say, "our culture is gone." Or "the practices of Hawaiian people are a thing of the past, a relic." I just don't buy that. There are so many lessons to be learned from doing things slowly. Everyone is moving so fast—fast and furious—and we just want to be slow. We are big fans of "the process": we've been doing this for 12+ years, and will probably be doing it for at least another 12 to 15 more.

I WAS RAISED IN A FISHING FAMILY

I really feel like the reason I'm here is because this path is in my DNA. It's part of my ancestral memory. I was first introduced to the pond through the University of Hawaiʻi at Mānoa, through the Mālama Loko Iʻa course at Kamakakūokalani Center for Hawaiian Studies. Prior to that, I didn't know that this pond even existed, even though I grew up in this community. That in itself is kind of amazing to me. You can't see the loko iʻa from the road, so many people don't know that it's here.

I came to find out, after working on the pond, that my great-great-grandpa helped to construct the pond down in Kahaluʻu that they call "Senator Fong's pond." It's a small pond between Heʻeia and Kahaluʻu Fishponds that was partially filled in. They call it Senator Fong's pond because he was the property owner for that area. My great-great-grandpa on my Hawaiian side, John Kawelo—who was actually from a place called Kapalilua in Kona Hema—lived and worked on that pond, at the residence of Robert Parker Waipā, who was his wife's brother.

On my Chinese side, my great grandfather and his family, the Ching family, were taking care of a fishpond called Kahanahou fishpond in Kāneʻohe, which is now Kahanahou Circle, a residential area. My other part-Chinese family took care of a pond in what is now Pearl Harbor. So I think ancestral DNA applies not only to my Hawaiian, but to my Chinese side as well, and I feel that me ending up here at Heʻeia fishpond is nothing out of the ordinary. I've come to realize, having been at Heʻeia for many years now, that it's probably just engrained in me to be doing what I'm doing.

I was raised in a fishing family at the Kawelo family compound in the ʻili ʻāina of Pākole right on the water there in Kahaluʻu. Our families were and are gatherers and hunters. Although I am thirty-six years old, I am still being raised in a fishing family; I still have so much to learn. We often have these kinds of conversations: what is your favorite fish? What is your favorite way to prepare that fish? Well, my favorite fish is Kole. Fried, of course. In general though, I love to eat my fish raw. I am a Lomi ʻOʻio and Awaʻaua connoisseur. Awaʻaua is what we catch in Kāneʻohe Bay and is comparable to ʻOʻio. What makes the lomi so ʻono? Texture? Limu Kohu? Niʻoi?

I have not tasted lomi that is better than the one made by my dad or me. Why? You just can't buy a really great lomi in the store or from your local poke counter. The same goes for poke! It really boils down to where the fish comes from; I caught it myself. Where the limu comes from; I gathered it myself. Where the paʻakai comes from; I got it from Uncle on Kauaʻi because we gave him heʻe. The process of making the lomi: keeping your fish fresh on ice, scraping the flesh away from the bone, taking care not to let any go to waste, saving the bone, head, and guts for crab bait. There is a silent reciprocity with the fish, a reciprocity we have with the resource. We maintain these relationships as skilled kānaka, confident in our specific practice.

We grew up cleaning fish, gutting fish, scaling fish. I used to love digging out the fish eyeballs and eating them. Or going down the beach when everyone came in with wana and having to clean wana for a family party. Everybody slept in the same room in my grandma's house. We wake up Saturday morning, the first thing we had to do was string a kui of ʻilima. We had to rake all of the rubbish in the yard—mango and puakenikeni leaves all over the ground—and bag it before we could go swim across the street in the ocean. I had such good, clean fun when I was a kid. And I thought that everyone lived the way I did! But the uniqueness of my upbringing became apparent when I went to Punahou. There were very few Hawaiians and Polynesians at the school. In addition, the Hawaiians who were there didn't grow up the way that I grew up. So I'm so thankful for my upbringing.

My upbringing taught me to see a difference between recreational fishermen, commercial fishermen, and subsistence fishermen. As clearly defined and differentiated as they are in my mind, the lines get blurred by the masses who might not understand fishing. Don't get me wrong, my time fishing as a subsistence practitioner is very enjoyable, but it's not the same as a recreational fisher. Let's use my time fishing with my dad for example: When I go holo-holo, I want to be with just my dad. It may sound selfish, but that's our time. While this time is enjoyable, and I love it, there's a definite level of seriousness to it. How am I to pass on our family traditions to my unborn children, to my niece and nephew, if I don't make the time to learn all there is for me to learn from my dad? Raising the new generations in a fishing family is part of that continuum. Growing up in that way—depending on the resource, gathering pretty much everything you need for family parties, or home consumption, or for bartering purposes—instilled in me an innate respect for the resource and an ability to have a reciprocal relationship with that resource.

MAKE IT REGULAR, NOT A NOVELTY

My experience growing up had everything to do with osmosis and diffusion. Nobody ever said "Eh, you better do this!" (Ok, maybe they said that about raking rubbish in the yard.) But nobody ever said "Eh, go help your uncle clean fish!" You just gravitated that way, and you did it, not because you were asked to do it. That kind of learning and practice was just regular in our fam-ily. There was no novelty about it.

Nowadays, what we are producing at the fishpond is a novelty. People are like "ooh, Samoan crab." "Ooh, he'e." "Ooh, kole." But those foods should be regular in our lives as islanders. In the past few years at Paepae o He'eia we have found ourselves not only doing cultural revitalization. If you had to cre-ate a label for it, we have found quite a niche in the larger community and in the *food sovereignty* movement. But the people who buy our products are of-ten gourmet chefs and restaurateurs; people turn our fish into beautiful dishes and are often catering to people who think of these foods as a novelty.

Among our staff at the fishpond, we often wrestle with this: "Okay, we're gonna sell this stuff to this restaurant for the enjoyment of people who live in downtown Honolulu, for people who are not from here. Yet our own people right here in our own community aren't consuming that which is grown in the pond. So what are we doing? And what do we want to be doing?" It's a challenge because we're in [a capitalist society where everything is monetized.] Paepae o He'eia operates as a non-profit: we have employees, and we have to pay them. We write grants to do so, but we'd rather be more self-suffi-cient and also less dependent on Kamehameha Schools, the landowner. So, to make ends meet, we sell our fish and limu and we charge school groups to come to our pond. It's a double-edged sword. But, on the other hand, I feel like the place that we have, this pond and this practice of revitalizing it: that is for us. We share the place and our practices with whomever comes, but not everybody is gonna come back. With that approach, we're not gonna see a tremendous amount of capital return. But that's alright because we're doing what our kūpuna practiced. We're teaching ourselves and others what it is like to become fishpond practitioners again.

In these times, we are redefining what it means to be a fishpond practitioner. There is no book that was written, no equation you can follow to tell you how to build wall. No guide that tells us how much fresh water versus salt water to allow into the pond, or what kind of fish to grow given the current environmental conditions. And there are so many environmental and ecological challenges we are facing, including invasive species. Our "native voice" means having the ability to be in this place, and practice, and evolve, evolve the practice—to define and redefine.

For instance, we take no issue with making use of modern equipment. The process and our methods and our approach are very Hawaiian because we are Hawaiian. As Native Hawaiians, we can change or slightly alter the practice. In its simplest form, "practice" is defined by your resource. So, why are you gonna limit yourself by saying "it's not traditional fishing practices if you're using a monofilament net. You should be using olonā"? Or, "your mākāhā should be lashed together with pieces of 'ōhi'a or 'ōhi'a 'ai or lama." Well, you know what? Go find me enough olonā to make a whole net. You go find some 'ōhi'a or lama that's accessible on the island of O'ahu, enough where you wouldn't feel completely guilty about harvesting it. So at He'eia we use mangrove wood. It is plentiful, and there's no harm in using it. We have adapted to the available resources, using what is plentiful and conserving what is scarce or threatened.

RECONNECTING AND ACTING AS "ISLAND PEOPLES"

The 'āina allows us to maintain a reciprocal connection. For some people, that connection has been severed completely. For some people, it's just a loose connection. People have been displaced and disconnected in multiple ways. First, I am talking about physical displacement: people don't have opportunities to connect with the ocean and fisheries because they don't have a place to practice. Second, I'm also talking about cultural disconnection. There are still spaces and opportunities for our people to reconnect. Mahalo i ka mea loa'a. Some people don't even know what it is that we still have. They don't know that they have an 88-acre fishpond that they can come and visit anytime they want. We still have our forests; we still have our ocean. These are public domain.

At Paepae o He'eia we provide opportunities for folks to reconnect. And that is not easy to do! You get them for a couple of hours and then they go back to their regular life, and it gets all undone. It is also a challenge for teachers who utilize the pond, because they are required to pay attention to bureaucratic, educational "standards." Many teachers don't even come out to the fishpond because they are inundated with standards and testing. We could create curriculum that's aligned with standards if we wanted to. But I think what attracts teachers and schools to come to the pond are not those reasons. I think the teachers or the schools that come and make use of the fishpond are often the ones who don't buy into the idea of standards. Instead, what's important for them is to give kids an experience out here and have them work on the land, learn by doing. [Reconnect to the resources that sustain us.]

To create the possibility of a better future for Hawai'i, on one level it's simple: we need to know, understand, acknowledge, act, and react as island peoples. Most of the people who live on O'ahu behave like they live on the continental US: "Our water comes from the pipe, that's where the water comes from. An aquifer? What is that?" We are so disconnected from the sources that give us life.

One of my biggest criticisms of our own people is that we see changes in our surroundings and our environment, and yet we don't adjust. We continue to do business as usual. That could be the downfall of us. Take climate change, for instance. We are gonna have to do what our kūpuna have always been doing: adapt and adjust. We see it already. Last year, my 'ulu tree fruited three times. Funny weather patterns are happening. So we're gonna have to try and be as in touch with our surroundings as possible and make decisions accordingly. If that means that we're not gonna be able to use fishponds anymore, then we're not gonna use them; we'll move ma uka. If we need to build our walls higher, then we'll build our walls higher.

In addition, we should be producing more food. Our agricultural land needs to be used to grow food. Not for research to grow seed corn. Our peoples did not eat corn. They ate kalo and 'uala and 'ulu. I would love to see a large majority of the food we consume being produced locally. The trend is shifting but we need to do more.

For one thing, I would love to see a larger number of fish we consume being grown, caught, or harvested locally. In the past, we had upwards of 400 fishponds or more throughout our pae 'āina, our archipelago, but the numbers now are bleak. Hawai'i is the largest consumer per capita of seafood in the US, and we import 67–69 percent of what we consume. Most of the seafood that we're harvesting gets exported. That is straight-up ridiculous. One simple solution would be to not export, right? Keep all of that in-house. I'm most concerned about food. Food speaks to everyone. In our family, we don't have conversations except over food or while making food. Food is power. If you want to start a good dialogue, do it over food. Better yet, have that food be something you caught or grew yourself. No one is going to reject food that's given to them, and that is a powerful way to begin a conversation.

NOTE

1. See Paepae o He'eia's website, at http://www.paepaeoheeia.org.

RESOURCES FOR FURTHER INFORMATION AND INSPIRATION

1. The Paepae o He'eia website, at http://www.paepaeoheeia.org.

HUAKA'I: FINDING YOUR POSITION AND YOUR WAY

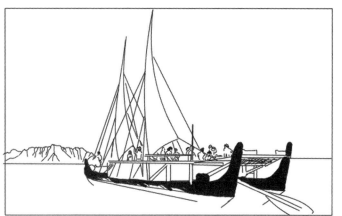
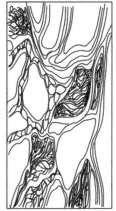
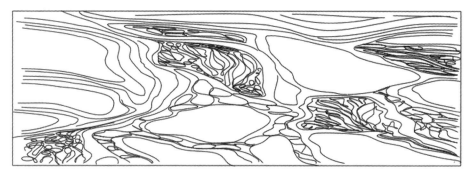
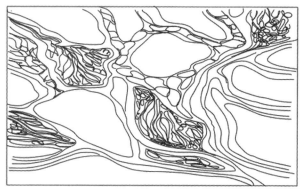

HALEY KAILIEHU

SAILING THE ANCESTRAL BRIDGES
OF OCEANIC KNOWLEDGE

BONNIE KAHAPE'A-TANNER

CONNECTING WITH THE OCEAN

When I was in the fourth grade, my dad got a boat so he could go fishing on the weekends. He would go out fishing with his friends, and we would go to the sandbar. We grew up out there at Ahu o Laka in Kāne'ohe Bay. Every Sunday it was the same routine: the dads would go out fishing, while the moms and the kids hung out on the sandbar. We swam and played all day. Sunburnt with sand in my bathing suit, I would go straight to sleep when we got home in the evening.

As my sister and I got older, my dad would take us trolling in the deep sea outside Kāne'ohe Bay. It was scary; the boat was only seventeen feet long, and he would go in anykine weather. We would stay out for hours, until nighttime. We would beg him to take us in, but he wouldn't go back just to drop us off. So, my sister and I would sleep in the fish bag on the deck.

My dad was never a great deep-sea fisherman, but I remember him catching a few big marlins, ono, and 'ahi. And he loved fishing. He worked hard at his job as a stevedore, worked seven days a week most times. When he had time off, all he wanted to do was be on the ocean.

When I got to high school, my dad would let me take the boat out with my friends. We were less interested in fishing and more into water skiing and hanging out. Through high school, I also got into paddling and kayaking. Later, when I was going to Windward Community College (WCC), I started diving, snorkeling, and got SCUBA certified. But it was when I started fishing and laying net with some friends from WCC that I really began to see the ocean as a place for more than just fun and recreation.

"STAY TOGETHER"

At one point during my studies at WCC, I thought I wanted to become a marine biologist. I worked out on Moku o Loʻe (aka "Coconut Island"), and part of my job was to count coral cells in a microscope. It was interesting, but what I really enjoyed was working in the shop and driving the shuttle boat. I would pick up scientists on the main island and bring them out to Moku o Loʻe for research. It was a great job, but I didn't yet know where it would lead.

I transferred to the University of Hawaiʻi at Hilo to study ʻŌlelo Hawaiʻi, an experience that proved to be foundational. I met some of my closest friends and became involved with the Hawaiian Leadership Development Program. The program, led by Manu Meyer, was empowering because it put us in the position to teach younger Hawaiians. Manu, and many other amazing people in Hilo, such as Pualani Kanakaʻole-Kanahele, Gail Makuakāne, and Pila Wilson, inspired us to further our studies and continue mentoring and teaching others.

Not long after I graduated from UHH in 1995, I was hanging out in Kona with friends for a weekend that came to change the course of my life. A new voyaging canoe, *Makaliʻi*, had just completed her maiden voyage to Tahiti and was touring the Kona coast. I had always dreamed of sailing on a voyaging canoe, but never had the opportunity. My friend and I were standing on the pier, when I saw her. I was in awe. All I could think about was, "How am I gonna get myself on there?" After standing there for awhile, I asked my friend, who was kamaʻāina to some of the crew, to get us onboard. We couldn't just board but had to be given permission by the captain. "Ask the two men standing over there," someone said. Glancing down the pier, I saw two large men: Clay Bertelmann—the captain—and crew member Chadd Paishon. Looking at them, it was like the fear of God ran through me. Their presence commanded respect. I figured I was outta luck, since I was WAY too chicken to ask. I must have been standing there for a long time, or maybe they saw something in me. They just chuckled to each other and called out, "You like go on? Go!" Once I stepped aboard, that was it. I don't think I ever really stepped off since. The waʻa has been my whole life.

The *Makaliʻi* crew is like a family; this is what makes a waʻa a waʻa. Clay Bertelmann was a no-nonsense guy. He demanded excellence. He was rough and harsh, but if you hung around long enough, he was a softy too. We called him "Cap." His dream was to honor Papa Mau Piailug properly by sailing him home to Satawal on *Makaliʻi*. You see, Mau had come to Hawaiʻi to teach us how to sail again. For over twenty years he had given his time and his sacred knowledge; he sacrificed his own family to teach us Hawaiians. Cap was determined to honor him properly, and we all believed in his dream. We trained over the next two years, sailing *Makaliʻi* around Hawaiʻi. It was during this time that I met Mau. I was amazed by his presence and his ability to point out stars on the other side of the earth!

In 1999, for the first time, Hawaiian navigators and sailors whom he trained honored Mau by taking him home to Satawal on a Hawaiian canoe. I quit my job so I could be a part of that journey. He had been coming to Hawaiʻi to teach since the 1970s, sailing on *Hōkūleʻa* all over Polynesia, but until then the Hawaiians had not sailed to his home in Micronesia. We got to see Mau in his own waters. We also made that trip because it was important for us to honor Papa Mau in front of his own people, so that they could see with their own eyes what he had been doing in Hawaiʻi all those years. Many of us were young and some of us were women, and that was different for them. But Mau never made that an issue for those of us who were women. He would say, "For Hawaiian women, it's no problem." But then if you ask him about Micronesian women, he would say "No, No." He was willing to make that stretch against his own culture and embrace our ways of doing things. He said it was "OK, because the very first navigator was a woman."

As that trip back to Mau's home came to a close, he told us that our responsibility was to teach what we learned and share what we experienced. "You just keep your culture strong. You just keep doing it. Make Strong," he urged us. That trip also gave me this sense of an Oceanic community. When you're voyaging, you kind of forget that you are Hawaiian, or Micronesian, or these various categories that mark our difference. You realize that there is a globalness to the world that is not as scary as globali*zation*; it's more about realizing the commonality of human beings. You are together, and you have to rely on one another for everyone to be safe and to make the journey. Mau always said, "Stay together." So simple, yeah? But how challenging. How do we learn to live with each other? How do we stay together? And we have to, because with climate change already impacting Oceania, there's not enough space for everybody. So, we have to learn how to live together and share the resources we have. It sounds kind of scary sometimes, but we don't have a choice.

Mau took a lot of heat in his homeland for coming to Hawaiʻi and teaching navigation here. But his choice was prophetic in many ways. It's like he had the foresight to see what was going to happen in the future. It's like he knew that his people were going to eventually end up being here. Back in the '70s, who would have thought that eventually there would be waves of migration from Micronesia to Hawaiʻi? Maybe he didn't foresee the specific forces that we are living under today, the forces that push Micronesian people here, but he connected our peoples. Now we are here together, and we need to learn how to live together and to share. As much as we Hawaiians are trying to fight for our sovereignty and independence, we have to share with others, especially Pacific peoples. When I hear people saying negative things about Micronesian people, I think, "How can you hate on a Pacific people that has had the same fate as us?" We have to stay together.

SACRIFICES, KULEANA, AND THE VALUE OF OCEANIC KNOWLEDGE

In March 2013, our *Kānehūnāmoku* crew learned that Papa Mau's son, Plasito, had moved to Hawai'i. He had already been here for six months, but not many in the Hawaiian voyaging community knew. Plasito, like so many other people from smaller islands with a limited economic base, had come to Hawai'i for health reasons and to find a job. So, he and his six-year-old daughter made their way here, and he found a place to rent out in Mākaha. Within a couple months, Plasito found a full-time job cleaning tour buses. But with the high cost of housing on O'ahu, he was barely making it. After our crew had been hanging out with him for a while, he told me, "My rent is too high." All I could say was, "Well, you're not gonna find any rentals cheaper than what you have now." He came for the promise of a Western lifestyle, but he is now realizing that it really sucks.

And yet, he has *all* of this knowledge. With *Kānehūnāmoku*, the educational voyaging canoe that I captain, we don't have the financial resources to hire Plasito (or any of our crewmembers) on a regular basis. But we have found ways to stipend him for workshops, and many of the same things we learned from Mau, Plasito is teaching our students. However, these workshops can't sustain him, so he maintains his other job. It's just absurd to me! The son of Mau Piailug, who gifted his knowledge to us and sparked the rebirth of Hawaiian long-distance voyaging, is making a living by cleaning tour buses? There is something wrong with this picture. The expertise and traditional knowledge Plasito brings is so valuable, yet he is marginalized in the greater community. Nobody knows or cares. That's a problem, and it's not just a problem about one person. It's a larger problem with the way the dominant society in Hawai'i today fails to value fully Oceanic knowledge and even the ocean itself.

For Plasito, the marginalization he has experienced since coming to Hawai'i was cutting him off from the ocean and its centrality in his life. The first time our crew met him, we took Plasito sailing with us, and I think it was the first time he had been out on the water sailing since he had arrived in Hawai'i six months earlier. He was as happy as a clam: smiling ear-to-ear, sitting back steering with one knee bent toward him and a cigarette in hand, so content. Needless to say, he's pretty much been with us ever since that day, and it's been a mutually beneficial relationship. He can see another part of life here on Oʻahu, not just the ghettos, the highways, and the city he sees on a daily basis.

Most people in Hawaiʻi never consider the sacrifices that were made so that Mau could come here to teach us navigation for all those years. When Mau first came in the '70s, there were doubts and distrust about his abilities, but those closest to him quickly realized that he was like a living ancestor. He didn't just know navigation, he was a healer, a fisherman, a farmer, everything—a complete man. He told us that the canoe is our mother and he is our father. When on the canoe with Mau, like a father, he cared for our safety and well-being. All those years in Hawaiʻi and in Polynesia he was a father to many voyagers.

Plasito, who is now fifty-one, tells us that when he was young, people in his own community criticized his dad. Mau was spending long periods with the Hawaiian voyagers here in our islands or on the ocean, and away from his family.

One evening, we were hanging out after a workshop in which Plasito taught a local hālau hula how to make cordage. Plasito shared that his first name, which he does not use often, means "my father is not a navigator." We were all speechless. Plasito explained that his grandmother gave him the name because of the controversies over Mau's decision to go outside of the culture and come to Hawaiʻi and teach this sacred knowledge. I was astounded. I could not imagine growing up with my father away teaching others and, on top of that, having the criticisms of him memorialized in my very own name.

We don't consider the sacrifices that others have lived with so that we in Hawaiʻi could have the opportunity to revitalize our voyaging traditions. But now that we know more of the story, it is our kuleana to ask ourselves how we are going to live differently because of it.

A SENSE OF OCEANIA

In the years that I have been teaching sailing and navigation skills to young people, one of the most powerful things I have seen is the way the waʻa makes kids feel like they're a part of something, part of a crew where everyone has each other's back. The canoe can help to bring about a better sense of Oceania. It can be a bridge to help young people understand that we come from similar cultures. This past year, we have been working on a program called "Ka Holo Waʻa," where we bring Pacific Islander students together through waʻa learning. On our first round, we had ten students from throughout the UH system: many from Micronesia, Marshall Islands, and Polynesia.

We have also connected with youth from Pālolo Housing, where there are a lot of Micronesian and Polynesian families. Just like our urban Hawaiian kids, they are plugged in with their earphones under their hoodies. They are urban, but the ocean is in their DNA. It's just that most kids in the housing are not getting the opportunity to connect with the ocean, with that part of themselves and their legacy. Like our own experience as Kānaka Hawai'i growing up disconnected from who we are and from the genius of our ancestors, so many Pacific Islanders living in Hawai'i have been displaced from their own lands and cultures.

With these programs we are running, the point is not to teach Oceanic students to become navigators. Rather, we try to expose them to the possibilities of the wa'a. We are trying to remind them about the value of their own voyaging traditions. When young people come from various cultures and islands that have rich legacies of seafaring, it's not our place to teach them our Hawaiian ways as *the* way. But we can show them, "Eh, you guys can do it!" In sharing what we are doing with *Kānehūnāmoku*, we can provide inspiration to Oceanic youth—who are now first, second, or third generation in Hawai'i—to practice their own wa'a traditions and build their own vessels. In the long run, we can provide help and a place for them to do it. The rebirth of long-distance voyaging in Hawai'i has paved the way for others throughout Oceania to reestablish their own wa'a. As of 2013, over a dozen wa'a throughout the Pacific are actively sailing and voyaging

TURNING AGAIN TO THE OCEAN

 We still have a long way to go, and we can learn a lot from others. Most importantly, we have to remember that traditionally, canoes were not for recreation: they were functional and utilitarian. In Hawai'i, we are still stuck in the "sunset sails" mode, and every couple years there is a big international voyage. In other Pacific islands, people have figured out ways to rebuild their lifestyles around the canoe, how to make it a functional part of their day-to-day lives and economies. For example, in the Cook Islands, they have had to think about how to maintain large voyaging canoes in a small economy, without mass tourism. So, they have begun to intertwine the canoe with government and conservation practices. A number of atolls in the area were designated as conservation, and they use the wa'a to run supplies and personnel out to these islands. These large canoes are being used in a traditional sense: to get people where they need to go for work, and to take food, water, and supplies to remote places. We too need to make our wa'a a more regular part of everyday life and find modern versions of traditional functions, like transit and education.

As island people, we know that most of our trade happens on the ocean. For Hawaiʻi, the shipping lines and our ports are our lifeline. In terms of education, we can be training students in waʻa knowledge, but it does not have to stop there. Many people have been dreaming of a Hawaiʻi-based maritime training school that would draw on our historic strength, not only on canoes but also on all kinds of seafaring vessels. In taking steps toward that, we are piloting a program in maritime training for high school juniors and seniors, introducing them to various career and academic opportunities connected to the maritime industry. Using the waʻa as our cultural foundation, we will then expose students to the range of respectable careers that are associated with this important industry: deck hands, tug boat operators, engineers, captains, harbor pilots.

There is so much educational potential. We could have canoes functioning to teach science, engineering, and leadership. Successful educational canoes, like *Hōkūleʻa*, *Makaliʻi*, or *Kānehūnāmoku*, are only possible when there is an ease of accessing and using the waʻa.

A real resurgence of canoes into our daily lives would require a shift. There are a few things we could do in Hawaiʻi to nurture the revitalization of our canoe culture:

1. We can allow canoes with an educational purpose to have free docking space at public harbors and beaches.

2. We can allow more shoreline access for paddling canoes, providing incentives for canoe clubs that have strong educational, rather than just recreational or competitive, missions.

3. We can more fully support maritime training, such as the program offered by Honolulu Community College's Marine Education Training Center.

4. We can encourage and support more outdoor marine education in the K-12 school system. This includes basic skills that allow new generations to have a safe connection with our ocean. The drown-proofing classes that were initiated decades ago have been slowly eroded from our public schools, as those programs were cut to prioritize a continental-derived approach to schooling and core curriculum. By not assuring that students have basic water safety skills, we are disconnecting young people from a huge resource surrounding us. If we cut this generation off from the ocean, they will not develop a relationship with it and they will not know how to care for it.

AN OCEANIC FAMILY

"I put the stick between Micronesia and Polynesia, now you walk on the stick, like a bridge. I like we make one family."

I had the honor of hearing these words directly from Mau. Pius Mau Piailug was more than a navigator; he was a philosopher and a prophet. His teachings are timeless and timely. In today's world, what is old is new again. We are the people of the Pacific, Moananuiākea, connected infinitely by the waters that touch each of our shores and flow through our veins.

Our canoe, *Kānehūnāmoku*, is only small, but we are committed to his legacy. We will do our part to walk on this bridge and teach what we have learned. The canoe connects us. Sail across the ancient bridges of our ancestors. We are, in fact, one family. Eō, e Moananuiākea!

RESOURCES FOR FURTHER INFORMATION AND INSPIRATION

1. The *Kānehūnāmoku* website, at http://www.Kanehunamoku.org. Like us on Facebook and Follow us on Instagram@kanehunamoku.
2. Sam Low, *Hawaiki Rising: Hōkūleʻa, Nainoa Thompson, and the Hawaiian Renaissance* (Waipahu: Island Heritage, 2013).
3. Ed. K. R. Howe, *Vaka Moana: Voyages of the Ancestors: The Discovery and Settlement of the Pacific* (Honolulu: U of Hawaiʻi P, 2007).
4. The Polynesian Voyaging Society website, at www.hokulea.org.
5. Take a voyaging course at Windward Community College, Honolulu Community College, Kauaʻi Community College, or UH-Mānoa.

MICRONESIAN DIASPORA(S)

EMELIHTER KIHLENG

I: INTERVIEW

EK: *Ahmw tepin kohla Seipan oh dah ke wia? Ke doadoak?*

When you first went to Saipan what did you do? Did you work?

IR: *Ehng. Doadoak nan factory.*

Yes. I worked in a factory.

EK: *Hmm. Dah ke kin wia nan factory?*

What did you do in the factory?

IR: *Wil kopwe. Re kin dehkada likou irail kin kidohng kit, wilikada kilahng ekei, song ko, koakoadihla.*

Fold clothes. They sew the clothes and give them to us, fold them up and give them to others, like that, as it goes down.

EK: *Doadoak laud?*

Hard work?

IR: *Ehng. Apw seh reirei eh, kin kiden aramas apw ngehi ongieh udahn ih kin pwangadah, ih kin lok.*

Yes. But we were long, lots of people, but for me I really got tired, exhausted.

EK: *Awa depeh?*

How many hours?

IR: *Ih kin tep kulok isuh nek kulok isuh nisoutik.*

I start at seven and finish at seven in the evening.

EK: *Aoooo. Werei ieu.*

Wow. That's a long time.

IR: *Werei ieu mwoh. Pweh tepda nimenseng eh, kohditehieu kulok isuh ni soutik, nek, klous.*

That was a long time. Because we start in the morning and go all the way till seven in the evening till closing.

EK: *Ah ih kak idek rehmw ke kin ale tala depeh awa ehu?*

And can I ask how much you made in an hour?

IR: *Ehng. Komplihdla week riau oh, ih kin aleh talah silipwukih limeisek isuh.*

Yes. Completing two weeks, I get $357.00.

EK: *Aooo. Sohte itar.*

That's not enough.

Ah kumwail kin lunchbreak apeh?

Did you guys have lunch breaks?

IR: *Ehng. Eisek riau lunch, komoal lah oh kulok ehu tep, kohditehieu.*

Yes. 12:00 pm lunch, rest, and 1 o'clock start until finish.

EK: *Ah ko mehn ia kei?*

You and who else?

IR: *Mehn Pohnpei, mehn Ruk, mehn Kusaie, mehn Pilipihn.*

Pohnpeians, Chuukese, Kosraeans, Filipinos.

EK: *Wei eh, sohte mehn China iang?*

Oh really, and no Chinese?

IR: *Adkih mehn China meh kin deidei eng kit.*

The Chinese sewed for us.

EK: *Oh.*

IR: *Aht kaun ko mehn Korea.*

Our bosses were Korean.

EK: *Wei eh. Ehri mehn China kau mihmi nan ehu pereh?*

Oh really. So the Chinese were in separate rooms?

IR: *Reh kin mwohd nan sehr irekdihdoh ehri kin deidei dohng kit ah se kin uhd wilik kilahng emen koakoadi.*

They sit in chairs in a line all the way down to us, and they sew, and give it to us, and we fold them and pass it down and onwards.

(She spits betelnut juice.)

Reh kin dir nan ehu sehr oh kak meh siliakan samwah mie, pweh udahn kin reirei koadihla, apw kaidehn pil ehu te, ehu room oh udahn kin line mwein kak meh wenou, ah kohla nih ehu room kak pil line wenou de isuh wen dir.

They were so many on one chair, could have more than thirty because it is so long, all the way down, but not just one. One room would have a line of six to another room with six or seven, since so many.

II: DREAMERS

1

Ih koalauh, ei doadoak oh, ong ie ih mwauki ei kin aleh nei sent, wiahki nse-nei song koh eh. Ah ei mihmi Pohnpei eh, ih sohte kin aleh songehn lapalahn sentuwoh. Apw ih men pwurala likioh, apw ih sohte men kohla ngehi pwurala Seipan.

When I went, I worked, for me I liked it when I got my own money, doing what I want with it. But staying in Pohnpei, I never get that much money. But I want to go back out there, but I don't want to go back to Saipan.

my dream is to bring my two babies with me
to Hawaiʻi, there are lots of us there and
I hear it's the nicest
get a job and eventually bring my parents
to live with us too

2

they are lucky these Micronesians
coming from their impoverished islands
I've been there, they have no sewage system
Filthy, nothing for them to do all day
yea, so they might have to work a few extra hours
I give them the American dream

3

North Pacific give me job at SeaWorld
Janitor, I don't like but cannot leave
they stop paying the rent
my wife and baby at home
they took the TV and the bed
we sleep on floor

4

yes, they are my people therefore
I know the economic conditions on our islands
the FSM government encourages migration
I'm doing them a favor

2

you can import maybe a thousand a year,
and you don't have to worry about a quota system.
they can fill any labor shortage you can find.

5

these islanders are taken advantage of
literally bought for $5,500
they become indentured servants held in
debt bondage upon arrival
with no ticket home
we are trying to do whatever we can

2

Micronesians don't need a lot to
keep entertained, they play
bingo and drink all night and
on their days off they sleep
they are happy, they don't complain

6

when we came, me and my sister
we only have our slipper on our feet
no clothes and when we got to the
apartment we cry and cry
they said it would be nice
and we know they lie

III: WHITE HOUSE

they broke my body on the inside.
I walk into the big white house.
already I smell it, Pohnpei hospital smell but worse.
pwohn kent, piss, stink.
piss and old people smell.
new smell to me.
I see them sitting, quiet some of them,
some talking to themself but not crazy, just alone.
I feel scared and the tile was sticky like white stuff from *pwomaria* tree.

my head hurt because I so sad for them.
so sorry for the old white people and some black.
so sad. I wonder where are their children?
they must be dead.
I never knew old people by themself, no son, no daughter.
in wheel chair, in bed, shake back and forth.
I want to cry for the children gone.

I don't understand.
I cannot.
back home no piss smell on them.
no shit smell.
only coconut oil smell. nice smell.

Nohno Pahpa Nohno Pahpa Nohno Pahpa Nohno Pahpa Nohno Pahpa Nohno Pahpa

LIMPOAK MEHLEL!

only love we show to grandma, grandpa, uncle, auntie.
all of them our mom and dad, we love them all.
sweet smell.

AMERIKA.
in this rich country, I so surprise.
so much french fries and cheeseburger,
so much Safeway, WalMart, Mall, SUV,
big house with fence, nice yard with flower.
I think oh, must be so much happiness and so much love.

I don't understand.
why grandma and grandpa alone?
no one visit, no one bring happy meal, no one talk to them.
I talk to them, even in my language.
I know they don't understand.
I don't care.
they want to hear my voice.

I tell them:

mah ke mihmi sapweioh ke sohte pahn loleid,
ke sohte pahn kelekelepw.
seh pahn apwalihiuk. kamwengeiiuk.
kiht nomw seri limpoak.

I tell them:

if you from my island. you never be lonely. you never be alone. you no scream
late in the night time. no cry. no piss smell, never. I am your child and I feed
you. the children you feed and their baby too.

DECOLONIZATION AND
PUBLIC EDUCATION IN HAWAI'I

TINA GRANDINETTI

Every day in Hawai'i, behind the red-dirt stained walls of our public schools, thousands of students participate in a tremendous exercise of cross-cultural interaction, tolerance, and understanding, between peers of different ethnic groups and varying economic backgrounds. The unfaltering routine of each morning renders invisible just how powerful this daily exchange truly is, that Hawai'i's public school system has long been a driving force behind our unique island culture. At one point or another, or several simultaneously, our public school system has served as an agent of American cultural imperialism, helped laborers pull themselves out of exploitative jobs, oppressed and devalued Native culture, and fostered a political revolution that challenged a powerful planter oligarchy.

I have always been proud to be a product of the public school system, and it wasn't until I left home that I became aware of these complexities mirrored in my own experience. While my education helped me develop cultural literacy and appreciate diversity, it also failed to teach me about my home, its history, and my place within it. Hawai'i's public schools play a critical role in defining our island identity, and yet have been rooted in a colonial ideology that positions Natives and non-Natives alike as inferior to the continental US. Perhaps it is time now to imagine a new role for our schools, as powerful tools for decolonization and empowerment, as vehicles for defining our island experience on our own terms.

My belief in this decolonizing potential grew from my personal experience within Hawai'i's public school system and my continued educational journey. When I was in the second grade, my parents pulled me out of a small private school and enrolled me at Mililani Uka Elementary because they believed that the lessons I would learn from a socioeconomically diverse classroom were just as important as those I would learn out of a book. From my first day at Mililani Uka, till my graduation from Mililani High School in 2007, I felt proud of my education. After moving to the US continent for college, however, I encountered a creeping feeling of confusion. Growing up hapa in Hawai'i, I never felt that my self-identity was an issue—being "local" had always meant the most to me. On the continent though, I wasn't Hawaiian, as people often assumed; I wasn't haole; and I didn't identify with being "American." I knew that Hawai'i was different, but I didn't know what that meant. It was then that I began to recognize that my education was, in many ways, lacking.

After returning to the islands to complete my BA in Political Science at the University of Hawai'i at Mānoa, I stepped even farther from home on a fourteen-month trip around the world, driven largely by a desire to place Hawai'i's complex history within a global context. While traveling often leaves me with more questions than answers, it has also made clear that there were holes in my schooling, and that filling these holes would have enriched my education and my subsequent experiences in the world.

In the conversations I had with other travelers during my journey, I found myself struggling, time and again, to explain that while Hawai'i is proud of its distinct identity, our children take only one compulsory Hawaiian History class in their entire time in school. I hesitated to admit that while I am passionate about Hawai'i's culture and history, I do not speak the Hawaiian language and had very few opportunities to learn it. While brainstorming for this essay in a village in Nepal, I spoke with a young couple from the Faroe Islands. They talked about how establishing their native Faroese as the language of instruction in public schools was an important milestone in the struggle to achieve "home rule," or political autonomy, from Denmark. They, like many other travelers from countries where bilingualism is the norm, commented on how typically American it is to portray bilingualism as unattainable. And I began to recognize this monoligualism as just one symptom of US cultural imperialism—homogenization of a uniquely heterogenous society.

Exchanges like this one, repeated so many times with people from so many places, gradually made me aware that my education remained rooted in a colonial past. By failing to ground students in the history and culture of the place we call home, our public school system continues to contribute to the marginalization of Hawai'i's indigenous people and to the disempowerment of all of us.

Now, as I write about Hawai'i from a refugee camp in the West Bank, I realize that sometimes it is easier to recognize the larger picture once you've taken a step back. Feelings of confusion, questions of identity, and guilt over my own ignorance are by no means unique problems. All over the world, colonizing powers have sought to assimilate populations and legitimize colonial authority by implementing a form of schooling that devalues native cultures and knowledge. Here, in the occupied Palestinian territories, I have had the good fortune of learning from a group of young refugees participating in an experimental higher education program focused on "unlearning" the ideology of occupation. They seek to redefine their identity as refugees—not passive victims, but architects of a vibrant community that has maintained a level of autonomy and sociopolitical independence through the harsh conditions of occupation. In their refugeehood, they have created an alternative space that challenges not only the occupation of Palestine, but also global issues of consumer capitalism and imperialism. Simultaneously, they use these intellectual explorations to fuel community projects that enhance life in the camp and nurture a strong, freethinking refugee community.

Learning alongside these young people, I witnessed the power of an education that is centered in place, experience, and indigenous ways of knowing. Their intellectual growth has brought them so far beyond the cramped alleyway of the refugee camp, while at the same time rooting them within it. I will never forget sitting with a friend one night, after being confronted by armed soldiers at an Israeli checkpoint, and telling him how Hawai'i's history of occupation has largely been ignored. He looked at me and said, "in some ways, it seems that we are more free here in Palestine, because at least we can see what we are struggling against." Ultimately, it was my time in Palestine that truly illuminated the potential to reimagine our education as one that could similarly liberate and empower the people of Hawai'i.

A COLONIAL LEGACY

To understand the potential for the education system to reclaim our identity, it is important to understand the ways schools have been used in the past to erase it. School curriculum is "never simply a neutral assemblage of knowledge. . . . It is always part of a selective tradition, someone's selection, some group's vision of legitimate knowledge."[1]

While Native Hawaiians played an integral role in establishing literacy and schooling in the Hawaiian Kingdom, under the growing influence of plantation interests in the late nineteenth century, public schools increasingly moved towards an assimilationist model. Just three years after the illegal overthrow of the Hawaiian monarchy, Act 57 declared English the official language of instruction in public schools. In subsequent years, as the population became increasingly dominated by foreign laborers, instilling US values and beliefs became even more important to the planter oligarchy.[2]

Education was used to maintain a plantation labor force from within the Native Hawaiian and Asian immigrant populations, and educators were charged with ensuring that the lifegoals of their students were kept in line with US planter interests.[3] Teachers were expected to be "thoroughly American," and in 1920, the territorial legislature passed a bill that required teachers to hold a certificate confirming that they "possessed the ideals of democracy, knowledge of American history, and institutions."[4] Foreign language schools set up by immigrant communities faced opposition, as American interests viewed them as a threat to US authority in the islands, and in 1914, *The Hawaii Educational Review* boldly proclaimed the Department of Public Instruction's conviction that "The schools of Hawaii stand foremost among the agencies at work for the Americanization and uplift of this important part of the United States."[5]

RECLAIMING OUR PRESENT

This complicated legacy is still present today. While public education later came to serve as a powerful equalizer that challenged the plantation hierarchy of the territorial era, schools today continue to perpetuate an ideology that legitimizes US authority and marginalizes the Hawaiian experience. For instance, they serve as recruiting centers for a military that continues to occupy and abuse precious Hawaiian lands. They are dominated by capitalist interests, as evidenced by the overwhelming presence of business leaders, lawyers, and political elites in DOE and BOE leadership. Native Hawaiian studies are still shamefully absent from the daily lives of our students. My experience with Hawaiian education in the mainstream public school system was often simplistic, and still limited to sporadic Hawaiian studies lessons through the kūpuna program in elementary school, a class in the seventh grade where we memorized a chant and learned a hula, and one Modern Hawaiian History course in the tenth grade.[6]

Ultimately, education is treated as a subtractive enterprise; as though teaching our keiki about Hawaiʻi's unique history and complex relationship with the United States detracts from more pragmatic educational goals and is detrimental to the students' ability to succeed in a globalized world. Instead, indigenous epistemologies should be regarded as valuable knowledge that can help us to confront the social and environmental challenges that we face in our islands, and as a planet.

MAKING STRIDES TOWARD A POSTCOLONIAL FUTURE

The educational victories of the past few decades show that there is potential for transformational change. Though my access to Hawaiian education was severely limited, my sister's experience, just six years later, was markedly different. As a student at Mililani High School, she attended the same classes I did, but was exposed to a curriculum that allowed her to engage critically with Hawai'i's past, as well as its present. Thanks to educators who took it upon themselves to incorporate these weighty issues in their curricula, she interacted with recent scholarship on the overthrow, occupation, and annexation of Hawai'i, and she had the opportunity to translate this learning into direct action by travelling to Kaho'olawe with the Protect Kaho'olawe Ohana. These examples, as well as the successes of Hawaiian charter schools and language immersion schools, demonstrate that gains have been made in rooting our students in place and history. These cultural kīpuka have given rise to a generation of students who have grown up with Native Hawaiian knowledge as a means of preparing for life in a global world.[7] We can continue to cultivate connections between 'Ōiwi and non-'Ōiwi to transcend neocolonial relationships and create "a community that comes to understand and define itself as a collective that makes Hawaiian culture foundational to its day-to-day life."[8]

Like my friends in Dheisheh refugee camp, we must realize that while our education has been used to limit our growth and bind us to unequal and unjust power structures, it can also be reclaimed. It can give us the tools we need to regain autonomy over our island home, and create a future that remains true to indigenous values. In the past, the centralization of Hawai'i's public school system made it easy for colonial interests to implement assimilationist policy. Today, this same centralization can enable us to implement widescale change and make meaningful strides towards decolonizing the minds of future generations. Here are just a few suggestions for action:

1. Work towards meeting the goals of the Hawai'i State Constitution. The 1978 Constitutional Convention mandated the state to "insure the general diffusion of Hawaiian history on a wider basis, to recognize and preserve the Hawaiian culture which has contributed to, and in many ways forms the basis and foundation of, modern Hawai'i, and to revive the Hawaiian language, which is essential to the preservation and perpetuation of Hawaiian culture."[9] This mandate should be regarded as a serious legal obligation to the people of Hawai'i, and steps should be taken to ensure that this promise is made a priority.

2. Teach Hawaiian language to all of our keiki. The immense power of language should not be underestimated. As one 'Ōiwi friend of mine shared, while learning to 'ōlelo Hawai'i, the very structure and syntax of Hawaiian language reflect values vastly different from dominant, Western thinking. In English, the subject is typically placed at the start of the sentence. In Hawaiian sentences, the verb comes first, placing the importance on the action. My friend said, "Think how a lifetime of speaking by leading with the words 'I,' 'You,' 'We,' shapes a particular mindset as to the subject always being most important. Now think how a lifetime of beginning your sentences with and emphasizing the verb will shape a particular mindset that focuses first on our actions."

3. Take a critical eye towards existing curriculum. Curriculum that *essentializes* culture can do more harm than good. School curriculum all too often reduces Native Hawaiian and other longlived, dynamic cultures to "museum cultures" that appear to be of little relevance to a modern, globalized world. For cultural studies to contribute to decolonization, they must have at their core a commitment to challenging the status quo and changing exploitative colonial power relations.[10]

4. Provide teachers with rigorous and meaningful training in Hawaiian studies. When Modern Hawaiian History was added to public school curriculum as a required course in the 1980s, no additional training was provided to the teachers who would be implementing this new program. In many cases, this has led to misguided curriculum that can exacerbate, instead of challenge, our disconnections from Hawai'i's past and its ongoing relevance. We must provide teachers with the training, instructional resources, and funding needed to support a rigorous Hawaiian studies curriculum.

5. Make structural changes that will allow more Kānaka Maoli to become teachers. Though students of Hawaiian ancestry make up the largest proportion of our school population,[11] Native Hawaiians are severely underrepresented in public school as teachers and administrators. The colonizing effects of our education are deep, and the conditions of colonialism are reproduced by the education system itself. We must confront these structural inequalities in order to break this cycle and nurture a true exchange within our classrooms.

6. Address issues of multilayered identities in Hawai'i. Teaching about Hawai'i's culture and colonial history can be difficult because it often disrupts our image of multiethnic harmony.[12] We should recognize that there are multiple layers of oppression at play in Hawai'i. Cultural and historical education should help non-'Ōiwi students root themselves in a more honest and responsible understanding of our own identities. History tells us that various ethnic minorities were oppressed in the process of the Americanization and colonization of Hawai'i, and today, all residents of Hawai'i live under the burden of American imperialism and militarization. As we learn about Native Hawaiian struggles, we also connect with our own histories of struggle, and by coming to terms with our role as Asian or haole settlers in a Native land, we can begin to understand our responsibility to our Kanaka Maoli brothers and sisters. We all share in this struggle against US imperialism.

7. Push for educational reform on a systemic level. While state-level reforms are crucial to reclaiming our public education system, many public school educators will recognize these suggestions as inadequate, given the far-reaching effects of federal educational policy. Neocolonial education is not just an issue here in Hawaiʻi, it is a deeply rooted, systemic problem that demands that we take this challenge much farther than our islands. Neoliberal education policy across the United States is increasingly placing public education within a market-centric framework, turning students into commodities instead of creating intellectual community. Federal initiatives like No Child Left Behind and Race to the Top reduce education to standardization and a narrow conception of learning, while ignoring the structural conditions that so often determine educational opportunities. Transformational change will require us to decolonize Hawaiʻi's education system and consider the larger political and institutional framework within which it operates.

Education need not be subtractive; learning about Hawaiian culture and Hawaiʻi's past should be regarded as a key step in the process of building more just relationships between Native and non-Native people of Hawaiʻi. Many of us trace our roots to peoples from the Asia-Pacific region, and all of us are subjects of US imperialism. Raising our level of political consciousness through the lens of Native Hawaiian knowledge can give us valuable tools for dealing with pressing issues: from the corporatism invading our public education system and most other aspects of our lives, to the dire environmental crisis that we face together across the planet.

We need to shift our attitude away to recognize that Hawaiian cultural education is relevant and necessary in a globalized world. Native Hawaiian education should be elevated from an ethnic issue to a means of empowerment for all people of Hawaiʻi. We should all feel invested in the culture at the root of contemporary, multiethnic Hawaiʻi. We must work to unlearn the kind of thinking that devalues our unique heritage or seeks to define it as irrelevant. Whether our roots in Hawaiʻi are traced back to Kānaka Maoli, Asian plantation laborers, or US haole, fostering a deeper connection to our past—a past that begins with the Hawaiian people—will help us to better understand ourselves. Hawaiʻi's struggle belongs to all of us.

NOTES

1.   Michael Apple, "The Politics of Official Knowledge: Does a National Curriculum Make Sense?" *Teachers College Record* 95.2 (Winter 1993): 222 (222–41).

2.   As one school administrator in Puerto Rico wrote in a 1902 annual school report: "Colonization carried forward by the armies of war is vastly more costly than that carried

forward by the armies of peace, whose outpost and garrisons are the public schools of advancing nations" (Pablo Navarro-Rivera, "Understanding the American Empire," *Colonial Crucible: Empire in the Making of the Modern American State*, ed. Alfred W. McCoy and Francisco A. Scarano [Madison: U of Wisconsin P, 2009]: 164).

3. Maenette K. P. Ah-Nee Benham and Ronald H. Heck, *Culture and Educational Policy in Hawai'i: The Silencing of Native Voices* (Hillsdale, NJ: Lawrence Erlbaum, 1998): 148–234.

4. Qtd. on 204 of B. K. Hyams, "School Teachers as Agents of Cultural Imperialism in Territorial Hawaii," *Journal of Pacific History* 20.4 (1985): 202–219.

5. See Hyams 207, for its discussion of *The Hawaii Educational Review* 2.4 (1914).

6. Julie Kaomea's critical comparison of Hawaiian Studies textbooks and tourism pamphlets demonstrate that what little Hawaiian studies curriculum is present in public schools all too often reinforces stereotypes of Hawaiian culture. Just as plantation interests co-opted public education as a way to track Hawaiian and Asian students into agricultural livelihoods, this misrepresentation supports an economy dependent on tourism and military by co-opting the "aloha spirit" to prepare students to accept and participate in our islands' largest industries. See Julie Kaomea in the Resources for this essay.

7. Kīpuka are areas of old-growth vegetation that survive lava flows and regenerate barren lava fields. Davianna McGregor calls stands of cultural survival and growth "cultural kīpuka," alluding to the regenerative potential of these spaces and communities. See Davianna P. McGregor, *Nā Kua'āina: Living Hawaiian Culture* (Honolulu: U of Hawai'i P, 2007).

8. Noelani Goodyear-Ka'ōpua, *The Seeds We Planted: Portraits of a Native Hawaiian Charter School* (Minneapolis: U of Minnesota P, 2013): 31. As Goodyear-Ka'ōpua chronicles, culturally-based education has not only been used to challenge the institutionalization of colonizing education, but also to benefit indigenous students who have long suffered in a system that devalued their heritage and often imposed negative self-perceptions of Hawaiian identity. See Goodyear-Ka'ōpua's book in the Resources for this essay.

9. From a committee report that developed the Hawaiian education mandate of the 1978 Constitutional Convention, qtd. on 99 of William H. Wilson, "The Sociopolitical Context of Establishing Hawaiian-medium Education," *Indigenous Community Based Education,* ed. Steven May (Philadelphia: Multilingual Matters, 1999): 95–108.

10. See Jeanette Haynes Writer, "Unmasking, Exposing, and Confronting: Critical Race Theory, Tribal Critical Race Theory and Multicultural Education," *International Journal of Multicultural Education* 10.2 (2008): 1–15.

11. According to Kamehameha Schools' *Native Hawaiian Educational Assessment Update,* Native Hawaiian students comprised 27.6 percent of public school enrollment (*Native Hawaiian Educational Assessment Update 2009: A Supplement to Ka Huaka'i 2005* [Honolulu: Kamehameha Schools, Research & Evaluation Division, 2009]).

12. See Candace Fujikane, "Introduction: Asian Settler Colonialism in the U.S. Colony of Hawai'i," *Asian Settler Colonialism: From Local Governance to the Habits of Everyday Life in Hawai'i,* ed. Candace Fujikane and Jonathan Y. Okamura (Honolulu: U of Hawai'i P, 2008): 1–42.

RESOURCES FOR FURTHER INFORMATION AND INSPIRATION

1. Noelani Goodyear-Kaʻōpua, *The Seeds We Planted: Portraits of a Native Hawaiian Charter School* (Minneapolis: U of Minnesota P, 2013).This book provides an intimate look at the challenges of carrying out indigenous cultural education under a system of settler colonialism, and exposes the oppressive power of federal education policy. Read it to get a taste of how our very narrow conception of education can be reimagined, and the obstacles that stand in the way.

2. Julie Kaomea, "A Curriculum of Aloha: Colonialism and Tourism in Hawaii's Elementary Textbooks," *Curriculum Inquiry* 30.3 (2000): 319–44. This work shows the shocking parallels between Hawaiian studies textbooks and tourist brochures and materials, and demonstrates the need for a critical examination of Hawaiian cultural curricula in public schools.

3. Kevin K. Kumashiro, *Bad Teacher! How Blaming Teachers Distorts the Bigger Picture* (New York: Teachers College P, 2012). Making meaningful changes on a local level demands that we understand education policy within a national context. In this book, educator and author Kevin Kumashiro demonstrates how market-based reforms and the privatization of public school systems have created overwhelming obstacles to an equitable education system. This book is a great resource for understanding the larger systemic issues shaping the educational environment in ways that harm students and teachers alike.

4. A TED talk by Nigerian author Chimamnda Ngozi Adichie, "The Danger of a Single Story," brings to light the danger of allowing any place, person, or peoples to be dominated by a single story. In many ways, Hawaiʻi's culture and history are being dominated by a single story that silences other very important ones. The idea of Hawaiʻi's single story can be a great starting point for discussions on how to make these other voices heard. This talk can be viewed online at http://www.ted.com/talks/chimamanda_adichie_the_danger_of_a_single_story.html.

5. "Campus in Camps" is an experimental education project in Dheisheh Refugee Camp in Palestine, which fueled my excitement over the potential to decolonize Hawaiʻi's public education system. On its website, http://www.campusincamps.ps/en/about, you can follow along with the ongoing efforts to deconstruct the colonizing and occupying powers that permeate life in Occupied Palestine.

ALTERNATIVE ECONOMIES FOR ALTERNATIVE FUTURES

DEAN ITSUJI SARANILLIO

As a child growing up on the island of Maui, I remember my mother, Eloise Saranillio, singing a funny song to the tune of the McGuire Sisters' 1958 hit "Sugar Time." Changing the word "sugar" to "cabbage," she sang, "cabbage in the morning, cabbage in the evening, cabbage at suppertime." She told us that when she was growing up at the McGerrow plantation camp on Maui, her mother, my grandmother Masako Inouye, went on strike at the Hawaiian Commercial & Sugar Co. (HC&S) sugar plantation and served as a strike captain. In 1958, International Longshore and Warehouse Union (ILWU) laborers went on strike to seek a living wage, and cabbage farmers from Kula helped to feed the workers and sustain their strikes. I suppose the song made us laugh because as opposed to a romantic white American life of eating sugar all day, we were more accustomed to thinking of sugar as something that caused bitterness, like forcing a family to eat cabbage for three months.

My father, Dick Saranillio, told us about how his oldest brother, my uncle Fred "Junior" Saranillio, worked in the school garden while they attended Lanai Elementary School. When my Uncle Junior could not scramble enough lunch money for himself and his siblings, he would forgo lunch at the cafeteria and eat the vegetables he helped grow. My father only found out when he caught his older brother eating carrots by himself. When my brother and I were in elementary school, my father took us every weekend to Olowalu to dive for fish and tako (octopus) with three-prong spears. He taught us what was "good eat" and to catch only what we needed. Before we were born, upon his return to Hawai'i after serving in the Air Force during the Vietnam War, he would go diving to feed himself and stretch what money he had. He also did this when he went out on strike as an ironworker. By teaching us to dive, and to clean and prepare fish, he said that no matter what happened, we would always have the ability to feed ourselves in healthy ways.

These family stories regarding food and poverty arose from the deliberate strategy of Paul Isenberg, a prominent leader of Hawai'i's sugar industry in the nineteenth century. Isenberg argued that arranging workers' wages so that the "Chinese and Japanese had to *work or be hungry*" made them easier to control.[1] Like many have argued before, capitalism benefits the rich at the expense of the poor. Throughout history, to stave off getting deeper in debt, many have had to rely on alternatives to a capitalist economy—such as fishing, diving, hunting, planting, gathering, and sharing. Sometimes illegal economies are used to supplement otherwise meager incomes. In this way, capitalism cannot function without the existence of alternative economies.[2] These alternative economies, especially land-based Indigenous economies, also offer the "material conditions of resistance"—the ability to sustain resistance via autonomy that makes a community less vulnerable and controllable by employers, creditors, developers, and potential thieves.

Like my three older siblings and many other working-class students, I worked after school and on the weekends at a series of part-time jobs, often pulling twelve-hour days. By seventeen, I had worked at three jobs, including Taco Bell, Kay-Bee Toy Store, and Pizza People Paukukalo, delivering (and eating) pizzas. As a student at Maui High School I was thought of, and saw myself as, a "bad student." I viewed school as something that I was forced to do. Diving for fish still remained a passion, and I often cut school to go diving with my friends. But there was one class I never missed, with a teacher who broadened my world by teaching history as a guide to endless possibilities.

Walking into Mr. Andrew G. Klukowski's classroom portable, you would have noticed the Bob Marley banner overhead: "Emancipate yourselves from mental slavery, none but ourselves can free our minds!" You would have seen hung on the wall a series of black-and-white photos from the Vietnam War, of US soldiers dragging Vietnamese soldiers and civilians behind US tanks. His classroom was a place where seemingly taboo topics were openly discussed. Indeed, it was where I learned of the 1893 US military-backed overthrow of the Hawaiian Kingdom. The topic had been "taught" to me before, but this was the first time I learned this history in a manner that was not dismissive. In Mr. Klukowski's class, this topic was open to discussion, debated, and created the basis for imagining new possibilities for Hawai'i.

It is in the same spirit of Mr. Klukowski's classes, where there were no ready-made answers and no topics considered taboo, that I write this piece. While we often think of the history of different Asian groups on the sugar plantations and the US occupation of Hawai'i as separate and unrelated histories, I wish to place them in conversation by using food—a basic necessity of life—as a space for overlap. Indeed, low wages to make the poor "work or be hungry" are connected to a longer history of eliminating Indigenous foodways, often by seizing water, in order to coerce Kānaka ʻŌiwi into a capitalist economy. I write this piece as a member of a family who has been in Hawaiʻi for five generations because of the needs for exploitable labor by a sugar industry, an industry whose leaders were intimately involved in dismantling Indigenous land-based economies, leading to the 1893 US military-backed overthrow of the Hawaiian Kingdom. In this way, to riff off of recent scholarship on settler colonialism, haole settlers established a system of economics that generally seized Hawaiian land and exploited Asian labor to create haole property.[3] This colonial system, however, has changed so that it is no longer just haole who benefit.[4]

In his 2009 memoir, Benjamin J. Cayetano, former governor of Hawaiʻi (1994–2002), casts a Kanaka ʻŌiwi movement for self-determination as an "exercise in futility, an impossible dream," working at the expense of "all of Hawaiʻi's people."[5] While Cayetano paints this future Hawaiʻi as dangerous, the actions of the US government and the future it has in store for us are conveniently never questioned. Against Cayetano's warning for "all of Hawaiʻi's people" to *fear* a future Hawaiian nation, I would like to argue the opposite. I believe that what is *most valuable* in Hawaiʻi is the Hawaiian movement that aims to deoccupy Hawaiʻi from the United States, consequently creating alternative futures to an increasingly unsustainable, war-obsessed way of life. This is an alternative to exporting death from Hawaiʻi's shores via the US military, which is tied to the over 725 acknowledged US military bases outside of the United States—a network of bases that Chalmers Johnson explains "is a sign not of military preparedness but of militarism, the inescapable companion of imperialism."[6] An alternative to our current capitalist economy, based on dominating people and families through wages that leave the majority of people in massive debt, thus making them easier to control. Fundamentally, these alternative futures are absolutely crucial in a world facing increasing environmental catastrophe.

A HISTORY OF OUR PRESENT

Placing the enormity of our current environmental moment in context, Nobel prize-winning chemist Paul J. Crutzen, and his collaborator Eugene F. Stoermer, a marine science specialist, argue that we are moving into an altogether new geological moment. The last ten to twelve millenia have been referred to as the Holocene era—a period of general warmth. This new geological epoch—the Anthropocene era—is defined by the fact that humans are now considered a geological force on the planet, capable of producing environmental catastrophe. Crutzen and Stoermer point out that air containing high concentrations of carbon dioxide and methane and trapped in polar ice can be traced to the design of the steam engine in 1874.[7] Today, carbon emissions among developed nations are far higher than the rest of the world—the United States possesses 5 percent of the world's population but uses 25 percent of its resources. At the 2009 Copenhagen Climate Summit, the Indigenous president of Bolivia, Evo Morales, pointed out that the United States had spent $2.6 trillion for the Iraq war yet contributed only $10 billion to address climate change.

It would of course be a western culture prioritizing humans, especially western culture and people, above all other life forms that would lead us to the Anthropocene era. In the very creation of the United States both labor and Indigenous peoples became vulnerable, often through environmental degradation. The United States is a settler colonial nation: a nation that aims to expropriate Indigenous territories and eliminate their economies in order to replace Indigenous peoples with settlers who are made out to be superior, and thus more deserving of these contested lands and resources. As such, settler colonialism "destroys to replace."[8] The United States, like other settler colonial nations, is premised on establishing capitalism as the only way of life. It is accountable to neither nature nor people, only to the accumulation of profit.

There is a common misunderstanding that capitalism simply liberated communities from land-based barter economies; that capitalism was gradually welcomed and peacefully accepted by the masses.[9] In actual reality, akin to the use of wages to make plantation workers "work or be hungry," capitalism prior to this needed to violently break Indigenous economies by first eliminating the ability of Indigenous peoples to feed themselves. This process of primitive accumulation, and its ongoing process of "accumulation by dispossession," privatizes areas that were once used freely to provide food through a variety of commons—in Hawai'i the ahupua'a system functioned this way. Instead, communities are forced to sell their labor to acquire money to buy their food at the market. Once their food sources were gone, many formerly autonomous peoples were forced into positions of dependency, and thus became easier to colonize. For example, take the Lakota and their sacred relationships to the buffalo, not unlike Kanaka 'Ōiwi sacred familial relations with kalo. Buffalo herds numbered 15 million in 1871, but were hunted by US settlers to such an extent that by 1903, only 34 buffalo remained. Once the buffalo were killed, the Lakota became vulnerable. The US military saw this as strategy, as Brigadier General Philip Sheridan argued: "The best way to get rid of the Indian is to destroy the buffalo by which he lives. The more buffalo killed, the better, and what good is a buffalo anyway except for slaughter.[10]

A HISTORY OF THE FUTURE

In 1897, Liliʻuokalani writes in *Hawaii's Story, by Hawaii's Queen* about the differences between Kanaka ʻŌiwi economies and capitalism: "I have always said that under our own system in former days there was always plenty for prince or for people. The latter were not paid in money, nor were they taxed in purse."[11] In her work, Candace Fujikane discusses the arguments made by longtime Hawaiian activist Walter Ritte, who provides a similar comparison, that an Indigenous economy is based around abundance, restoring the resources to be ʻāina momona, while a western capitalist economy is based around scarcity:

> We all understand the cash economy; we all part of that and we all know where that goes. If you don't have money, you cannot feed your face. And that's the cash economy. So for us, it was like, whoa, we gotta eat, man. So we also have a subsistence economy, and that economy keeps us in a position to yell at people, to tell people to go to hell, get off our island, I mean, we can tell them anything because we don't need them to feed our faces.[12]

In order to sustain resistance, one must be autonomous and anticipate the pitfalls of capitalism. Ritte argues that looking deeply into Hawaiian culture and recognizing the true genius of a Hawaiian economy, not looking to others, is what provided an abundance of food for an entire population of people for eons while still maintaining the health of those resources. This argument reflects the difference between food sovereignty and food security.[13] As Candace Fujikane elegantly states: "As we are faced with manufactured conditions of scarcity, the people of Moana Nui are working to restore ʻāina momona and abundance, and in this pathway lies a future beyond empires."[14]

To offer an example of a history of primitive accumulation and the use of food as resistance that can benefit both Hawaiians and settlers, we can look to the island of Maui. Four valleys with four streams comprise Nā Wai ʻEhā (the Four Great Waters)—Waikapū, Wailuku, Waiehu, and Waiheʻe—and they irrigated the largest continuous area of loʻi kalo (wetland taro fields) in all of Hawaiʻi, considered one of the pinnacles of Hawaiian agriculture. Loʻi kalo enable a sustainable mode of Hawaiian farming that makes use of intricate ʻauwai (irrigation canals) to irrigate a diversity of wetland kalo and an array of other plants and animals. This nutrient-rich water is then channeled back to the stream or river. For centuries, the vast cultivation of different varieties of taro—the food staple and genealogical ancestor of Kanaka ʻŌiwi—nourished one of the largest and densest populations on the island.[15]

In the later half of the nineteenth and early twentieth centuries, however, sugar planters claimed ownership of these rivers. White settler planters diverted water away from Kanaka 'Ōiwi communities to arid areas of the island in order to expand the industrial production of sugar sold on the US market.[16] Kānaka 'Ōiwi were no longer able to access the required amount of water necessary for Indigenous foodways to continue. The historical robbing of a way of life, however, did not succeed in eliminating the memory of another way of organizing Nā Wai 'Ehā.

In 2004, taro farmers calling themselves the Hui 'o Nā Wai 'Ehā, together with environmentalists of Maui Tomorrow and Earth Justice, petitioned for the restoration of these four streams to replace rapidly depleting ground water and to support non-industrial local agriculture in the area.[17] Hawaiian Commercial & Sugar Co. (HC&S) and Wailuku Water Distribution Co. (formerly Wailuku Sugar Co.), the two companies responsible for the original water diversions from Nā Wai 'Ehā, argued that without continued access to up to 70 million gallons of water a day, their already declining industry would be in jeopardy and 800 HC&S workers would be at risk of losing their jobs. Organizing themselves into a group called Hui 'o Ka 'Ike, workers argued desperately, "Our jobs are at stake, our very livelihood and the ability to support our families."[18]

In June 2010, the water commission ruled to return only a third of the stream flow for which the groups petitioned, and to only two of the four streams—Waihe'e and Waiehu. Hōkūao Pellegrino, whose family lo'i sits along Waikapū stream, which did not receive any of the petitioned water, responded: "I may not be able to employ 800 people, but I can feed 800 people—if I was able to grow on all of my land."[19] Hōkūao Pellegrino's response forces one to consider a preceding moment in time, a different arrangement of land and resources, and a way of life that predates the settler state: one that can create the conditions for mutual respect between these different communities. Although not relying on wages to support one's family is often imagined as illogical or impossible, Pellegrino's community work shows that lo'i kalo in Nā Wai 'Ehā are viable foundations for Hawai'i's future. Together with his father, Victor Pellegrino, they have used their farm named Noho'ana, which translates as "way of life," since 2004 as a community resource to teach traditional subsistence, organic, and sustainable farming techniques to students from preschool to the university level. Such knowledges are, in fact, grounded in centuries-old ongoing creative practices. Not so much a process of "going back," this work brings Maui's present environmental and economic problems together with ongoing Indigenous technologies and knowledges, particularly a deep historical knowledge of the specific environmental features that are essential to the health of Nā Wai 'Ehā.

In her thought-provoking and inspirational book *The Seeds We Planted: Portrait of a Native Hawaiian Charter School*, Noelani Goodyear-Kaʻōpua illustrates just how Indigenous knowledge and economies can materially transform the structures of settler colonialism:

> The marginalization and suppression of Indigenous knowledges has gone hand-in-hand with the transformation and degradation of Indigenous economic systems and the ecosystems that nourish us. Conversely, settler-colonial relations might be transformed by rebuilding, in new ways, the Indigenous structures that have historically sustained our societies.[20]

Land-based economies have the possibility of creating new non-capitalist and non-colonial ways of relating to each other. Goodyear-Kaʻōpua sets the conditions for cultivating mutual respect by promoting what she refers to as "land-centered literacies" that "attend to the health of the environmental systems of which we are a part. They create the space and give Indigenous and settler participants the intellectual tools to reckon their genealogies and positionalities in relation to history, land, and the diverse peoples with which one lives."[21] As opposed to Benjamin Cayetano's arguments that Hawaiian sovereignty is dangerous, this economy, what Kumu Danny Bishop calls "taro patch economics," would require an average person to labor for fifteen to twenty-five hours a month. Cultivating this Indigenous knowledge and know-how might lead to a completely land-based, or hybrid economy, that could feed all of us. I say this not because there are ready-made answers, but to challenge our sense of what is possible. As a former worker in the tourism industry and the son of parents who often held three jobs at a time, I know many who work for more than fifteen hours in a single day.

ALTERNATIVE FUTURES

Prominent philosopher Takeshi Umehara, who is a part of the Japanese government's Reconstruction Design Council responding to the 2011 nuclear disaster in Japan, argues that seemingly "developed" nations should learn from Indigenous peoples and, similar to Ritte, Pellegrino, and Goodyear-Kaʻōpua, should look to their own history for answers to current problems. Recounting the earthquake and tsunami that hit Sendai, Japan, in March of 2011, he says that the nuclear fallout from the Fukushima Daichi plant—where my great-grandfather Kumakichi Abe is from—has made him consider that the western way of organizing society is a "dead end."[22] He instead argues that to chart new principles for a future civilization, Japan needs to return to its ancient ways of thinking, primarily around its relationship to nature. Umehara states that he was born during the US nuclear attack on Nagasaki and Hiroshima, and at the end of his life is now concerned with nuclear fallout. Umehara asks: "Is it so hard today to see that modernity, having lost its relationships to nature and the spirit, is nothing other than a philosophy of death?"[22] Umehara states about Japan: "By learning more about early civilizations, I believe we can better transform ours from one that uses technology to conquer nature to one that employs technology to coexist with nature."[23]

Industries that aim to profit off of food are making alternative futures impossible. Thinking about the connections among food, war, colonialism, and the environment, ecofeminist Vandana Shiva points out that 40 percent of all greenhouse gasses contributing to global warming are from industrial agricultural models, which require exporting foods across long distances and increasingly transporting genetically modified seeds to farmers. This is Hawai'i's current way of producing food and Hawai'i, besides being one of the most militarized places in the world, is also the GMO (genetically modified organism) capitol of the world. Shiva argues that GMOs are themselves producing a militarized food industry: "War and agriculture came together when the chemicals that were produced for chemical warfare lost their markets in war, and the industry organized itself to sell those chemicals as agrochemicals."[24]

At a rally at the State Capitol to get the Hawai'i State Legislature to label GMOs, on the eve of the 120th anniversary of the overthrow of the Hawaiian nation, Shiva stated clearly that militarized food via GMOs is about dominating life for profit, but also: "In the making of your own food is the making of freedom. . . . The human hand and the human mind have been made to look primitive. And the primitive minds of violence and war, have been made to look like our future. *We do not accept it.*" Nature, not profit, needs to determine the conditions of possibility for Hawai'i. By taking seriously Indigenous knowledges and economies, we can create another future, and in the creation of an alternative future, more space for mutual respect can occur. Settler states have no interests in non-Natives identifying with Native movements, as such identification opens our world to alternatives that the settler state denies are possible. But we can oppose this system that, while the prices we each pay are *different*, comes at the expense of *all of us.*

NOTES

1. As cited in Ralph S. Kuykendall, *Hawaiian Kingdom 1874–1893: The Kalakaua Dynasty* (Honolulu: U of Hawai'i P, 1967): 637.
2. See J. K. Gibson-Graham, *The End of Capitalism (As We Knew It)* (Minneapolis: U of Minnesota P, 1996); and J. K. Gibson-Graham, *Postcapitalist Politics* (Minneapolis: U of Minnesota P, 2006).

3. Patrick Wolfe, "Settler colonialism and the elimination of the native," *Journal of Genocide Research* 8.4 (2006): 388.

4. See Candace Fujikane, "Introduction: Asian Settler Colonialism in the U.S. Colony of Hawai'i," *Asian Settler Colonialism: From Local Governance to the Habits of Everyday Life in Hawai'i* (Honolulu: U of Hawai'i P, 2008): 1–42.

5. Benjamin J. Cayetano, *Ben: A Memoir, From Street Kid to Governor* (Honolulu: Watermark, 2009): 445.

6. Chalmers Johnson, *The Sorrows of Empire: Militarism, Secrecy, and the End of the Republic* (New York: Metropolitan Books, 2004): 24. For the acknowledged number of US military bases, see Johnson 4.

7. Dipesh Chakrabarty, "The Climate of History: Four Theses," *Critical Inquiry* 35 (Winter 2009): 197–222.

8. Patrick Wolfe, "Settler colonialism and the elimination of the native": 388.

9. David Graeber, *Debt: The First 5,000 Years* (Brooklyn: Melville, 2009): 29.

10. Sharon O'Brien, *American Indian Tribal Governments* (Norman: U of Oklahoma P, 1993): 70.

11. Liliuokalani, *Hawaii's Story by Hawaii's Queen* (Honolulu: Mutual, 1991): 24–25.

12. As cited in Candace Fujikane, "Asian American critique and Moana Nui 2011: Securing a future beyond empires, militarized capitalism and APEC," *Inter-Asia Cultural Studies* 13.2 (2012): 18.

13. The food security model for combating hunger is driven by the United Nations, the World Bank, the International Monetary Fund, and other organizations that have long failed to achieve their stated goals. Instead, food sovereignty bases its economies around local farmers and knowledges, and more effectively challenges the corporate monopolization of the food industry. See William D. Schanbacher, *The Politics of Food: The Global Conflict between Food Security and Food Sovereignty* (Denver: Praeger Security International, 2010).

14. Candace Fujikane, "Asian American Critique and Moana Nui 2011: Securing a Future beyond Empires, Militarized Capitalism and APEC," *Inter-Asia Cultural Studies* 13.2 (2012): 19.

15. E. S. C. Handy and E. G. Handy, *Native Planters in Old Hawaii: Their Life, Lore, and Environment* (Honolulu: Bishop Museum, 1972): 272.

16. See Carol Wilcox, *Sugar Water: Hawaii's Plantation Ditches* (Honolulu: U of Hawai'i P, 1996); see also "Tunneling for Water: A New and Important Industry Being Developed on Maui," *The Maui News*, February 2, 1901: 3, at http://chroniclingamerica.loc.gov/lccn/sn82014689/1901-02-02/ed-1/seq-3.

17. For more information, see http://earthjustice.org/our_work/campaigns/restore-stream-flow.

18. Chris Hamilton, "Na Wai Eha: HC&S speaks. Jobs, fields at risk in stream water dispute," *The Maui News*, October 9, 2009, at http://www.mauinews.com/page/content.detail/id/524576.html.

19. Chris Hamilton, "Na Wai Eha: Decision in but dispute lingers," *The Maui News*, June 13, 2010, at http://www.mauinews.com/page/content.detail/id/532430.html.

20. Noelani Goodyear-Ka'ōpua, *The Seeds We Planted: Portraits of a Native Hawaiian Charter School* (Minneapolis: U of Minnesota P, 2013): 127.

21. See Goodyear-Ka'ōpua, *The Seeds We Planted*: 246.

22. *Fukushima NHK Documentary: "Civilizational Disaster"—The Cons of Nuclear Power,* March to Recovery Series, NHK World TV, aired October 28, 2012.

23. Takeshi Umehara, "Ancient Postmodernism," *New Perspectives Quarterly* 26.4 (Fall 2009/Winter 2010): 40–54, at http://www.digitalnpq.org/archive/2009_fall_2010_winter/06_umehara.html.

24. See Umehara, "Ancient Postmodernism."

25. Jon Letman, "GM Seeds and the Militarization of Food: An Interview with Vandana Shiva," *Earthfirst Newswire,* March 22, 2013, at http://earthfirstnews.wordpress.com/2013/03/22/gm-seeds-and-the-militarization-of-food-an-interview-with-vandana-shiva.

RESOURCES FOR FURTHER INFORMATION AND INSPIRATION

1. *Asian Settler Colonialism: From Local Governance to the Habits of Everyday Life in Hawai'i,* ed. Candace Fujikane and Jonathan Okamura (Honolulu: U of Hawai'i P, 2008).

2. Noelani Goodyear-Ka'ōpua, *The Seeds We Planted: Portraits of a Native Hawaiian Charter School* (Minneapolis: U of Minnesota P, 2013).

3. David Graeber, *Debt: The First 5,000 Years* (Brooklyn: Melville, 2009).

4. Candace Fujikane, "Asian American critique and Moana Nui 2011: Securing a future beyond empires, militarized capitalism and APEC," *Inter-Asia Cultural Studies* 13.2 (2012): 189–210.

5. Raul Zibechi, *Territories in Resistance: A Cartography of Latin American Social Movements* (Oakland: AK P, 2012).

BACKYARD KULEANA

KEONE KEALOHA

Aloha kākou, ʻo Keone Kealoha koʻu inoa. I currently live and work on Kauaʻi with a non-profit, Mālama Kauaʻi, I helped found in 2006. The following is a brief history of how I came to be here, some of what I've learned, and where I see things going. I hope my experience can provide another facet to your worldview and a meaningful insight for your future choices.

COMMUNITY ORGANIZING

I was raised in California for the earliest portion of my life. At thirteen, I came to live on Oʻahu, where I attended Kamehameha through my high school years. It was there that I came to have a deeper connection with Hawaiian Culture—the history and stories, events and traditions. Pushing boundaries and sometimes getting into trouble, I was finding my place in the world and coming to understand myself as a youth and as a kanaka.

After traveling and living abroad for some time, I returned to the islands in 2005 to raise my children. We landed on Kauaʻi in Kīlauea, a small sugarcane town on the northern coast of the island. Multigenerational and ethnically diverse, Kīlauea was reminiscent of my earlier home in Kahuku on the North Shore of Oʻahu. The roads were single lane, not much going on past 6:00 p.m., and everybody knew everybody's business. This made for some drama, but it also made for a strong community. When big things happened, people came out, together, and could put their differences aside for the good of the town.

I was inspired to be a part of such a place and to assume my kuleana as a town resident. I started by volunteering on the neighborhood board, one of the oldest and most well-respected boards on the island. This position helped me make connections and eventually led to my helping found a community-focused non-profit called Mālama Kauaʻi.

My intention was the same: support the community and the ʻāina; respect culture and history; leave things better than you found them. Mālama Kauaʻi was a vehicle to make a difference. We organized meaningful gatherings, educated ourselves, and collectively had a more unified voice—one that said there were other ways of doing things, ways that put the best interest of our community first. Our approach has focused on sustainability through local culture, and we developed many programs and partnerships to realize that, including:

- Hawai'i's first Green Map, highlighting green businesses and sustainability-oriented non-profits for island visitors and residents alike

- The Kaua'i Green Business Program, in which locally owned companies agree to adhere to responsible baselines in energy usage, waste practices, and procurement options

- Cultivate, a 100 percent-local food distribution service that helped expand access to local healthy food, increase income and markets for producers, and provide more options to grocers, restaurants, and hotels

- The Kaua'i School Garden Network, which has installed or revamped gardens at many of Kaua'i's pre-K–12 schools

- The Kalihiwai Community Garden, forty-two individual plots organically planted and maintained by local residents

- The Kalihiwai Permaculture Food Forest, a two-acre living library of propagation material with over a hundred species of climatized staple fruit and food trees purposefully in-planted with nutrient-rich companion plants, with the goal of localizing as much amendment material as possible

- The Eco-Roundtable, a quarterly meet-up of Kaua'i-based environmental and sustainability organizations, providing a forum for relationship-building, updates on each other's work, and outreach to the public on important issues and ways to impact change

Our members also took a stand on local issues, sometimes as an organization and sometimes as individuals. In nearly all of these cases, we found the crux of the issue to be the duel between corporations and the community—profits versus people.

For instance, at Naue, an ancient cemetery was paved over by a housing developer when the notorious SHPD, or State Historic Preservation Division, failed in dynamic fashion. We stood against the Superferry, when public funds were being used to test an ocean transportation system for a multibillion dollar military contract concerning a Joint High Speed Vehicle (JHSV). More recently, we opposed the Public Lands Development Corporation (PLDC), a tool that would have increased the control and influence of private interests over Hawai'i's state-managed lands.

In each instance, we made a big push in local media, including newspaper articles, letters to the editor, newsletters, blog postings, live broadcasts of events on our community radio station, and direct action in the form of protests and sign waving. Our aim was to get people talking about the issues. We even traveled to other islands to build relations—a much-needed step in bridging communities, especially on larger issues. For example, during the Superferry struggle, we organized delegation trips to Oʻahu to meet with legislators and Navy leadership, and we held press conferences to grow public understanding. Statewide rallies on the PLDC helped raise awareness and pressure leading up to the 2012 legislative session. While each of these issues demonstrated how community organizing can make a difference, they also highlighted how the existing systems of law are used by a powerful minority to circumvent the health and best interests of subject communities; we have a broken system of representation.

GLOBAL PRIVATIZATION AND PUBLIC-ASSUMED DEBT

We need to understand our local struggles in the context of a larger global system of control. Here, I focus my comments on some of these control mechanisms and a few ideas that might allow communities to better address them.

A primary means of community control is through money, and within the global monetary system we see an increased blending of corporate and government interests. The currency system has gone global and is so highly evolved that it is now based on, well, nothing at all. Silver, gold, and oil standards have disintegrated, or are fast disappearing. Working in tandem, the US Treasury Department and the Federal Reserve continue unabatedly printing money and creating credit, with no connection to any real assets. We have pictures on paper; enormous ghost loans, and the Maiden Lane shells that receive them, are invented with a few keystrokes, yachting the financial markets off into the sunset with sails that would impress even an emperor's greatest tailor. The warped work of 401(k)s, home equity, and college savings accounts weft with stocks, funds, and other financial instruments forms the tapestry that is "too-big-to-fail." Proponents of the too-big-to-fail idea argue that when some financial institutions are so big and interconnected, their failure would be "disastrous" to the economy. They use this assertion to call for government support, or bail-outs, with taxpayer monies.[1]

Yet this status quo only persists because we, ordinary people, buy into the psyche of money. We measure our own worth in terms of it. What we do for a living (aka, how we make money) defines our position. Our society believes this because we, individually, believe it—so we colonize ourselves and conform ourselves into acting as the "good citizens" needed for this hierarchy to continue.

An important aspect of the current monetary system is debt. Debt is provided in exchange for things we are told, and somehow believe, will make us happier. Surrounded by credit cards, mortgages, and various loan options, we understand how debt works and accept these things as normal. Our money/debt habit is a dysfunctional and abusive relationship. Yet we continue to endure this domestic violence because breaking up just seems too impossible to imagine.

The debt dynamic isn't limited to the individual level; it works just as well on entire countries. The model is this: the public assumes the debt, money is paid to corporations, and resources are now open for exploitation. Institutions like the International Monetary Fund and the World Bank offer loans in exchange for submissive economic policies and structural adjustment clauses that promote privatization, deregulation, and exploitation of natural resources and real assets. When forceful military approaches won't fly, transnational corporations (TNCs) put on a civilized, peacetime face. The loans function as payouts to corporations, to build things like dams in India, road systems through the Amazon rainforest, and pipelines in central Asia. International trade agreements facilitate capitalistic predation, placing corporate interests above even the constitutions of sovereign governments and creating special world courts in which cases are heard and decided.

The Public Lands Development Corporation (PLDC) illustrates a local version of this model of privatization. Act 55 of the 2011 Hawai'i State Legislative Session established the PLDC as a corporate entity intended to enter into partnerships with private companies to develop State-entrusted lands in Hawai'i. The problem is that the lands controlled by the State are Hawaiian Kingdom and Crown lands. Such lands could be used as collateral to enter into business agreements or to float loans related to proposed projects.

The PLDC was governed by a five-member board of directors, the majority of whom were appointed by the governor. Three state agencies were represented on the board either by their director or their designee: the Department of Business, Economic Development, and Tourism; the Department of Budget and Finance; and the Department of Land and Natural Resources. One member was appointed by the Speaker of the House of Representatives, and one member was appointed by the President of the Senate.

"Sounds great!" they said, unless of course the projects don't work out. Then the State would have to make good; in other words, the State (you and I) would be required to relinquish the collateral. Corporate banks would still receive real assets in exchange for nothing more than computer numbers. The general public would be left to clean up whatever was left behind, much like the Superferry's $40M barges, set to be auctioned in 2013, with starting bids as low as $250K—1/160th the original cost.[2] Guess who pays? Not the government officials who made those decisions. You pay. And that's how it works.

We saw this model surface in 2013 on Kaua'i, where the county water department (DOW) was proposing to drill a four-mile hole through Mount Wai'ale'ale and extract the water out of the heart of the island. This is the same water department that in 2012 agreed to settle a class action suit involving the pesticide Atrazine, which studies have associated with a number of health problems, including birth defects, cancer, and reproductive issues. Syngenta, a GMO company operating on Kaua'i who manufactures the pesticide, would pay less than $10,000 and be immune to related lawsuits for the next ten years.[3] While the DOW maintains no Atrazine has been found in the drinking water supply since 2005, a 2011 study by the USDA showed its presence in the water at Waimea Canyon Middle School.[4] Yet the DOW wants the public to float over $50M in public debt to support more development on an untested, experimental drilling technology and associated pipeline. And who profits again? Private corporations. Who gets access to the water? Once there's access, history says whoever lobbies the system better gets the access. And so it goes. This global model of public-assumed debt, with money paid to private, transnational corporations and access to resources opened for exploitation, is at work all over the world and in our islands, even here on Kaua'i.

LOCAL COMMUNITIZATION: THE OLDEST NEW STRUGGLE

What is most ironic is that we ourselves are the biggest hurdle standing in the way of what we say we want. But we can be agents of change. Real change involves commitment. You have to feel it, and it has to matter. Nothing changes if nothing changes. I'm not talking about thinking outside the box; we must widen our frame and realize that, actually, there is no box. We must unplug from globalized control systems, such as the money/debt model, and put our energies into building strength and resiliency in our own communities. This can be done personally and at the next level of community that one feels one can influence.

- Organize your community's voice and push that voice up to the higher levels of social decision-making, to government representatives and lawmakers

- Disallow corporate takeovers, government debt agreements, contract payouts, and the exploitation of your community's real assets—land, water, etc.

- Elevate *local* management, oversight, and use of those real assets for the betterment of your community

Let's look locally at (1) money/debt, (2) governance, and (3) real assets to see how communities can get a step up.

MONETARY COUP D'ETAT: FINANCIAL EXPENSES AND REINVESTMENTS

The value of a dollar is not up to you; it's up to the central banking system. To avert a monetary collapse, real or manufactured, we must unplug. As daunting as this might seem, it's possible! Start by looking at (1) your expenses, biggest to smallest and (2) how frequently you make transactions in the globalized monetary system.

List all of your expenses: mortgage, loans, car payments, credit cards, etc. How many transnational corporations are you supporting? Surprised? You have to switch to local options, otherwise you are shipping your money right out of your community. Eating local and organic is essential, but we have to get smarter and think deeper. Who owns the organic company? Did you know pesticide and GMO giant Monsanto has been buying up the organic seed providers market?[5] Go beyond the label and know what you are supporting with your purchases.

If you have a bank account, mortgage, or loan, move them to a community bank or credit union. They reinvest locally. In essence, this reinvestment enables you to build equity in your local economy. There is a movement to localize the financial sector, and a few notable thinkers and innovaters include Stacy Mitchell with the Institute for Local Self-Reliance and Michael H. Shuman of Cutting Edge Capital.[6] Other powerful tools include community currencies, or barter and "hour exchange" models. Ithaca Hours, BerkShares, and the Hour Exchange in Portland, Maine are good examples to look at.[7]

Consolidate all credit cards and only use one, primarily for emergencies. Interest payments are corporate giveaways. Don't support a system designed to exploit you. Keep your purchases local. Even items made from imported materials use local labor. If you are dependent upon imports for your basic needs like food and energy, eventually the price will go up and you will be stuck. Insulate yourself from volatile fluctuations by living a lifestyle that has built-in safeguards. For example, Kauaʻi has experienced many "black-outs" that we did not find out about until a day later. How? Our off-grid solar voltaic system meets our ongoing needs while supplying clean energy that is under our direct cost control. Invest in systems that have built-in redundancy; they can help to insulate you from global currency and market fluctuations.

As you localize, you will see a decline in your expenses. The less you need to make money to pay someone else, the better. This includes, well, everything! In our household, we have narrowed our food expenses to meat, bread, dairy, and alcohol, and we are finding ways to source these locally and sustainably. We trade greens with local hunters. We are experimenting with alternative grains and flours. We are looking at a dairy share for milk, cheese, and butter, and experimenting with home brews. With less expenses, we spend more time developing homesteading solutions and are sharing techniques among our friends and neighbors.

The solution is not just simple action alone; it's acting toward the end game of "think global, act local"—achievable, community-based choices to decrease the power of transnational corporations and increase community wealth.

COMMUNITY CONNECTION

Civic engagement is another important aspect of community wealth building. Often, communities only come together when a perceived emergency happens, such as when a developer wants to build a sub-division or resort. We must realize: if we don't have a plan, someone will make a plan for us.

If we only rise up in opposition, we'll never create the community we want; we will only be saying "no" to what we don't want. We must proactively direct our energy into our own plans for how we want our communities to grow. Then, if developers want to come in, they will have to consider our plans and explain how they will provide what the community has agreed is important. This is the aikido of proactive civic engagement. When the community has an organized voice, the systems can work for the community's benefit.

POLITICAL SAVOIR FAIRE

There has always been a need for representation that reflects community voices. In government, these voices are too often drowned out by corporate lobbyists, but government is dependent upon the people to function. Without your energy (taxes, obeying laws, elections, etc.), government just doesn't work.

What happens when our representatives are no longer representing our needs, but rather those of private corporations? There must be repercussions. If the senators behind the PLDC—Donovan Dela Cruz (Wahiawā) and Malama Solomon (Hāmākua/Waimea)—had career-ending campaigns mounted against them, other office-holders would definitely be on notice. Political karma is one of the most important areas to be developed in local community organizing.

BE THE SOLUTION

Why has it been so hard to bring people together for what we want, yet so easy to bring them together for what we don't want? If we can engage people in actions that are the solution, then people naturally tend to support the change. If conditions and relationships can be sustained collectively, they will begin to take root and grow. I am seeing more of this on Kaua'i.

As of mid-2013, Kaua'i County is moving to require more accountability from the corporations that do business here. Take Bill 2491, introduced by Council members Gary Hooser and Tim Bynum, and crafted in consultation with community stakeholders and organizations.[8] The main focus of this bill is to require the disclosure of restricted-use chemical pesticides and to create buffer zones around public facilities like schools, hospitals, and water ways. The largest pesticide and GMO companies in the world dump tons of poisons on Kaua'i every year with little to no oversight. This bill is a culmination of many tactics discussed in this essay. The use of local media and direct-action protests have raised awareness and engaged the public. Community groups and local government representatives have collaborated to draft policy solutions that bring our laws in line with our values. I am encouraged to see the level of activism happening here on Kaua'i and feel confident it will continue to evolve.

To recap: local communitization requires working together with your community, your friends, and family, to make a proactive plan. How do you want tomorrow to be? What do you want your home, neighborhood, and community to look like and represent? Don't be colonized. Remember that money is not your source of self-confidence. Make a personal commitment to invest your energy only into things that reflect your values. Listen deeply and follow your instincts. Your intuition is, and always will be, your best guide.

NOTES

1. Andrew Sorkin's book, *Too Big to Fail: The Inside Story of How Wall Street and Washington Fought to Save the Financial System—and Themselves* (London: Penguin, 2010) can be accessed for free at http://openlibrary.org/works/OL15300574W/Too_big_to_fail.

2. Duane Shimogawa, "Hawaii Superferry barges, docks to be sold at auction," *Pacific Business News,* July 8, 2013, at http://www.bizjournals.com/pacific/blog?2013/07/hawaii-superferry-barges-docks-to-be.html.

3. See the Board of Water Supply, County of Kaua'i, special board meeting minutes of August 28, 2012, at http://www.kauaiwater.org/AgendaAug12sm.pdf.

4. Chris D'Angelo, "Atrazine pollutant concerns draw DOW response," *The Garden Island,* March 13, 2013, at http://thegardenisland.com/news/local/atrazine-pollutant-concerns-draw-dow-response/article_671443f0-8ba9-11e2-96bb-0019bb2963f4.html.

5. Brenda Wagner, "Monsanto in Your Garden: Why You Need to Buy Organic Seeds," *Organic Consumers Association,* June 15, 2010, at http://www.organicconsumers.org/articles/article_21049.cfm. See also Matthew Dillon, "Organic Vegetable Farmers—WARNING—you may be engaging in contract agreements with Monsanto," *Organic Seed Alliance,* March 16, 2010, at http://blog.seedalliance.org/2010/03/16/organic-vegetable-farmers-warning-you-may-be-engaging-in-contract-agreements-with-monsanto.

6. You can learn more about the Institute for Local Self-Reliance at http://www.ilsr.org. You can read some of Michael H. Shuman's ideas on his *Huffington Post* blog, at http://www.huffingtonpost.com/michael-h-shuman, or at http://www.cuttingedgecapital.com. His most recent book is *Local Dollars, Local Sense: How to Move Your Money from Wall Street to Main Street and Achieve Real Prosperity* (White River Junction, VT: Chelsea Green, 2012).

7. For more information on Ithaca Hours, see http://www.ithacahours.org; on BerkShares, see http://www.berkshares.org; and on the Portland Hour Exchange, see http://www.hourexchangeportland.org.

8. For the full text of this bill, see http://www.stoppoisoningparadise.org/#!bill-2491/c1994.

RESOURCES FOR FURTHER INFORMATION AND INSPIRATION

1. Gene Sharp, *From Dictatorship to Democracy: A Conceptual Framework for Liberation*, 4th ed. (East Boston: Albert Einstein Institute, 2010).

2. Nana Veary, *Change We Must: My Spiritual Journey* (Honolulu: Institute of Zen Studies, 1990).

3. Rob Hopkins, *The Transition Handbook: From Oil Dependency to Local Resilience* (Totnes, Devon.: Green Books, 2008).

4. John Seymour, *The Self-Sufficient Life and How to Live It: The Complete Back to Basics Guide* (New York: DK, 2003).

5. Mālama Kaua'i website, at http://www.malamakauai.org.

MY JOURNEY AS AN ALLY
FOR SOCIAL JUSTICE

ERI OURA

In February of 2012, I traveled to Vieques and Puerto Rico for the eighth gathering of the International Women's Network Against Militarism. Paying attention to the landscape of Puerto Rico and the struggles those women shared really taught me to think about the connections between militarism, global capitalism, and land use. There were many military installations, and the cult of corporations—McDonalds, Walmart, K-Mart, Burger King, Taco Bell, PetCo, etc.—saturated many towns, and billboards were everywhere to be seen. Tens of thousands of personnel were brought in or hired locally to work the bases, stores, and restaurants. I saw that welcoming a US military base into your community is like welcoming a big city of people to be your neighbors. It means giving up land to house and support all of the personnel and their dependents, along with the necessary military infrastructure. In places where environmental and economic resources are limited, this can be a tremendous burden.

According to a 2007 study, there are over 1,000 US military bases and installations across the globe, occupying over three million acres of land.[1] They are scattered across North and South America, Europe, Australia, Southeast and East Asia, and many islands in the Pacific. Each year, billions of our US tax dollars get funneled into military and civilian government issued (G.I.) jobs for the Department of Defense, for the development and maintenance of these US bases and installations. In Hawai'i, the US military controls over 236,000 acres of land in the state, and has had a presence in the islands for over 200 years, since the arrival of the first warship in Hawaiian waters in 1814, and permanent rotations of warships since 1867.[2] As the decades have passed, each generation in Hawai'i has normalized both the presence of the military and the ideals of "militarism."

"Militarism" is a broader way to think about how military ideals, the glorification of military might and violence, and the assumption that we need a military to have a strong and secure nation, seep into all other parts of our society and lives. How does the military affect our lands, our resources, our families, our jobs, our future possibilities? How are we impacted differently and disproportionately by the military, depending on our gender, race, and class? What kinds of communities rely on the military for careers and education, and what costs are these communities paying for the dream of a better life? How is the global military presence connected to global capitalism, and how does this web affect sustainable local economies?

Through my life experiences, education, and work with a variety of activist groups, I have become an advocate for demilitarization. The damage the military has done to all of us over generations far outweighs the benefits. The exploitation and commodification of local and Native communities around the world. The environmental damage and resource drain. The gender violence. Demilitarization means saying "no" to militaristic ways of thinking and economic investments in militarism that take away our abilities to determine our own paths in life. I grew up in a militarized setting, and I have also spent time with people whose lifestyles have as little to do with this system as possible—out in Waiāhole on the windward side of Oʻahu, and in the rural areas of Lānaʻi and Molokaʻi. They grow their own food, build their own shelters, consume as few imported resources as possible, and focus on raising their families to be caretakers of the land. They do these things because they understand that knowledge is an intergenerational asset and that if they don't take the time to teach their values to the next generation, this lifestyle could be lost forever. Being an advocate for demilitarization has allowed me to form really strong relationships with folks who not only envision sustainable futures, but also have worked to create the conditions for that sort of existence. My friends and allies in this movement for social change in Hawaiʻi are farmers, fishers, folks who have gardens in which they grow food! As an ally, I have made it a point to take time to lend a hand in helping out in whatever ways that I can.

WHAT DOES IT MEAN TO BE AN ALLY?

The first time I learned the word "ally," it was in one of my high school history classes during our lessons on the two world wars. "Alliances" were made between nations at war, who sacrificed human lives to prove whose might was greater. When I started doing community work, I re-learned the idea of being an ally as being lovingly connected with other individuals and groups, and I moved away from the earlier, military-centered definition. When I use the term ally, it means being spiritually, politically, socially, and economically supportive of another person or group of people because we understand each other's struggles. Being an ally means doing actions in solidarity with each other to address issues within our communities. It means to be there for each other in small, simple, loving ways—having strong relationships, being homies, being good friends, being part of a family.

There are many different ways to be an ally. One way I am an ally to others in my local and global communities is through story sharing. Over the years, I've learned that story sharing is one of the most important and powerful ways to be in solidarity with other people because it helps us to understand where we each come from and gives us the opportunity to imagine alternative futures together. When you share stories, you give the stories life so that they are not forgotten, and you lend the strength of your stories to those you are sharing them with.

FACING GUILT

Kalama Valley is a lush valley on the southeast side of Oʻahu, and was once rich with agriculture and piggeries. The residents were primarily working-class landless[3] people whose community was described as "Hawaiian" or "local."[4] In the early 1970s, Kalama Valley was the site of major protests after the Bishop Estate served eviction notices to the pig farmers in the area in order to build a suburban neighborhood. Activist-scholars like Haunani-Kay Trask and George Kanahele considered the Kalama Valley protests the birth of the modern Hawaiian movement, also known as the Hawaiian Renaissance. Trask and Kanahele wrote about how people banded together to support the pig farmers and others who were being displaced for the sake of developing Hawaiʻi. The protesters were non-violent, but several of them were still arrested. In the end, the farmers were forced to move, and the housing subdivision was built.[5]

I grew up in a suburban neighborhood in Kalama Valley, on a quarter-acre lot with a four-bedroom house, swimming pool, yard, and a two-car garage. Though I went to the local elementary and high schools, it wasn't until much later that I learned about the history of the place I grew up in, including the contested development of that suburban housing I lived in. "This land used to be pig farms," my dad used to tell me: "I stood in line for three days to buy this property."

My dad never shared any details with me about the evictions of the pig farmers. I think it's because he didn't share their perspectives. Instead, he believed in the American Dream. My dad was born in 1936 and grew up in Lāhainā on the island of Maui during the years of martial law, 1941 to 1944. In his youth, descendents of immigrants, like him, were heavily encouraged to assimilate to US culture. Otherwise, he might have faced prison time or deportation back to the land of his ancestors, Japan, which he had never stepped foot on before. When my dad graduated from high school, he enlisted in the US Army. His G.I. benefits helped him graduate from college and later become a civilian employee of the Department of Defense as an accountant. According to the script he was given, following the rules, assimilating to US culture, and working for the government allowed him to have money, middle-class resources, a family, and a house in Kalama Valley.

During my junior year at the University of Hawai'i, when I first learned about the evictions and history of injustice in Kalama Valley, I felt ashamed to be someone whose family settled in that contested area. I did not know how people would react to the fact that I spent most of my life in Kalama Valley, post-evictions. The fact that my family was a part of a process that displaced people was such a daunting thing. I was not sure how the people I wanted to learn from would receive me if they knew this about my family and me.

Even though I felt shame and guilt, I still decided to share this story with people whom I looked up to as mentors—people who were part of these protests I learned about. They were unexpectedly kind and told me that it took courage to take ownership of that part of my family history. "You were just a baby," one of my mentors, Aunty Terri Keko'olani, told me. "You can't control where your parents settled."

Aunty Terri's words really helped me to overcome my feelings of guilt and shame, which had been a barrier to my participation in the movement for justice. Living and growing up in a middle-class setting in Hawai'i had not pushed me to be conscious of the struggles of different folks in my community, but once I heard these other narratives of struggle, I could not pretend that they did not exist. I also could not sit idly by, knowing that people continue to be displaced without proper reparations, all for the benefit of people who would not even know or care about the stories of those who lived there before them. This part of my personal history is the root of my passion for social justice and my desire to be an ally to everyone who has experienced injustice in their lives.

INTERCONNECTED CURRENTS OF MILITARISM

When I was in college, I learned how to contextualize my life within the broader narratives of war and military presence through reading narratives shared by progressive scholars.[6] These stories helped me make connections between my family's story and the larger context of militarization by the US empire. Thinking about my own family history within that larger context opened my eyes to thinking about how the US military impacts men and women across the world in ways that are often violent and damaging. Understanding these connections also helped me to become a better ally to other people because my own narrative of struggle was something that other people could relate to and empathize with.

As a child, I spent three of my formative years in the city of Seoul in the southern part of the Korean peninsula, in an area called Namsan. This move was made possible by my dad's job with the US Department of Defense. He moved us there in 1988 to be closer to our step-mom's family. See, my birth-mom passed away from cancer in 1987, and my dad then married the niece of his Korean coworker. My step-mom had a curable form of hepatitis and needed medical treatment, and my dad had two young motherless children and access to the resources my step-mom needed. I suspect that the marriage was arranged because my parents never talked about how they met or the idea of falling in love. Instead, they made a deal: she would get the medical attention her condition required if she married my dad and helped with raising his children.

The choice that my step-mom made was not an uncommon one. I could understand her story with more compassion once I could place it within a larger context of global US militarism. Stories of "war brides" run throughout histories of war and militarism. War brides are women who marry men with the intention of gaining material resources and better living conditions, because they struggle to live due to war or occupation where they come from. Sometimes the marriages work out and they learn to be with each other. Other times, the brides escape their marriages because of the lack of autonomy or control over their own lives and bodies. For my step-mom, the codependent nature of her relationship with my father was overwhelming. She left when I was sixteen; she wanted to fall in love. Once I realized that she left to seek happiness, I learned to admire that about her.

Thinking about my own family also teaches me to appreciate the complex effects of militarism in all facets of our lives, even love. It's hard to say who is an "enemy." My dad was not a bad guy. He comes from a generation that was brought up to want the American Dream, which structured family relations in patriarchal ways. The head of the household, the breadwinner, the decision-maker in a heterosexual nuclear family was always the husband/father. You could imagine the frustration my dad felt when he couldn't control the stubborn Korean woman he married and *his* two children whom she raised. He worked for the US Department of Defense, which the military falls under, for over thirty years. The rigid hierarchies set up by global capitalism and militarism were all he knew. My dad saw his relationships in terms of competitive hierarchies, and he needed to be the one on top. He retired as an accountant. His work had maintained and contributed to global capitalism, as well as supported his family, while all other politics fell to the wayside.

INTERCONNECTED CURRENTS OF RESISTANCE

The existence of military bases planted all over the world has created a global movement of resistance against the US military and US imperialism. My life and my work are situated in these interconnected currents of resistance. Choosing this path was one of the easiest choices I had ever made because this path is all about sharing aloha with each other. Sharing aloha doesn't mean always being pleasant and undisruptive. No, in fact, it is quite the opposite. It means being an ally and taking action to address oppressive behavior, with the intention of keeping things pono (right/balanced). This is important because resisting violence and oppression helps us to heal ourselves and to make life better for future generations.

The International Women's Network Against Militarism (IWNAM) is a space for women working to end different forms of violence in our home communities, and to take action as an international network to address the injustices our communities are experiencing. Violence against women is a major problem in the military itself and in communities that are in states of war or military occupation. According to the military's Sex Assault Prevention and Response Office, one-third of women in uniform experience some sort of sexualized violence, whether it is harassment or rape or something else, which goes unprosecuted or even unreported the majority of the time.[7] In countries such as Okinawa, South Korea, and the Philippines, or war zones like Iraq and Afghanistan, there is a shameful history of US military personnel raping civilian women and escaping sentencing or prosecution.

As of 2013, IWNAM is represented by women from Okinawa, Japan, Korea, Guåhan, the Philippines, Marshall Islands, Hawai'i, the US, Vieques, and Puerto Rico. At our eighth gathering, convened in Puerto Rico and Vieques in 2012, we traveled around the two islands and shared our stories. Community allies were brought in to translate for those who needed translation. Sexual assault, AmerAsian babies, murder, prolonged imprisonment, weapons testing that rapes and poisons the land—these were some of the concerns we addressed in the statement we created together. It was a beautiful meeting. We discussed the tragedies so that we could envision futures that are genuinely secure. We boldly choose to imagine "genuine security," as opposed to "national security," which is frequently overused by the military, other government officials, and the media to justify waging war and continued occupation of lands and lifestyles.

There are four principles that IWNAM members feel are necessary for genuine security to be realized:

- The physical environment must be able to sustain human and natural life

- People's basic needs for food, clothing, shelter, health care, and education must be guaranteed

- People's fundamental human dignity should be honored and cultural identities respected

- People and the natural environment should be protected from avoidable harm[8]

How these principles become reality will look different in every community and for each individual, but getting there will be a collective effort. Examples of how we are currently working toward genuine security in Hawai'i can be found in the intergenerational actions and event organizing to raise awareness about militarism. For example, Hawai'i Peace and Justice, the organization that I work for, has initiated various petition drives to address military recruitment in our local high schools and to prevent the Osprey helicopters from being stationed at Kāne'ohe. We also organize DeTours, in which we take groups of visitors and locals around to different contested sites on the island, like 'Iolani Palace, Ke Awalau o Pu'uloa (aka Pearl Harbor), and Mākua Valley, to share stories of the land and our alternative, demilitarized visions for these places.

VISIONS FOR THE FUTURE

Militarism affects all our personal lives in complex ways. It impacts how we relate to each other and our environment. The current coupling of militarism with capitalism is a dangerous combination; there is no dignity in being commoditized and stripped of our values to fit an economic system that does not see the integrity of our way of being. We have become less able to relate to each other because we no longer see each other as humans. Conversations with our families about critiques of militarism become contentious because so many of us are connected to and enmeshed in these institutions and hierarchies that militarism promotes and perpetuates. That is why it is important for us to envision futures without militarism!

Envisioning futures without militarism will require an intergenerational conversation across communities and struggles. It will require alliances and relationships based on care and genuine security, not on fear and national security. We must also share stories so that we can understand and gain strength from each other's struggles. There are big, future-altering events that are coming up, like the renewal of land leases for the military bases in Hawai'i, which could lead to significantly reducing the military presence in our islands. What kind of future could we see for Hawai'i if our communities decided not to renew those leases? For example—Pōhakuloa consists of nearly 109,000 acres of land being used for live-fire training on Hawai'i Island. What could we do with that land if it was returned to the people of Hawai'i? What other possibilities would be open to our young people if our high schools did not allow military recruiters on campus, or if joining the military wasn't the only way for some of them to get a job and an education? Could we live in a rape-free society? What does genuine security look like in Hawai'i? Perhaps we can envision a demilitarized future together, as allies.

NOTES

1. Nick Turse, "The Pentagon's Planet of Bases," *TomDispatch.com,* January 9, 2011, at http://www.tomdispatch.com/blog/175338/tomgram%3A_nick_turse%2C_the_pentagon's_planet_of_bases.

2. Kathy E. Ferguson and Phyllis Turnbull, "The Military," *The Value of Hawai'i: Knowing the Past, Shaping the Future*, ed. Craig Howes and Jon Osorio (Honolulu: U of Hawai'i P, 2010): 47–52.

3. I use the term "landless" here to mean having no ownership of land within the conventional US understandings of land ownership.

4. Haunani-Kay Trask, "The Birth of the Modern Hawaiian Movement: Kalama Valley, O'ahu," *Hawaiian Journal of History* 21 (1987): 126–53.

5. George Kanahele, "The Hawaiian Renaissance," *Polynesian Voyaging Society Archives*, Kamehameha Schools Archives, 1979, at http://kapalama.ksbe.edu/archives/pvsa/primary%202/79%20kanahele/kanahele.htm.

6. As an undergrad and graduate student, I read work by Cynthia Enloe, a scholar of militarism and globalization, that helped me to understand the larger global context and impact of US militarization. I also learned a lot from reading Nora Okja Keller's novel *Fox Girl* about two Korean teenagers who worked as prostitutes for an American soldier.

7. For more information, see the United States Department of Defense Sexual Assault Prevention and Response (SAPRO) website, at http://www.sapr.mil.

8. "What is Genuine Security?" *Women for Genuine Security*, at http://www.genuinesecurity.org.

RESOURCES FOR FURTHER INFORMATION AND INSPIRATION

1. Demilitarize Hawai'i (DMZ) website, at http://www.dmzhawaii.org.

2. Women's Voices, Women Speak blog, at http://wvws808.blogspot.com.

3. Ellen-Rae Cachola, *Mapping Histories: Militarization of the Asia-Pacific and US*, 2008, on the ellenraec YouTube channel, at http://www.youtube.com/watch?v=3RBQsOWFFUs.

4. Kamakako'i, "Pohakuloa: Now that you know, do you care?." 2013, at http://kamakakoi.com.

5. "Na Wahine Koa II: The Impact of Militarism on Hawai'i" can be viewed on the wvws808 YouTube channel, at http://www.youtube.com/watch?v=HaIvb57kHfw.

CULTIVATING FORESIGHT AND EMPOWERMENT

AUBREY MORGAN YEE

The best way to predict the future is to invent it.

—*Alan Kay*[1]

Here we sit, at the outset of the twenty-first century, wirelessly connected to the world and increasingly disconnected from our communities. We have more stuff than ever before, but our generation is faced with overall worse health and fewer economic prospects than our parents and grandparents. We import over 90 percent of the food we eat in the islands, and we are losing our remaining open and productive agricultural space to continued development and housing. Hawai'i is a place of intense natural beauty and yet Honolulu recently ranked fourth among US cities for the number of high rises crowding our skyline. In rushing to keep pace with the present, we are rarely left with time to creatively imagine and envision our future. What I would like to offer is a thought, a challenge, and a question: what would Hawai'i look like, feel like, sound like, and smell like in fifty or one hundred years from now if *you* could paint the picture? If that sounds like a daunting or even idealistic endeavor, consider this: if you are not part of actively creating, envisioning, and planning for the futures, you, your children, and their children will be destined to live someone else's vision.

I believe that the process of cultivating foresight is a radical way of cultivating empowerment. If there is to be a shift, a systemic change, a turning, a breakthrough, I believe it will come on the wings of empowered people who have nurtured and shared the tools of foresight.

One of the biggest misconceptions about futurists is that we predict the future. No one can predict the future. As my mentor Jim Dator, one of the founding fathers of the modern-day academic discipline we call Futures Studies, always reminds me, "The future does not exist." That is because there is not just one future, there are an infinite number of *futures*, all of which are *equally possible* though some may *seem* more plausible for one reason or another. This line is often followed by his second "law" of the futures, "Any useful idea about the futures should appear to be ridiculous," to which it is critical to add: but not every ridiculous idea will be useful. Foresight is not meant to be fantasy.

If we can agree that *the future* doesn't exist, shouldn't we be wary of those who claim to predict it? Predictions, by their nature, *disempower.* They ask us to sit back, safe in the "knowledge" of what the "experts" tell us is going to happen. Predictions lay out a path that we feel compelled to follow, and they often become self-fulfilling prophecies. In contrast, foresight allows us to scan the horizon for possibilities and to be prepared for a variety of potentials. Foresight *empowers.* A healthy practice of foresight enables each and every one of us to become experts because we all have powerful experiences to share; we are rich with wisdom and insight that is completely unique to our lives. That is a priceless reservoir of knowledge that must be shared. It is our kuleana to do so.

The problem is no one is teaching us how to cultivate foresight. We are taught the power of history, but we are not taught the power of productively and creatively envisioning alternative or preferred futures. Instead, when challenged to envision the world as we wish to see it, we often become entangled in utopian visions of perfection or dismayed and stuck in dystopian visions of what we fear.

Idealistic in my youth, I have always believed that clarity of intention, mixed with focus and hard work, are keys to building the life you want to live. I found myself at the center of the Futures Studies program at the University of Hawaiʻi at Mānoa after a long journey through conflicting internal narratives derived from, on the one hand, my desire to change significantly the world, and on the other, my complicity in the state of things as they are. We often get mired in this holding pattern between aspiration and survival, and as the forces of capitalism, consumption, and disconnection from the natural world grow stronger, the mire often seems to deepen.

Futures Studies is a field with tested methodologies that help people, communities, companies, governments, non-profits, and others creatively and productively imagine, plan for, and begin *crafting* alternative and preferred futures. Futures thinking can help organizations to uncover and prepare for blind spots that may seem unlikely but could be catastrophic. It can also help people collectively create a vision for a preferred future, and craft realistic steps toward achieving goals that may have once seemed too audacious. The most amazing part of facilitating groups through futures-thinking exercises is how closely aligned our preferred futures usually are. We all basically want the same things: peaceful interactions, a sense of physical and economic sufficiency and safety, to be surrounded by community, to have contact with the natural world, and to participate in meaningful and fulfilling work.

We all feel the pace of technological, social, and environmental change accelerating. There are powerfully entrenched and overwhelming forces at work, leading our islands down a pathway of increasing inequality, environmental degradation, political apathy, and economic instability. While it seems that some form of systemic breakdown is inevitable, I find in this possibility the hope of renewal. Where one thing breaks, there is a vacuum, a space for potentiality, and if we are ready, we will be able to fill it. Significant change is often preceded by significant disruption.

The growing consensus is that we have entered what is being called the Anthropocene era. First popularized in 2000 by the Nobel-prize winning atmospheric chemist Paul Crutzen, the Anthropocene era is a new geological epoch characterized by the understanding that human influence on the planet is now ubiquitous, from the macro- to the micro-level. We are affecting everything from the climate, to biodiversity, the earth and ocean chemistry, and the microbiotic realm, in ways that we do not yet fully understand. And truthfully, we may never fully understand the full effects of our influence. This new reality heralds great new challenges. As Jim Dator aptly describes it, in the face of these great challenges posed by the Anthropocene era, we must be ready to "surf the tsunamis of change" that inevitably lie ahead. Which means that despite the potentially awe-ful and destructive power of these portending changes, we must do our best to surf these waves with all the foresight and grace we can muster. And who is better at surfing than Hawaiians?

FUTURES IN PLACE

At any rate, a good forecast is not one that comes true, but one that stirs people to action.

—Michel Godet[2]

My work in futures studies has always been with an eye towards the future of these islands in particular. We live on the most isolated islands in the world. We are unable to feed ourselves in the case of natural or manmade disaster. Many of us are disconnected from our communities; we barely know our neighbors. The strain of economic survival creates emotional and physical stress in our families. Large and powerful corporations are trying to control land, water, and food in Hawai'i at a time when we should be striving for local sustainability and resilience. Our physical isolation and our dependence on the outside world for basics like food signal a perilous situation where we are no longer, by any measure, self-sufficient. This present reality has been crafted over time by a series of decisions and visions that have privileged certain values, namely economic growth, at almost any cost.

To envision a different future, we must more clearly understand our past and the choices that created our present reality. This process requires an honest reflection on both our indigenous and colonial heritages in Hawai'i. These unique histories have shaped our present in distinct ways.

Like many of the people I know here in Hawai'i, I am a settler, an immigrant, the first generation of my family to be born in the islands. My father came here with the Marine Corps in the mid-1960s, and my mother followed soon after. They married and decided to stay. I was raised in Niu Valley on lands originally under lease, which my family was able to purchase in the 1980s. These changes in land tenure are what Candace Fujikane describes when she writes:

> a "Maryland-type" law was used in the 1980s to target the landholdings of Bishop Estate, a perpetual charitable trust for Native Hawaiians. Such measures sought to take this patrimony from Hawaiians by forcing them to sell trust lands that they were leasing to middle- and upper-class Asians and whites in east and windward O'ahu.[3]

I attended Punahou School, which was founded by many of those complicit in the colonization of the islands and the overthrow of the Hawaiian kingdom: Dillingham, Dole, Bishop. These were the names of the buildings where I studied and learned about the world. Many of my close friends carry these family names in their genealogies. All of these associations and entanglements make it more difficult for me to imagine Hawaiian sovereignty, as much as I believe it is possible.

I now sit on the board of Kanu Hawai'i, a grassroots non-profit founded by people who care about Hawai'i's future and who believe that we need to redefine what we mean by the "good life." Kanu was founded by passionate people who understand the power of foresight. There have been many great visions for the future set forth for Hawai'i, but what has been lacking is a keeper of the flame. Kanu seeks to fill that critical role for the long haul. Over a series of weekends in 2005, and under the guidance of futurist Kaipo Lum, the forty founders of Kanu laid out their vision for a future Hawai'i. Understanding that foresight is an ongoing process, not a one-time event, we continue to revisit this work every five years, remembering our core values and our history, evaluating our failures and successes, digesting the current state and potential futures of Hawai'i, and discussing and reimagining the organization's vision.

I joined Kanu because I can see that the political, social, environmental and economic systems we rely upon for surviving and thriving in Hawai'i are all in some state of disrepair. And the best way to change a broken system is to build a better one that makes the old way simply obsolete.

Around the same time that I joined the board of Kanu, I also began to study Indigenous Politics at UH Mānoa. That education has helped me to understand more clearly the legacy that I have inherited as a non-native settler in Hawai'i. I have been given better frameworks to recognize the injustices of the past, and all of this knowledge has strengthened my belief in the need for a shift away from current systems that are destroying the planet. I have more clarity than ever about the violence of the colonial heritage I have inherited. I can see the tendrils of history that delineate this struggle between privilege and suffering and that have led to the deep structural inequalities that persist today. I have come to comprehend the meanings of Patrick Wolfe's famous statement, "Invasion is a structure, not an event."[4]

And yet, after all of this intellectual endeavor, I am left uncomfortable because I also understand my own complicity, however innocent or circumstantial it may be. My complicity is that my life, my home, my education, my opportunities for earning a living, are all made possible as a result of settler colonialism. My comfort and ease is built on the past and present of others' displacement. I am also uncomfortable because I understand that in the daily task of survival, we cannot always be heroes. The systems within which we are entangled demand that we become numb to our quiet and persistent aspirational visions of a different future.

I struggle with my place as a settler in this tapestry. While Hawai'i is not my genealogical home, it is the only home I have. I believe that any substantive change will come from a deep understanding of Hawaiian values, or what we at Kanu call "island values." I think that many of us here in the islands share a similar anxiety, knowing that we are not genealogically tied to Hawai'i and yet we care deeply about the 'āina and the futures. The complications of our real lives and complicit entanglements keep us from imagining radical change despite the fact that we desire it, and despite the fact that we can look to history and see how often radical change occurs.

Radical change is almost always difficult to imagine. But throughout world history, we have seen radical political change happen again and again. The Berlin wall eventually crumbled; Myanmar is now a struggling democracy; East Timor gained independence from the Indonesian state. Something like Hawaiian sovereignty may seem ridiculous to some, but the futurists' role is to imagine the potentiality of seemingly ridiculous ideas. In order to shape meaningful futures, we must give these sorts of ideas their due share of discussion, and resist foreclosing radical openings in favor of seemingly more plausible avenues.

In the Spring of 2013, I listened to 'Umi Perkins defend his PhD dissertation in Indigenous Politics at UH Mānoa. He talked about the symbolic and literal erasure of claims to kuleana lands—those lands granted to Native Hawaiian makaʻāinana (commoners) during the Māhele land divisions of the late nineteenth century. Corporations established plantations on the very lands that were granted to makaʻāinana, and when family members returned to their ancestral lands, they found seas of sugar or pineapple with no fences, borders, or any physical way to distinguish where their small parcel might lie. Over time, this practice led to the erasure of land holdings from familial memory, and many kuleana lands succumbed to corporate ownership. Perkins then asked us, his audience, to imagine a radical possibility. Today, when the massive multinational Dole corporation is selling thousands of acres of former plantation land on the North Shore of Oʻahu, might it be possible to find the kuleana boundaries and require compensation to the existing relatives of those whose lands were taken by the plantations long ago? Could these sorts of radical ideas be actually not so radical at all? "Common sense" in a globalized, profit-driven world would call such ideas ridiculous. But perhaps delayed restorative justice—repairing the violences of our colonial past—is exactly what we need to build a more equitable future—a future grounded in values that honor ancestry, humanity, place, and the natural world over corporate profit.

Yet, trying to imagine radical change also leaves me disconcerted. I imagine the small blocks of land divided up for single-family residences all around me wiped clean of the homes that sit on them today. I imagine what this land may have been long before any of the current settlers were here. I imagine what it could become again one day. This is my crisis.

Realizing that I am a foreigner in the only land that has ever felt like home, I feel called to embrace a hybrid genealogy—one that will enable renewal, regeneration, and a radical rethinking of our place on the planet, our place as humans in Hawaiʻi. This hybridity requires an acceptance of what is, an understanding of what was, and a collective imagining of what can be for "us." Old grievances have no place in a productive future, but neither does an erasure of the past. Somewhere in the middle lies reconciliation and a way forward.

I believe that empowerment lies within foresight. It is critical to teach our youth that their stories, no matter how fraught with turmoil, pain, suffering, or privilege, are valuable parts of the tapestry. We need to learn how to live together and be better as a whole. Our need for renewable energy, our need for local food systems, our need for connected communities, open governance, grassroots social services, environmental renewal, balanced economies, and social justice—all of these challenges require that no one person or group works in isolation. We must do it together.

TRAVELERS ADRIFT ON AN ISLAND IN THE SEA

First we ask what needs to be done, then we do it, then we ask if it's possible.

—Paul Hawken[5]

This to me is the value of Hawai'i: the limited space of our land surrounded by the energy of the ocean forces us to bump into one another over and over again until it is impossible not to see the connections. We cannot hide in anonymity because everyone really is just two degrees removed. I see this as a true blessing because it forces us to take responsibility for our part in the greater picture. When we can clearly see how our decisions and actions affect others, we are more likely to consider those impacts. Our islands' physical isolation and resource fragility is both a challenge and opportunity.

To begin the process of imagining a better way, educate yourself on the good works being done by those in your community. Commit to getting involved and giving back in some way that makes sense for you. Commit to learning the real history of these islands so that you can better understand your place. Understanding how we have gotten to where we are will help us understand how decisions today may impact the future. Remember that ridiculous ideas can be useful. If you had told someone fifty years ago that they could video call a loved one halfway around the world on a small hand-held wireless telephone, they would have thought you were dreaming up science fiction. But there were those then who believed it was possible, and now it is so.

What vision do you have for the future of Hawai'i, and how can you plant the first seed of that grand vision today? Futures-thinking only requires that you truly open your mind and begin to think about how any one thing affects many others, how systems are interrelated. Start noticing the patterns around you: what words, phrases, happenings, ideas are you noticing popping up in multiple, diverse places? Those signals may be important, emerging trends; pay attention to them. You can find resources and exercises to engage in futures-thinking at the Hawaii Research Center for Futures Studies website, and don't hesitate to contact us, we're here to help you, it's what we love to do.[6] Following this essay is an example of a futures-crafting exercise for you to try.

Audacious as it may sound, the futures will be composed of a conglomeration of ideas, thoughts, and aspirations held by various people who understand their capacity to create change. Your thoughts, aspirations, dreams, and visions are part of that building wave. Every action matters and influences others, in ways that ripple out and in ways you may never know. Each one of us is part of a family, community, workplace, school, government. Bringing the tools of foresight and creating conscientious conversations around preferred futures to our everyday lives will have ripple effects on everything that we do here in Hawai'i. It is our kuleana and our blessed gift to participate actively in that process of envisioning and enacting the futures.

NOTES

1. Comment made at a PARC (Palo Alto Research Center) Meeting in 1971.
2. Michel Godet is an economist and professor at Conservatoire National des Arts et Metiers.
3. Candace F. Fujikane, "Introduction: Asian Settler Colonialism in the U.S. Colony of Hawai'i," *Asian Settler Colonialism: From Local Governance to the Habits of Everyday Life in Hawai'i,* ed. Candace F. Fujikane and Jonathan Y. Okamura (Honolulu: U of Hawai'i P, 2008): 28.
4. Patrick Wolfe, *Settler Colonialism and the Transformation of Anthropology: The Politics and Poetics of an Ethnographic Event* (London: Cassell, 1999): 2.
5. As quoted by Lester Brown in *Plan B 4.0: Mobilizing to Save Civilization* (Washington, D.C.: Earth Policy Institute, 2009).
6. You can contact the Hawaii Research Center for Futures Studies at www.futures.hawaii. edu.

RESOURCES FOR FURTHER INFORMATION AND INSPIRATION

1. Jose Ramos, "Why Future Studies: An Interview with Jim Dator," *Action Foresight* July 16, 2012, at http://actionforesight.net/media/2012/07/16/why-futures-studies-an-interview-with-jim-dator.
2. The Hawaii Research Center for Futures Studies website, at http://www.futures.hawaii.edu. For a list of publications and readings about futures studies, see http://www.futures.hawaii.edu/publications.html.
3. TEDx Noosa talk by Sohail Inayatullah on "Causal Layered Analysis" (a foundational futures method), on YouTube, at http://www.youtube.com/watch?v=LGOnJDek5To.
4. The Institute for the Future in San Francisco, at http://www.iftf.org.
5. The *Journal of Futures Studies,* at http://www.jfs.tku.edu.tw.

The Three Circles Exercises

These Three Circles Exercises were created by fellow futurist John Sweeney and graphically designed by colleague Aaron Rosa. Directions: choose an issue or topic you want to think about (food, water, governance, the future of your organization/school, etc.). In the first exercise, place yourself in the shoes of your grandparents, you today, and your grandchildren, and think about the greatest challenges and opportunities for each generation in relation to your issue. For the second exercise, take that perspective of your grandchildren and imagine a preferred future for them in relation to your issue. The preferred future is an ideal world but it is not perfect or fantastical. Imagine this preferred future in terms of values (ethics, ideals, etc.), structures (physical structures, economic systems, political systems, etc.), and behaviors (daily practices, relationships, etc.) that would be part of their reality. For example, if you were concerned with increasing food security in Hawai'i, you might imagine that community would be strong (value), local markets would be ubiquitous (structure), and people would regularly participate in growing at least some of their own food (behavior). Good luck and have fun!

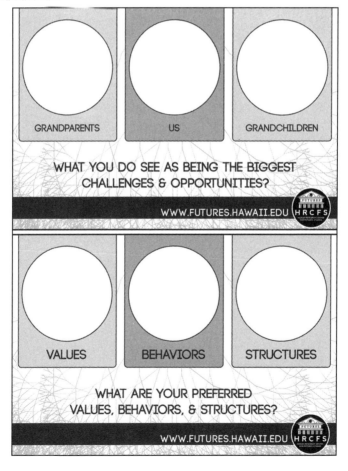

PU'UHONUA: CREATING SAFE AND SACRED SPACES

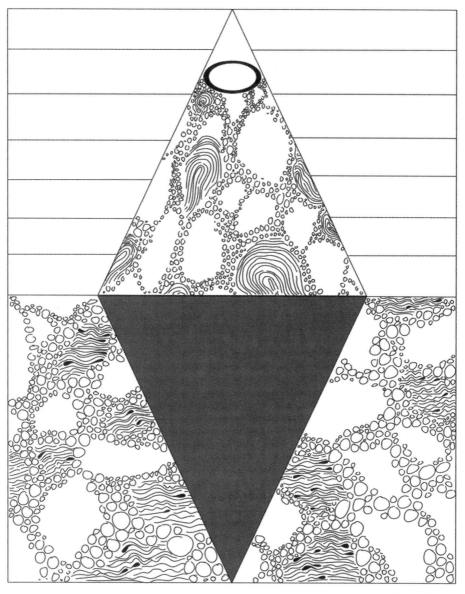

HALEY KAILIEHU

TRANS**FARM**ATION

CHERYSE JULITTA KAUIKEOLANI SANA

I ʻāina nō ka ʻāina i ke aliʻi, a i waiwai nō ka ʻāina i ke kānaka.
[The land remains the land because of the chiefs, and prosperity comes to the land because of the common people.[1]]

THE EXPERIENCE

I have always loved ʻāina. Her beauty, strength, and energy raised me to be the person I am today. Early morning pinks, oranges, and yellows peeking over the Waiʻanae range reassure me that my kūpuna also experienced the same beauty. The Kaiāulu wind brushes against my body to imprint the magnitude and function of the mountains before me. The soft smell of early morning dew on fresh vegetables wakes me for the soon-to-be-intense workday of harvesting. Organically grown produce gives me energy, nutrients for my body, and a love for life itself.

FINDING FARMING AND FOOD SOVEREIGNTY

Growing up, I wanted to mālama ʻāina and make sure that she was cared for, but never did I think that one day I'd be growing food with her. Once I began farming, I realized soon that growing food and loving the ʻāina also meant loving myself so that I could be in service to my family and community. As I have learned from Bentham Ohia, CEO of Te Wānanga o Aotearoa: "We are only here for two reasons: To love and to serve."[2]

I was a student in the Hawaiian Studies program, which was part of the Natural Resources Academy, one of four academies at Waiʻanae High School. The other academies are Business and Industrial Education, Health and Human Services, and Searider Productions (Arts and Communications). These academies were created to contextualize education so that students can relate and learn subjects in their field of interest and be given specific options to start their career paths. In the Natural Resources Academy, there are four programs: Hawaiian Studies, Agriculture Science, Marine Science, and Food Science and Nutrition.

Within the Hawaiian Studies program, I was in the archaeology tract. We would go up to Kaʻala Farms in Waiʻanae valley to excavate ancient loʻi systems. In the early '70s, the founders of Kaʻala Farms began the process of clearing and returning water back to these loʻi kalo. Their water had been diverted to feed a local sugar plantation. Over the course of its thirty years in existence, Kaʻala Farms has served as an education center, immersing participants in the ancestral sciences and spirituality surrounding communal food production. To assist with this aim, Kaʻala Farms continues to maintain a relationship with Waiʻanae High School's Hawaiian Studies program.

I was always interested in my Hawaiian culture and how my ancestors thrived a thousand years in the Pacific ocean. Questions would often come to mind: How did they grow so much food? What did the ʻāina look like at its full potential? Why aren't we using these loʻi today? Where are our traditional foods like kalo and ʻuala today?

So my interest in food and the connection to ʻāina came at a young age. But it wasn't until I got accepted into the MAʻO Organic Farms Youth Leadership Training (YLT) program that I was exposed to the idea of food sovereignty in Hawaiʻi.

MALA ʻAI ʻŌPIO

MAʻO is an acronym for Mala ʻAi ʻŌpio, which translates to Food Youth Garden. The YLT is a college program that offers an internship so that young adults from the Waiʻanae community have an opportunity to work on an organic farm, gaining entrepreneurial, agricultural, and educational experiences. This internship provides a full-time tuition scholarship to Leeward Community College for two years and a monthly monetary stipend starting at $500. While attending LCC, the interns are also required to take four classes to receive a certificate in Community Food Security.

At MAʻO I met Kukui and Gary Maunakea-Forth, who became my mentors and teachers for growing fruits and vegetables. At first I thought that I was just going to be a part of this internship to get me through LCC, but it soon became more than that. I learned more about our food system and how corrupt it has become for our people and our ʻāina. We are literally eating junk. The American diet consists primarily of fast foods that are unhealthy and/or processed. I did not even realize this, and worse, I had never thought to question it.

At the time, I had no idea what food sovereignty was. I knew nothing about our present food systems in Hawaiʻi, so in high school, when I first heard about the idea of food sovereignty it scared me a bit. It felt strong, and I was not used to hearing the word "sovereignty." I felt sovereignty was bigger than something I could help or make a difference in. I imagined people fighting for food in order to survive; little did I know that is *exactly* what we are already doing. My experience working on this organic farm helped me understand the relationship between food and 'āina and people. Food sovereignty is when people take control of their food systems and return them to a living practice.

BECOMING A LEADER

After my first year interning at MA'O, I received an opportunity to be the first intern in the Step-Up Internship. In this internship, I was given more responsibility to manage and motivate my peers while interacting with our coproducers. This internship also gave me more time to learn about farm operations, and paid a little extra cash. Little did I know I was getting trained to become a leader.

I realized that being a youth leader to my peers was key in growing more young leaders for our generation and those to come. One of the graduated YLT interns, Puanaupaka Williams, said "You can't be what you can't see." I took this very seriously and made a commitment to be a role model for the youth in my community, to show them that we can do anything together.

Some people thought that young adults from Wai'anae interning on an organic farm was nonsense and wouldn't work. We were already stereotyped. But being stereotyped gave us more freedom and creativity to do what we wanted. If we were to believe other people's thoughts about what we could accomplish, then we would only have limited ourselves, just as other people's stereotypes limited their belief in us. They, not us, created this box for us to fit into. But we refused to trap ourselves in those boxes, and as we busted those stereotypes, we became 'āina-tending artists. The sheer variety and quality of our produce made us look like geniuses. In all actually, it was just our ancestral knowing placed into action. All my friends and I wanted to do was to grow food! We were on a mission to feed Hawai'i the best local organic produce.

I am currently the Farm Manager at MA'O Organic Farms, and I would not have gotten to this position without the friendships that I have made along the way. The people that I have met and worked with on this farm helped me to be the person that I am today. We were with each other every day. We worked together, we went to school together, and we cruised together on our days off. My friends became my second family. Heck, I was seeing them more than my family at home! MA'O is not only a work place, but also a space for 'ohana or family values to be put into practice.

We are future ancestors, and once we are awake to that idea then our kuleana can be accomplished. Working on the farm gave us a mission, and helped us believe in our ancestors, our future descendants, and ourselves. There is nothing like working with people you love while doing something you love. While working with my friends, all we feel is aloha. There is aloha between people, between foods, and between ourselves. It was while working on the farm that I learned to love myself.

Through leadership within ourselves and with each other, all we are doing is following the practices that our ancestors left for us. We are building healthy communities and building kauhale—interconnected and caring family systems. Sonny Kinney, a beloved teacher and haku for hoʻoponopono, was in service to the liberation of the Hawaiian people through Hawaiian culture and values. He talked about "knowledge as a sequence of immortality," and I believe when I express this knowledge I become a link between past and future. Our kuleana is to live in this present with active knowledge. This is key to building kauhale. All we are doing is prepping these gracious spaces for future generations. I am only a manifestation of my kūpuna. Providing opportunities for these upcoming practitioners is going to provide Hawaiʻi and the world new ideas for true sustainability.

"IT'S A PRACTICE, NOT A JOB"

We live in a group of islands in the vast Pacific Ocean surrounded by thousands of miles of water. Do we really understand the reality of our living situation? We have been deceived to believe that we have everything we need to survive here in Hawaiʻi. Truth be told: we do not.

According to an article from the College of Tropical Agriculture and Human Resources at the University of Hawaiʻi at Mānoa, Hawaiʻi is still importing more than 85 percent of our food.[3] If a disaster occurred and those ships and planes stopped coming to bring us food, what could we rely on to feed us? Better yet, who can we rely on? That is why it is important to grow our own food here in Hawaiʻi.

Over 150 years ago, the introduction of the sugar cane and pineapple industries changed the understanding of growing food in Hawaiʻi. The plantations made us think that farming is about mono-cropping for business. This type of farming was hard work that never paid enough to those who did the hardest labor. It was during this type of farming in Hawaiʻi that we started to lose our connection with food.

Food should be rewarding for the ones growing it. Farmers should be eating what they grow. Once there is no connection between the farmer and the food, there is no relationship. And when we have a relationship with our food, farming becomes a practice rather than a job. When the word "job" comes to mind, you might think or feel that you *have* to do it. But if it is a practice, then you are *led* to do it. Growing food should also be a practice of a community. When a community binds together to grow food, the healing begins.

Working at MAʻO made it possible for me to deepen my relationship with the ʻāina. It gave me the space to think and reflect, and I started to take care of and eat the food that we produced together. The connection was growing, and I felt good. I felt fresh. I felt truth. I felt aloha. During the morning sunrises and late afternoon sunsets, I continue to be nourished and blessed with beauty. The ʻāina not only feeds me, she also nourishes me with images that my kūpuna experienced as well.

MAʻO has become a puʻuhonua, or a place of refuge for my peers and me. It has created space in Lualualei Valley to center myself and to find the puʻuhonua within. Working with the ʻāina made me realize that I am my puʻuhonua because I am the ʻāina. There is no separation; we just think there is.

I believe Hawaiʻi and other islands in the Pacific are going to be key in recreating food systems. We have thousands of years of knowledge within our peoples, and it should be acknowledged and put into action in new, knowing, creative, and innovative ways. I truly believe projects like MAʻO Organic Farms provide opportunities to gain this ancient knowledge and these practices. The earlier youth get exposed to this knowledge, the better our world will be. This is my vision for the food revolution.

NOTES

1.   Other ʻōlelo noʻeau like this one can be found in the collection by Mary Kawena Pukui, *ʻŌlelo Noʻeau: Hawaiian Proverbs and Poetical Sayings* (Honolulu: Bishop Museum P, 1983): 125.

2.   Te Wānanga o Aotearoa is one of the largest tertiary educational providers in New Zealand, with over eighty locations, providing a range of certificates and degrees guided by Māori principles and values. In March 2013, I had the privilege to be an intern under Dr. Manulani Meyer to help launch the first cohort of He Waka Hiringa, which is a Masters of Applied Indigenous Knowledge.

3.   PingSun Leung and Matthew Loke, "Economic Impacts of Increasing Hawaiʻi's Food Self-Sufficiency," *University of Hawaiʻi at Mānoa College of Tropical Agriculture and Human Resources*, December 2008, at http://www.ctahr.hawaii.edu/oc/freepubs/pdf/EI-16.pdf.

RESOURCES FOR FURTHER INFORMATION AND INSPIRATION

1.   Manu Meyer, *Hoʻoulu: Our Time of Becoming—Hawaiian Epistemology and Early Writings* (Honolulu: ʻAi Pōhaku, 2003).

2. MAʻO Organic Farms Website, at http://www.maoorganicfarms.org.

3. The documentary *Ingredients Hawaiʻi*, dir. Robert Bates, 2012. A segment on MAʻO Organic Farms can be viewed at http://vimeo.com/42736638.

4. Jason Ubay, "More than just farming, MAʻO Organic Farms combines ag with Hawaiian culture and youth education," *Hawaii Business Magazine* 56.5 (November 2010), at http://www.hawaiibusiness.com/SmallBiz/November-2010/More-Than-just-Farming.

5. Te Wānanga o Aotearoa website, at http://www.twoa.ac.nz/Home.aspx.

6. "What is Food Sovereignty?" *US Food Sovereignty Alliance,* USFSA, 16 Oct. 2012, at http://usfoodsovereigntyalliance.org/what-is-food-sovereignty.

TE LUMANAKI O TOKELAU I HAWAI'I[1]

SANIA FA'AMAILE BETTY P. ICKES

February 3rd, 2010, nine a.m. Lumanaki School is in session. As Bonnie Patelesio tunes her guitar, she competes with the crowing roosters, the wind whistling through holes in the exterior wall of the hall, and the excited banter of students settling into their seats. Mas Patelesio and other teachers and parents are setting up equipment for the classes that will share the hall's open space following the morning assembly. Mas and Bonnie belong to the declining handful of native Tokelauan-language speakers who call Hawai'i home.[2] This morning, as most Saturday mornings since 2004, the husband-wife team and other native speakers volunteer at Lumanaki School. The school's mission is simple: "to revitalize the language and culture of Tokelau." With guitar in hand, perched on the edge of the hall's deteriorating wooden stage, Bonnie leads the assembled group of thirty or so students, teachers, and parents in Tokelauan songs, occasionally taking requests from students seated facing her, and turning and nodding her head to acknowledge and guide newly-arriving students to a seat.

Non-learners come to socialize at Lumanaki School. Parents, uncles, aunties, curious neighbors, friends, and Elders sitting in the back of the hall join in occasionally but mostly talk among themselves and help discipline wayward students with verbal commands shouted from where they sit. In Tokelau, every woman is mother to every child. A twelve-foot table on one side of the entryway holds a five-gallon water cooler, cups, and a growing collection of peka (food gifts)—spam musubis, Kilani Bakery pastries, koko alaisa (sweet cocoa rice), and Costco chicken—for after school.

Like its homemade wooden tables and benches, the hall, built in the 1940s, is termite-ridden but functional. It is part of the Poamoho Camp accommodations built by the Del Monte Corporation for its immigrant—mostly Filipino—labor force. In the 1960s, Tokelauan men used Poamoho as a base for raising their resettled kaiga (family) from Olohega, Tokelau. In 2010, the pineapples and remnants of a once-thriving labor community had gone, casualties of globalization.[3] The sixty families still living here include four Tokelauan households. This morning, their second and third generation descendants use the hall for their language learning activities.

This morning's opening repertoire consisted of traditional fatele (songs), chants, Tokelauan Christian hymns, and Tokelauan-translated English standards like "Jesus loves Me" and "Twinkle, Twinkle, Little Star." Students between the ages of three and thirty-five often dance the songs sitting or standing in place. Some songs move the entire group to stand and dance in place, picking up the tempo, anticipating the typical fatele progression. Singing is interspersed with recitals of the Tokelau pi (alphabet), numela (numbers), aho o te vaiaho (days of the week), and mahina o te tauhaga (months of the year). With a blessing, morning assembly ends, and Bonnie sends the students to their respective classes.

Inspired by the tala (stories) of their tupuna (ancestors), the teachers and parents of Lumanaki School drive the revitalization of the Tokelauan language in Hawai'i. They established the non-profit Te Taki, Inc. to govern the school's activities. Of the approximately 1,000 Tokelauans in Hawai'i, roughly one-quarter are affiliated with Lumanaki School.

This is my talaaga (an account) of that community, told as an academically trained historian looking at the past and interpreting it through the lens of an observer and lifetime participant in these extended Tokelauan kaiga. The need to fill the gaps in the migration stories of my tupuna led me to graduate studies in History at the University of Hawai'i at Mānoa. There, immortalized in reels of microfilm, I found the voices of my tupuna. They offered a compelling counter-narrative of their forced relocation not found in previously published sources. In this talaaga, I remind my generation, and others that follow, of the journey taken by our tupuna so that we can have what Grandmother Tinā called olaga haoloto (life without repression). I honor their sacrifices by committing them to memory and text; and I honor their legacy by perpetuating, through thought and action, the values and traditions that strengthened them for the journey here. These values and traditions are encapsulated in, and transmitted through, the language of Tokelau.

In this essay, I consider the resettled Tokelauans as active agents whose culturally informed actions maintained a fragmented group of migrants in a quasi-informal community for decades. I trace some of the historical forces that caused Tokelauan migration from Olohega (Tokelau) to Sāmoa and then to Hawai'i. Finally, I conclude by exploring the host-guest relationship as it applies to Tokelauans (and other settler communities) in Hawai'i. It exposes a quandary. My residency and that of the Tokelauan community in the Hawaiian Islands was made possible through the colonial superstructure that illegally seized and continues to alienate Native Hawaiians from control of their lands and their future as a sovereign people. And as part of the growing settler population that relegates Native Hawaiians to a minority in the electorate, I participate in the empowerment of the system that continues to perpetuate this injustice. How can we, in the settler communities, perpetuate those practices that help us maintain our unique identities and still cultivate reciprocity and balance with our native hosts?

DEFYING THEORETICAL ODDS, SEEKING PU'UHONUA IN CONTESTED SPACES

If theories posited by prominent migration and diaspora scholars held true, there would be no formally organized, culturally-distinct community of Tokelauans in Hawai'i. According to these scholars, certain characteristics of the history of the Tokelauan migration and resettlement—i.e., small migrant enclaves, dispersed settlement patterns, exogamous marriages, and alienation and isolation from the homeland—placed this migrant community at high risk of losing its cultural identity.[4] Indeed, those distinctive characteristics of the early settlers challenged early efforts to organize as a resettled ethnic community.[5] But in their grandchildren—my generation—our tupuna instilled a love and respect for our Tokelauan heritage that moved some of us to celebrate and share our identity as a community of learners through Lumanaki School. Celebrating its tenth anniversary in 2014, Lumanaki School and the community that supports it prove academic predictions about the demise of Tokelauan identity wrong.

AGANUKU O TOKELAU / TOKELAU CULTURE AND WORLDVIEW

Although Tokelauans have lived in Hawai'i for over sixty years, our small numbers make us an invisible minority. People often confused us with other Polynesians. But while we may have similar physical characteristics, there are distinct cultural differences. I was often asked:
   "So what, you guys Sāmoan?"
   (Me) "No! We Tokelauan!"
   "Oh, is that like Tongan?"
   (Me) "No! Tokelauan! Tokelauans are from Tokelau!"
While it is impossible to encapsulate Tokelauan culture (or any culture for that matter) in a paragraph, it is important to understand the distinctive values and traditions that inform the cultural foundation of the resettled Tokelau kaiga, as they are founded in a physical environment different from that of Sāmoa, Tonga, and Hawai'i. Tokelauan worldview is rooted in the seascape of four low-lying atolls—Atafu, Nukunonu, Fakaofo, and Olohega. Comprised of 128 islets, the first three atolls have a total land area of 12.2 square kilometers, roughly the size of Mililani Town on O'ahu, scattered over 200 miles of sea. The nearest hospital and airport are south in Apia, Sāmoa, a

day-and-a-half away by boat. Olohega, the southernmost atoll, is a contiguous 800 acres with a brackish lagoon.

Most islets are a few meters above sea level with a soil base of mostly sand and coral. With no streams or rivers, Tokelau is scant in land-based resources, but its people enjoy an abundance of wealth from the sea—its most prominent physical feature, which also serves as a highway to additional resources in nearby Sāmoa, Tuvalu, the northern Cook Islands, Tonga, and Fiji. Tokelau's tala kakai (public stories) trace the travels and deeds of its heroic figures—Tinilau, Hina, Maui, and Lata—to all the islands of Central Polynesia. Tokelauans share with their Polynesian kin traditional navigational knowledge and technology; material culture; an Austronesian language base; and many of the traditional gods, legends, and cosmogonic genealogies.

To survive in relative isolation within a limited land base, Tokelauans developed traditions and institutions that avoided or minimized conflict. Of primary importance is māopoopo (of one heart), similar to the Hawaiian concept of lōkahi. Cultivated properly through fealofani (mutual compassion), māopoopo occurs when Tokelauans set aside individual concerns and commit to those of the group. Resources were managed through sustainable conservation practices such as hā (ban) on designated areas on both land and sea, and through inati (equal sharing), where communal resources, for example from village faiva (fishing expeditions), are equitably and institutionally distributed. Within the privacy of the kaiga, it is the eldest daughter or fatupaepae (stones of the foundation) who manages and distributes the kaiga resources. Those who endure the stringent education and training for master navigator and fishermen are honored with the kaukumete, a sacred ceremony that conferred the title of tautai (master navigator and fisherman). Highly-respected Uluhina (white-haired) or Toeaina (elder males) traditionally formed the council of elders that governed village affairs. This cultural complement of values, customs, and traditions accompanied the Tokelauan kaiga on their journey to Hawai'i.

Over time, living in Hawai'i challenged the abilities of the kaiga to practice some of the customs and traditions of the homeland.[6] But the essence of these practices and traditions lives on in Lumanaki School's curriculum and community.

TALA FAKAHOLOPITO O TE MALAGA / HISTORY OF THE MIGRATION (1860S TO 1960)

The forced migration of Tokelauans echoes the experiences of other communities in Oceania. In the nineteenth century, foreigners descended on the region in search of goods for trade, including humans. In the 1860s, shockwaves from the US Civil War reverberated throughout Oceania, and the increased demand for sugar and cotton led to vast exploitation of Native lands and peoples. In 1862, after decades of successfully repelling European and US explorations under the leadership of the Aliki (Chiefs) of Fakaofo,[7] Tokelau experienced multiple waves of rapacious assaults by crews of Peruvian-based ships who were scouring East Oceania for defenseless populations from which to "recruit," but mostly to kidnap, workers for their mines and plantations. Tokelau's population plummeted by 52 percent as a result of these raids.[8] A weakened Fakaofo, whose theocratic monopoly had ruled Tokelau for centuries, was no match for the ensuing waves of foreign weapons, foreign religions, and insatiable capitalism.

In the decades that followed, foreign land grabbers alienated Tokelauan lands controlled by the Fakaofo. Olohega was the first to be seized by New Englander Eli Jennings. As a paid interpreter for the Peruvian slave ships that raided the atolls in 1862, Jennings lured unsuspecting Tokelauans aboard the ships ostensibly to trade. Thereafter, he claimed Olohega for himself and his future heirs,[9] controlled inter-atoll travel, and forced the natives into compulsory labor for a profitable copra venture that capitalized Olohega's cultivated and natural resources for the next 100 years.[10] Unbeknownst to Tokelauans, Jennings—like the pro-annexation haole of 1890s Hawai'i—also pushed for the United States to annex Olohega, and succeeded. In 1925, with little fanfare, a representative of the US Navy planted the American flag on Olohega. None of the elders I interviewed in the 1990s remembered this event.

Parts of Olohega's colonial history have many parallels in the Hawaiian Islands. Like Hawai'i's annexation,[11] the legislation for Olohega's failed to garner enough votes in the US Congress; Olohega, like Hawai'i, was incorporated by Executive Order, in 1925.[12] The northern atolls of Tokelau became a protectorate of New Zealand in the same year. Olohega remains part of the Territory of American Sāmoa, and before 1952 was governed by an appointed officer of the US Navy stationed 200 miles away in Pago Pago. The Navy's own records show it was derelict in its oversight of Olohega. Its sparse reports of visits to assess the health and well-being of the people of Olohega were colored with condescending comments about the people's habits and attitudes, yet harsh labor practices and civil rights abuses imposed by the plantation management were whitewashed as "culturally-appropriate" discipline.[13] Under US Navy rule, the Jennings heirs answered only to themselves, and operated their business outside the legal arm of US territorial laws that governed American Sāmoa.

In 1953, forces collided that led to the forced relocation of Tokelauan kaiga from Olohega to Pago Pago, American Sāmoa. On a sweltering mid-July work day while loading copra, the workers' request for a water break was refused by a supervisor. Olohega's elders protested and all activities ceased. Jennings ordered participants in the fakatuikehe (protest) to leave Olohega. An investigation responding to a petition by workers found in favor of their complaints, but the acting Governor, at Jennings's request, dispatched a ship to remove them.[14] According to Paul Pedro, whose family was on board, men, women, and children were "dumped," like cargo, at Pago Pago harbor. Neither Jennings nor the acting Governor made arrangements for food, shelter, or transportation. Pedro and sympathetic colleagues hustled that evening to accommodate the Olohega refugees.

The displaced kaiga became second-class citizens in Pago Pago. As non-Sāmoans, they had limited economic opportunities and were legally barred from access to land. They arrived as the US Navy transferred rule of American Sāmoa to the US Department of the Interior. When the Navy left Sāmoa, the economy collapsed; local businesses that employed thousands of workers and provided support services for the military lost their biggest customer. The Tokelauans looked elsewhere. In 1959, Paul Pedro's younger brothers and sisters followed him to Hawai'i, where he was on scholarship at Church College of the Pacific in Lā'ie.[15] Their pooled wages eventually brought most members of the Su'a-Pedro-Tyrell puikaiga (extended family) to Central Oahu by the mid-1960s.

PU'UHONUA (REFUGE)

Grandpa Iosefa Su'a compares the forced relocation of Tokelauans to that of penu tafea (floating coconuts). Involuntarily dislodged from the homeland, a penu tafea can survive for months at sea before making landfall, where the hosting landscape will then invariably shape the growth of the foreign seedling. Su'a, his children and grandchildren, and other Tokelauan kaiga made landfall on O'ahu. The first seedlings survived due to the fertility of the new soil.

Poamoho Camp, a few miles north of Wahiawā, was our pu'uhonua. Back then, our Uncles and Aunties worked alongside other migrant laborers from Samoa, Guam, China, Japan, the Philippines, and Puerto Rico. Many of them did not return home, others could not due to indebtedness to the planter. Hawai'i has served as pu'uhonua for all of them. While some Tokelauans continue to struggle financially, others have been sustained and thrive here due to a defiant spirit of determination. This determination informs, for example, the activities of Lumanaki School. Where the community lacks skill and expertise, the staff and teachers have built an extensive network that includes professional colleagues, neighbors, fellow church members, and other non-profits who can help fill these needs.[16] Lumanaki School testifies to penu tafea thriving through collaborative relationships with Hawai'i's various communities.

It is customary for Tokelauan guests to honor their hosts with gifts of goods and/or services; this nurtures reciprocity and fosters respect by adding value to the relationship instead of draining the host's resources. Thus, an important issue for us to consider is the well-being of Native Hawaiians, whose lands and resources became our pu'uhonua. How can I, and others like me, add value to this relationship? In my limited professional capacity, I began by cultivating an appreciation of the host culture through building and sustaining a relationship between my communities and theirs. My aim was to close the gap that alienated one community from another, because despite living in Hawai'i most of their lives, many of my students knew very little about the history of the Hawaiian Islands and its people.

I teach at Lumanaki School, where we strive to promote our host culture by connecting our students and their kaiga to Native Hawaiian communities. Our partnership with Ho'oulu 'Āina, for example, exposes our students to Hawaiian cultural practitioners who presently lead the restoration of neglected and misused lands in Kalihi Valley. What they learn there—regard and respect for the environment, community, and nurturing relationships—affirms the importance of the Tokelauan values we teach at Lumanaki. As our students and kaiga join in the ongoing restoration, they benefit from the practical knowledge gained, the exposure to Hawaiian culture, and the "shared connections" they make with hundreds of other volunteers from diverse backgrounds.

The relationships being nurtured promote fealofani and māopoopo. More significantly, the experience results in a newfound appreciation for Native Hawaiians and their struggle to restore the health of their people and their lands despite the "history of illegalities" they have endured. For some students, there is a lasting impact. I continue to see them volunteer at Ho'oulu 'Āina without me. It is my hope that a cooperative spirit, born of this generation's intercommunity relations, will translate into cooperative pursuits for real solutions to the unresolved injustices that continue to harm the well-being of Native Hawaiians and other groups.

Lumanaki School testifies to our generation's commitment to honor the legacy of our Tokelauan tupuna by perpetuating their values and traditions. Lumanaki's community also honors our tupuna by pursuing a relationship of trust and reciprocity with our Native Hawaiian host culture, whose homeland offered respite and refuge to the penu tafea of Tokelau. This relationship, thus far, has helped Tokelauans in Hawai'i defy the odds that predicted the loss of our culture and identity.

NOTES

1. Te Lumanaki o Tokelau is roughly translated as "the future of Tokelau."

2. The community's sociolinguistic survey conducted in 2005 found only 8 percent of the 432 Tokelauans surveyed were fluent speakers.

3. Will Hoover, "Wahiawa Camp fights eviction," *The Honolulu Advertiser,* March 27, 2004, at http://the.honoluluadvertiser.com/article/2004/Mar/27/ln/ln11a.html.

4. Stephen Castles and Mark J. Miller, *The Age of Migration: International Population Movements in the Modern World,* 2nd ed. (New York: Guilford, 1998). See also Roben Cohen, "Diasporas, the Nation-State, and Globalisation," *Global History and Migrations,* ed. Wang Gungwu (Boulder: Westview, 1997): 117–24; and Michael D. Lieber, "The Resettled Community and its Context," *Exiles and Migrants in Oceania,* ed. Michael Lieber (Honolulu: U of Hawai'i P, 1977): 342–87.

5. Challenges included the cultural stigma of "banishment" as punishment for breaking village law, which for Tokelauans brings shame upon the family of the perpetrator. For many of the relocated adults, banishment and relocation were indistinguishable because the results were the same, despite the extenuating and differing circumstances. I discuss this issue further in my dissertation, "Expanding the Tokelau Archipelago," listed in the Resources of this essay.

6. For narrative and analysis of the early years of resettlement of the Su'a-Pedro-Tyrell puikaiga (extended clan), see my dissertation, "Expanding the Tokelau Archipelago," listed in the Resources of this essay.

7. See Judith Huntsman and Antony Hooper, *Tokelau,* in the Resources for this essay.

8. See H. E. Maude, *Slavers in Paradise: The Peruvian Labour Trade in Polynesia* (Canberra: Australian National UP, 1981).

9. Olohega continues to be controlled by descendants of the Jennings family; presently a family member is paid a salary to represent Olohega in the American Sāmoa Fono (Legislature).

10. See Ickes, "Expanding the Tokelau Archipelago."

11. See, for example, the 1898 Newlands Resolution: "To provide for annexing the Hawaiian Islands to the United States."

12. US Congress, 68th. "Joint Resolution 294," 1925.

13. Lt. Colonel L. W. Strum, "USN 1918 on Swain's Island, reports on treatment and conditions of Natives and gender conditions on the Island, Letter to the Governor [of American Sāmoa]," ed. US Navy, 1918.

14. There were efforts by Jennings and the acting Governor of American Sāmoa to transport the families to the northern Tokelau atolls, but entry was refused, citing the atolls' limited resources.

15. This became Brigham Young University, Hawai'i.

16. See the works by Betty Ickes, Akiemi Glenn, and Candice Steiner found in the Resources for this essay.

RESOURCES FOR FURTHER INFORMATION AND INSPIRATION

1. Akiemi Glenn, "Wayfinding in Pacific Linguascapes: Negotiating Tokelau Linguistic Identities in Hawai'i" (Diss., U of Hawai'i at Mānoa, 2012).

2. Judith Huntsman and Antony Hooper, *Tokelau: A Historical Ethnography* (Honolulu: U of Hawai'i P, 1996).

3. Betty Ickes, "Expanding the Tokelau Archipelago: A History of Tokelau's Decolonization and Olohega's *Penu Tafea* in the Hawai'i Diaspora" (Diss., U of Hawai'i at Mānoa, 2009).

4. *Matagi Tokelau: History and Traditions of Tokelau* (Apia: Office of Tokelau Affairs, and Suva: Institute of Pacific Studies, U of the South Pacific, 1991).

5. Candice Steiner, "Te Kauhiva Tokelau: Composing and Choreographing Cultural Sustainability" (MA Thesis, U of Hawai'i at Mānoa, 2012).

THE SECOND GIFT

BRANDY NĀLANI MCDOUGALL

FOR HAUNANI

The first gift of Western civilization was disease. The second gift of Western civilization was violence.

—Haunani-Kay Trask

1

I have no mercy or compassion for a society that will crush people and then penalize them for not being able to stand up under the weight.

—Malcolm X

For over four generations
they have said we are
a people with a history
of violence, accustomed to
the dark, cold cell, remedial
in mind and body. They write
of how we killed infants,
sacrificed humans, practiced
incest, how our kings and queens
were alcoholic, inept dictators,
how we owned slaves, how
disease comes with darkness,
how they must save us
from ourselves.

         And we take
the new tongue and its historical
revisions, the low test scores,

the longer sentences, the water
shortages, the paid-off politicians,
the third part-time job, the cancers
and the radiation, diabetes
and amputations, eminent
domain and adverse possession,
the overruling of all our objections
because now
their violence
is all we know.

2

We are not Americans! We are not Americans! We are not Americans!
—Haunani-Kay Trask

Violence is more than lodging
bullets into brown or black
bodies, but also burning
sacred valleys, stabbing tunnels
into mountains, damming streams,
dumping poisons into oceans,
overdeveloping ʻāina, bombing
and buying islands. Violence is
Arizona jail cells, GMOs,
and unearthed iwi waiting
under a Wal-Mart ramp, in boxes,
in museums, in a church basement.
Violence is what we settle for
because we've been led to believe
green paper can feed us
more than green land.

Violence is what we're used to
as they measure our blood
to wait decades for a dollar-a-year
lease, when we forget how we once
fed and healed ourselves, how
our mouths hold life and death.
We are no longer shocked
by raids on what is left
in the pitched tents and tarps,

our evictions from beach to beach
and park to park, the poverty
of unfurling fists open only
to the smallest of handouts.

Violence is believing
you are in the United States
driving on a highway
built over the sacred,
carrying artillery to scorch
the sacred so more sacred lands
can become the United States
through violence.

3

> *Don't let anybody tell you not to be angry. We have every right to be
> angry—This is our country.*
>
> —Haunani-Kay Trask

You were born
into captivity,
a native in a racist,
anti-Native world;
yet, they call *you* racist.
They hate you
like they have hated
every warrior before you.

This helps them bear
the weight of dominion;
helps them keep their vacation
houses, golf courses, hotels,
and bases; helps them feed
their children denial,
so as adults they, too,
can say, "Don't blame me
for what happened
a hundred years ago."
They must keep
believing that
the United States

is our country
and not just
the country
that occupies
our country,
Hawai'i.

4

It always seems impossible until it's done.

—Nelson Mandela

You tell us:
"You are not a racist
because you fight racism.
You are a warrior,"
and you train more warriors,
show us how to sharpen
and land words like spears,
how to catch their spears
and hurl them back.
You call us the spears
of our nation, assure us
"Decolonization is all
around us." You guide us
to the rope of resistance
so we can weave
the newest strands together
under a sovereign sun.

And so we tell our children,
our children tell their children,
and their children tell their children
until our words become
the chattering winds of hope
that erode the hardness of violence
from the earth, and we are sown
back into
                    and born from
                    Papahānaumoku
                            green and tender once again.

ACHIEVING SOCIAL AND HEALTH EQUITY IN HAWAI'I

JOSEPH KEAWE'AIMOKU KAHOLOKULA

Mōhala i ka wai, ka maka o ka pua.

[Flowers thrive where there is water, as thriving people are found where living conditions are good.[1]]

An event at the checkout counter of the Ala Moana Longs Drugs store has stuck with me for life. I was nine years old, standing with my mom as the cashier rang up the total for the woman in front of us. The woman wrote out her check. The clerk took it and handed the woman her bags. Although it was common practice at Longs in those days, the clerk did not verify the check against her I.D.

"Have a nice day," the clerk said, as the woman walked away. Our turn at the checkout wasn't so easy. Presented with her total, my mother too wrote a check, but this time the clerk stopped and called the store manager to verify it. I asked my mom, "Why she called the manager for your check and not the other lady's?" My mother, frustrated, replied, "Because we Hawaiian, that's why!"

It was not until thirteen years had passed, in 1992, as the centennial of the overthrow of the Hawaiian Kingdom loomed, that I understood what my mother felt that day in Longs and what her response meant. It would be another decade before I could fully appreciate what that moment, as a tangible example of larger social issues, meant to our health and well-being as Native Hawaiians.

Having good health is more than the mere absence of illness, disability, or disease. According to the World Health Organization, it is a state of complete physical, mental, and social well-being. Well-being is a person's subjective experience of how well he or she is doing physically, psychologically, socially, and spiritually. Although a subjective experience, well-being is influenced by many socially-construed realities (such as social ranking and assignment of privileges) that reflect society's collective perceptions, expectations, and aspirations. My mother's reply to me that day in Longs was an instance of her perception of her social reality as a Native Hawaiian.

SOCIAL REALITIES OF GROWING UP IN HAWAI'I

That day in Longs, my mother was communicating to me her frustration with what she saw as discrimination. "Because we Hawaiian," the clerk needed to call the manager to verify our check. This came with more than suspicion of Hawaiians writing bad checks; Native Hawaiians at the time (circa 1970s) were stereotyped as being untrustworthy and unproductive. Neither my mother nor I could have known the true intent of the clerk that day in her differential adherence to store protocols. All I know is that my mother was frustrated by that experience. Her frustration was probably fueled by years of having to confront these negative stereotypes, coupled with the economic challenges she and my father, also a Native Hawaiian, dealt with most of their lives, raising three kids on low wages in a state with one of the highest costs of living.

Looking back on my childhood, I recall many situations where my parents felt discriminated against or where there was ethnic tension between people in my lower Makiki neighborhood. Some were subtle, like that day at Longs. Some were blatant, like when our neighbor, an older Japanese woman, called my dad the terrible "n" word. A backdrop to all of this interpersonal tension was the poor economic condition we all, regardless of ethnicity, lived with and endured in our neighborhood. I can recount the many times we were on the verge of applying for welfare. Instead, my parents often opted to work more than one job each to make ends meet.

Now, as a health professional and behavioral scientist, I realize the toll these socioeconomic conditions were having on the health of my parents, my siblings, and me, and how social inequities and health inequities go hand-in-hand in society.[2] Native Hawaiians continue to feel discriminated against by other social groups in Hawai'i. My research indicates that 48 percent of Native Hawaiians strongly believe they were discriminated against over the past twelve months, while the other 52 percent reported being discriminated against sometimes. My research also shows that those who perceive more discrimination are more likely to have high blood pressure—a major risk factor for heart disease and stroke—and cortisol (a stress hormone) activity that is associated with heart disease.[3] Other researchers find that Native Hawaiians who experience more discrimination are more likely to be excessively overweight—a major risk factor for diabetes, heart disease, and certain cancers.[4] Research with Native Hawaiian, Pacific Islander,[5] and Filipino adolescents indicates that their perceptions of discrimination can increase their likelihood of cigarette, alcohol, and marijuana use.[6]

ETHNICITY AND SOCIAL DETERMINANTS OF HEALTH IN HAWAI'I

Social and health inequities parallel each other, and certain ethnic groups in Hawai'i bear a disproportionate burden of these inequities. Native Hawaiians, Pacific Islanders, and Filipinos are more likely to be undereducated, to be working in low paying jobs, to be incarcerated, and to be living in poorer conditions than other ethnic groups.[7] They are also the highest-ranking ethnic groups in terms of obesity, diabetes, cardiovascular disease, and certain cancers.[8] People from these groups are more likely to develop diabetes and cardiovascular disease at younger ages. Depression, anxiety, and substance abuse are also higher among these groups.[9] Consequently, they live an average of a decade less than people of other ethnic groups in Hawai'i.[10]

There is more than biology—such as genetic predisposition for disease—or lifestyle—such as poor eating and exercise habits—at play here. Even lack of access to good medical care, including poor insurance coverage and scarcity of medical services, doesn't explain it completely. The length and quality of our lives has a lot to do with our social conditions (such as where we live, work, and go to school) and the distribution of wealth and resources in our society. These forces are referred to as *social determinants of health*—the social and economic conditions people find themselves in and the underlying reasons for group differences in health status.[11] Social and health inequalities are particularly evident along ethnic lines.

In his book *Ethnicity and Inequalities in Hawai'i,* Jonathan Okamura contends that social and economic inequities follow along ethnic lines.[12] He argues that ethnicity drives both the social relations and the educational, economic, and political structures in Hawai'i so as to elevate or subordinate certain ethnic groups by regulating how resources, rewards, and privileges are distributed and obtained in society. The ethnic groups most at a disadvantage are Native Hawaiians, Pacific Islanders, and Filipinos—ethnic groups that are indigenous to the Pacific Region and who were subjugated by Western powers.

Here are examples of how social determinants of health intersect with ethnicity in Hawai'i. One of the highest areas for pedestrian and automobile-related fatalities is on the Wai'anae coast of O'ahu, where there are few usable sidewalks with curbs to prevent cars from driving up onto them, or median strips that separates lanes of traffic going in opposite directions. The Wai'anae coast is home to the largest concentration of Native Hawaiians in Hawai'i, and home to other Pacific Islanders. Contrast this to the more affluent neighborhoods of Kāhala and Hawai'i Kai, where formal sidewalks and median strips are the norm, and where the lowest pedestrian fatalities are found on O'ahu. Native Hawaiians, Pacific Islanders, and Filipinos comprise a much smaller proportion of the population living in Kāhala and Hawai'i Kai.

The neighborhoods with larger concentrations of Native Hawaiians, Pacific Islanders, and Filipinos are considered obesiogenic. These environments promote unhealthy patterns of eating and sedentary lifestyles, and they pose more stressors and health risks. They have more fast food restaurants and liquor stores, less access to fresh fruits and vegetables, few if any walking and biking trails, poorly maintained public parks, and more exposure to environmental toxins. Think about where most garbage dumps and industrial plants are located in the islands. Given such living conditions, it should be no surprise that Native Hawaiians, Pacific Islanders, and Filipinos have the highest rates of obesity, diabetes, and certain cancers.

The occupation of the Pacific by Western powers—the United States, Great Britain, France, and Germany—and the accompanying acculturation and racism have imposed an added health burden on Pacific Peoples, impacting their social determinants of health. For Native Hawaiians, the US occupation of Hawai'i brought compulsory assimilation and discriminatory laws and practices in education, employment, and housing. Traditional Hawaiian values and practices have been both devalued and exploited for profit.

In the wider Pacific, Western colonialism has created drastic, adverse economic and environmental changes—such as damage done by nuclear weapons testing and climate change. Many Pacific Islanders have been displaced from their island homes. Since the mid-twentieth century, people from Sāmoa, Tonga, and the island groups collectively referred to as Micronesia have been migrating to Hawai'i in search of a better life.[13] However, these Pacific Islanders are more often socially stigmatized and economically disadvantaged than other groups of settlers in Hawai'i.[14] These historical and contemporary injustices are associated with poorer socioeconomic and health conditions for these ethnic groups.

NĀ POU KIHI: A HAWAIIAN-INSPIRED FRAMEWORK FOR ACHIEVING SOCIAL AND HEALTH EQUITY

As a Native Hawaiian and health professional, I strive to improve the social position of Native Hawaiians in our ancestral home as a strategy to improving our collective health. In this section, I present a call to action. The waiwai (value) of Hawai'i is the indigenous people and culture of these islands. It is what makes Hawai'i unique and special. It is what the tourism industry uses to lure people to these islands in search of paradise. It is what big businesses use to promote their products and services. It is what politicians, educators, and employers often promote to build solidarity. But how is it that a people and culture with such great marketing value are among the most poor, disenfranchised, and sick in our society? How is it that Native Hawaiians make up nearly 25 percent of the state's population but do not enjoy the same social and health status as the other major ethnic groups, such as Caucasians and Japanese?

Social and health equity in Hawai'i needs to start with Kānaka 'Ōiwi (Native Hawaiians). This is a social justice *and* a public health imperative.[15] Our Kānaka 'Ōiwi population is expected to nearly double in Hawai'i by the year 2050, to roughly 537,000.[16] An increase in population size can mean an increase in political and economic influence, if Kānaka 'Ōiwi organize around shared aspirations to improve our collective socioeconomic and health conditions.

Inspired by the work of Sir Mason Durie, a Māori scholar and physician,[17] I have come to realize that improving the health of Kānaka 'Ōiwi requires systemic change—changes in our political, educational, economic, and social systems. A framework to guide this systemic change is needed. I propose *Nā Pou Kihi* (the corner posts) as a framework to achieving social and health equity for Kānaka 'Ōiwi. Formulated from a Kanaka 'Ōiwi perspective, and considering the diverse realities of Hawaiian communities and institutions, this framework should move us toward health equity in Hawai'i.

Like the four corner posts of a solid house, each of the elements of Nā Pou Kihi are essential for optimal health. Nā Pou Kihi is summarized in Table 1 and explained more fully in the subsections below.

KE AO 'ŌIWI

The first of Nā Pou Kihi is *Ke Ao 'Ōiwi*—creating and maintaining indigenous space. The optimum health of Kānaka 'Ōiwi can only be achieved in a society that values their social group and provides the sociocultural space for their preferred modes of living and aspirations. My research indicates that over 80 percent of Kānaka 'Ōiwi identify strongly with their indigenous heritage. Creating the sociocultural space that allows for the expression of that cultural identity is necessary to advance their health.

What might Ke Ao 'Ōiwi look like? The Hawaiian language and other cultural practices are highly visible and operating beyond the realm of tourism, entertainment, promotional ads, and ceremonies. Federal and state laws and policies are not barriers to Kānaka 'Ōiwi-preferred modes of living but are designed with them in mind. Non-natives are not filing lawsuits against Kānaka 'Ōiwi institutions in order to bar their existence. Kānaka 'Ōiwi have

Table 1. Summary of Nā Pou Kihi: A Framework for Achieving Social and Health Equity for Kānaka 'Ōiwi.

Nā Pou Kihi (the corner posts)	Principles/Strategies	Examples of Goals
Ke Ao 'Ōiwi (indigenous space)	Optimum health of Kānaka 'Ōiwi is achievable when society values their social group and provides the sociocultural space for their modes of living and aspirations.	• Positive cultural identity development • Hawaiian/English linguistic landscape • 'Ōiwi-focused media • Strong 'Ōiwi political influence • Cultural-based public education
Ka Mālama 'Āina (environmental stewardship)	Optimum health of Kānaka 'Ōiwi is achievable in safe and well-resourced communities that provide opportunities for healthy living.	• Economic self-sufficiency • Food sovereignty and security • Strong civic participation • Access to walking/biking/hiking trails • Expanded/synergized role of Ali'i-founded organizations in community development
Ka 'Ai Pono (healthy consumption)	Optimum health of Kānaka 'Ōiwi can only be achieved when healthy patterns of living are accessible, promoted, and practiced; contingent upon Ke Ao 'Ōiwi and Ka Mālama 'Āina.	• Community health promotion programs • Access to technology to enhance lifestyle goals • Affordable/accessible Hawaiian foods • Tax benefits to promote healthy living
Ka Wai Ola (social justice)	Optimum health of Kānaka 'Ōiwi is achievable through social justice (equitable share of the benefits and burdens of society) and indigenous rights; cumulative effect of Ke Ao 'Ōiwi, Ka Mālama 'Āina, and Ka 'Ai Pono.	• 'Ōiwi values/practices applied to legislative decision-making • Livable wages • Obesity prevalence < 15 %; diabetes prevalence < 5 %; average life expectancy 81 years • Kānaka 'Ōiwi equitably represented in business, education, politics, and media

united toward a common goal and developed the critical mass necessary to influence electoral voting outcomes, political agendas, and allocations of the state's resources, or even the obtaining of political self-determination.

'Ōiwi Television, *Mana Magazine*, and Maoli Arts Month (MAMo) are examples of how Kānaka 'Ōiwi leaders, thinkers, and artists are creating Ke Ao 'Ōiwi. They are making the Hawaiian language, culture, and perspectives available to all of Hawai'i in a positive light that will combat negative stereotypes and demonstrate the relevance and value of Kānaka 'Ōiwi perspectives and culture for contemporary times. We need to ensure that these forms of media that convey the beauty of Kānaka ʻŌiwi and our culture continue and grow. They are powerful tools to change public opinions and attitudes and to advance Kānaka ʻŌiwi aspirations. Other examples of creating Ke Ao ʻŌiwi in educational spaces are the cultural-based public charter schools and Hawaiian-language immersion schools.

KA MĀLAMA ʻĀINA

The second of Nā Pou Kihi is *Ka Mālama ʻĀina*—environmental stewardship and the maintenance of healthy environments. Optimum health can only be achieved in communities that are safe and provide equitable access to the necessary resources for sustainable healthy living. Consider how people who live in communities that have access to healthier food options, to walking, biking, and hiking trails, to safe and low density neighborhoods, and to opportunities for social networking and civic participation are less likely to be plagued by obesity or by violence and crime in their neighborhoods.[18]

What might Ka Mālama ʻĀina look like? Kānaka ʻŌiwi and other resource users have a say in what experts manage our natural and social resources. Hawaiian homestead communities are economically self-sufficient by capitalizing on renewable energy sources, aquaponics, and communal gardening. Imagine having a Hale Mua (men's gathering place) and Hale o Papa (women's gathering place) based on traditional Kānaka ʻŌiwi principles of child development and communal reciprocity in every Kānaka ʻŌiwi community. Environmental protection, resource management, and land-use planning initiatives are inspired by traditional Kānaka ʻŌiwi values and practices, and Kānaka ʻŌiwi are in positions of leadership in these areas.

MAʻO Organic Farms, Paepae o Heʻeia, and the Papakōlea Hawaiian homestead community provide examples of how Kānaka ʻŌiwi grassroots organizations are working to build healthier communities by providing healthy foods and contributing to sustainable, community-based economic development. These programs not only engage in organic agriculture and aquaculture, they provide leadership and job-training programs as well.

KA ʻAI PONO

The third of Nā Pou Kihi is *Ka ʻAi Pono*—healthy consumption. The term ʻAi Pono refers to eating healthy as well as exercising responsible consumption, whether that is consumption of food, natural and manufactured resources, technology, or the other conveniences of daily living.

Healthy islander ways of living have been pushed aside to make way for the artificial, processed, and manufactured world. For instance, paʻi ʻai (pounded taro) and 'ulu (breadfruit) have been replaced by white rice and bread. Fresh fish has been replaced by Spam. Lū'au (kalo leaves) and 'uala (sweet potato) have been replaced with macaroni salad and French fries. 'Awa has been replaced with alcohol and tobacco. The kapu system, which was essentially a public health system, has been replaced with laws promoting individualism and allowing wasteful consumption. The foods we consume are no longer the kino lau (physical representations) of our Akua (Gods). They are not fit for ho'okupu (sacred offerings), so why should they be fit to put in our bodies?

What might Ka 'Ai Pono look like? Poi is on every dinner table. High-fat and calorie-dense processed foods are replaced with fresh fish, vegetables, and fruits grown in Hawai'i. Kānaka 'Ōiwi are making daily use of their healthier community infrastructure realized under Ka Mālama 'Āina. Imagine a world where 'awa has eliminated the reliance on tobacco and alcohol to unwind and manage negative emotions. Kānaka 'Ōiwi and others have regained the belief that food is a way to commune with our spirituality and faith.

The PILI 'Ohana Project is an example of Kānaka 'Ōiwi, Pacific Islander, and Filipino communities taking control of improving their own health. Through the PILI 'Ohana Project, community members develop the capacity to improve their own health, within their own community context and using their existing community resources. Over the past nine years, I have worked closely with community leaders from Ke Ola Mamo Native Hawaiian Health Care System, the Hawaiian homestead communities of Papakōlea, Kewalo, and Kalāwahine, Hawai'i Maoli of the Association of Hawaiian Civic Clubs, and Kokua Kalihi Valley Comprehensive Family Services to develop several community-placed health promotion programs. The PILI 'Ohana programs address excess body weight and diabetes self-management. Participants have significantly reduced body weight and blood sugar levels, and improved blood pressure and physical functioning.[19] The programs are currently being disseminated to other Kānaka 'Ōiwi, Pacific Islander, and Filipino communities across Hawai'i.

KA WAI OLA

The fourth of Nā Pou Kihi is *Ka Wai Ola*—social justice, which encompasses and extends beyond the previous *Nā Pou Kihi*. It is about being afforded fair treatment and an equitable share of the benefits and burdens of society. Ka Wai Ola includes indigenous rights to self-determination, to quality education and healthcare, to natural resources and technology, to economic self-sufficiency, and to living in safe and healthy societies.

What might Ka Wai Ola look like? All children have access to the best educational opportunities, whether privately or publicly administered. Kānaka ʻŌiwi have a social status befitting a host culture and a people who have sacrificed so much to accommodate others. Non-natives appreciate the value of Kānaka ʻŌiwi and their culture, and support (rather than challenge) Kānaka ʻŌiwi rights, institutions, and aspirations. Kānaka ʻŌiwi and other disenfranchised groups in Hawaiʻi are equitably represented across government, education, business, and socioeconomic statuses. Imagine a world where Kānaka ʻŌiwi are local and global leaders in indigenous education, entrepreneurial activities, medicine and health, law and politics, and public health systems.

THE HEALTH OF ALL PEOPLE

In writing about the social determinants of health in Hawaiʻi, my intent is not to divide people of different ethnic groups, to "create victims" and "perpetrators," or to pit Natives against non-Natives. Certainly, people of all ethnic groups may find themselves in challenging social and economic conditions. Many of the disadvantages we see in education, housing, and employment today are perhaps remnants of discriminatory practices rooted in the past. Notwithstanding, ethnicity appears to play a key role in the social and health inequities of Hawaiʻi. So obvious is the role of ethnicity that it cannot be ignored. The less than desirable health of Hawaiʻi's indigenous people—Kānaka ʻŌiwi—cannot be ignored. Nā Pou Kihi, as a framework for achieving social and health equity for Kānaka ʻŌiwi, can also serve as a guide to the foci and strategies needed to improve the health of all people who call Hawaiʻi home.

NOTES

1. This Hawaiian proverb translates as "Unfolded by water are the faces of flowers." Its metaphorical translation is provided in the text. Both translations are from ʻŌlelo Noʻeau: Hawaiian Proverbs & Poetical Sayings by Mary Kawena Pukui (Honolulu: Bishop Museum P, 1983; ʻŌlelo Noʻeau #2178).
2. "Social and health inequities" refer to unjust differences between groups of people in terms of their social and/or health status. Poor access to quality education compared to another social group is a social inequity. Greater prevalence of diabetes in one ethnic group versus the general population is an example of a health inequity.
3. J. K. Kaholokula et al., "Association between Perceived Racism and Physiological Stress Indices in Native Hawaiians," *Journal of Behavioral Medicine* 35.1 (2012): 27–37. See also J. K. Kaholokula, M. K. Iwane, and A. H. Nacapoy, "Effects of Perceived Racism and Acculturation on Hypertension in Native Hawaiians," *Hawaii Medical Journal* 69.5 Suppl 2 (2010): 11–15.

4. L. D. McCubbin and M. Antonio, "Discrimination and Obesity among Native Hawaiians," *Hawaii Journal of Medicine and Public Health* 71.12 (2012): 346–52.

5. Pacific Islanders refer to people from other Polynesian islands (e.g., Sāmoa and Tonga) and the islands of Melanesia (e.g., Fiji) and Micronesia (e.g., Guåhan, Chuuk, and the Marshall Islands).

6. T. A. Wills et al., "Discrimination and Substance Use in Early Adolescence: Ethnic Differences in a Diverse Population in Hawai'i," *National Institutes of Health Summit: The Science of Eliminating Health Disparities* (2012).

7. Shawn Malia Kana'iaupuni et al., *Ka Huaka'i: 2005 Native Hawaiian Educational Assessment* (Honolulu: Kamehameha Schools/Policy Analysis & System Evaluation [PASE] Pauahi Publications, 2005).

8. M. K. Mau et al., "Cardiometabolic Health Disparities in Native Hawaiians and Other Pacific Islanders," *Epidemiologic Reviews* 31 (2009): 113–29. See also K. L. Braun et al., "Building Native Hawaiian Capacity in Cancer Research and Programming. A Legacy of 'Imi Hale," *Cancer* 107.8 Suppl (2006): 2082–90.

9. F. R. Salvail and J. M. Smith, "Prevalence of Anxiety and Depression among Hawaii's Adults Derived from HBRFSS 2006" (Honolulu: Hawaii State Department of Health, 2006).

10. C. B. Park et al. "Longevity Disparities in Multiethnic Hawaii: An Analysis of 2000 Life Tables," *Public Health Reports* 124.4 (2009): 579–84.

11. M. G. Marmot and Richard G. Wilkinson. *Social Determinants of Health*, 2nd ed. (Oxford: Oxford UP, 2006).

12. Jonathan Y. Okamura, *Ethnicity and Inequality in Hawai'i* (Philadelphia: Temple UP, 2008).

13. John F. McDermott and Naleen Naupaka Andrade, *People and Cultures of Hawai'i: The Evolution of Culture and Ethnicity*, new ed. (Honolulu: U of Hawai'i P, 2011).

14. S. Yamada, "Discrimination in Hawai'i and the Health of Micronesians," *Hawai'i Journal of Public Health* 3.1 (2011): 55–57.

15. J. K. Kaholokula, A. H. Nacapoy, and K. L. Dang, "Social Justice as a Public Health Imperative for Kānaka Maoli," *AlterNative: An International Journal of Indigenous Peoples* 5.2 (2009): 117–37.

16. G. K. Vincent and V. A. Velkoff, *The Next Four Decades, the Older Population in the United States: 2010 to 2050, Current Population Reports* (Washington, D.C.: US Census Bureau, 2010).

17. Mason Durie, *Māori Ora: The Dynamics of Māori Health* (New York: Oxford UP, 2001).

18. S. Srinivasan, L. R. O'Fallon, and A. Dearry, "Creating Healthy Communities, Healthy Homes, Healthy People: Initiating a Research Agenda on the Built Environment and Public Health," *American Journal of Public Health* 93.9 (2003): 1446–50.

19. For more information about the PILI 'Ohana Project, see their website at http://www2.jabsom.hawaii.edu/pili/index.html.

RESOURCES FOR FURTHER INFORMATION AND INSPIRATION

1. *Unnatural Causes* is a seven-part documentary series exploring racial and socioeconomic inequities in health. More information can be obtained at http://unnaturalcauses.org.

2. *Ola: Health is Everything* is a documentary exploring Hawai'i-specific examples of people and communities working toward improving our social determinants of health. More information can be obtained at http://www.olamovie.com.

3. For information on the social and economic inequities across ethnic groups in Hawai'i, read Jonathan Y. Okamura's *Ethnicity and Inequality in Hawai'i* (Philadelphia: Temple UP, 2008).

4. For information of how social status affects the physical and mental health of people, read R. M. Sapolsky, "Social Status and Health in Humans and Other Animals," *Annual Review of Anthropology* 33 (2004): 393–418.

5. Several excellent videos describing the social determinants of health and strategies to improve these determinants can be found on YouTube.com by using the search phrase "social determinants of health."

PRAYING FOR MENDEDNESS

JEFFREY TANGONAN ACIDO

I am an Ilokano-Filipino, born into a working class, farming community in the parched earth of the Ilocos in the Philippines. As far as I can remember, all of my ancestors have tilled the land, growing rice, garlic, and tobacco in order to sustain the difficult life under the five hundred-plus years of colonial occupation by Spain and then the United States. As a result, my soul inherited a language that has shaped the way I engaged the world—in the Philippines when I was young, and in Hawai'i as I grew older. Faith has been the source of my politicization, and locating my identity in faith has allowed me to participate in broader movements of liberation theology and critical education.

Although I speak about my faith as a Christian, I do not mean to equate faith with a religious institution. To have faith does not simply mean one attends church, temple, or synagogue, nor does it mean we derive our moral values solely from sacred books like the Bible, Quran, or Sutras. I speak of faith as a condition of being—a constant engagement with life that leaves us "open" to knowledge and wisdom that we receive from greater forces that we may not yet perceive. To have faith is to be open to the affirmative possibilities of life without the material evidence that we constantly look for.

And while many use religious traditions as a vehicle to receive knowledge and wisdom, belonging to an organized religious institution is not a prerequisite of faith. Instead, I believe one prerequisite of faith is the practice of being open to the many religious traditions that make up the spiritual tapestry of humanity.

Faith is a thread in my life that has grounded and rooted my soul in the struggles to liberate Hawai'i. This is the thread that I want to unravel in hopes that we better understand how people like myself are evoked and provoked by the role of faith and spirituality in caring for and valuing Hawai'i.

THE GENESIS OF MY FAITH

We are bundles of contradictions. How can a liberated Filipino believe so vehemently in the religion of his or her former colonial masters? There is absolutely no rational reason for the subjugated world to adopt a religion that has enslaved and colonized the indigenous peoples of this world. In secular-activist and academic circles I have, numerous times, been questioned about this obvious contradiction by people citing both historical and present injustices, especially among queer and indigenous groups. Whenever they bring this issue to light I always agree with their critique of Christianity; all the more they become frustrated and boggled by this complicated relationship I have with my faith. I can only respond with, "It is the religion that I was born into and the only religion that has moved my soul."

It was not easy coming to terms with my faith. I remember in my childhood years my mother, sister, father, and I would recite the rosary in the evening. Often, my sister and I were lulled into sleep by the rhythmic prayer of the *Hail Marys*. I did not know then the significance of faith and prayer in my mother's life. To my sister and me, this was an obligatory gesture, something that we had to do to appease my mother, to convince her that we were good, god-believing children. However, during my high school years I reached a point at which I could no longer utter words that I did not believe in, especially to something or someone that seemed so intangible, mystical in essence, and contradictory at best. I told my mother that I would no longer join her in doing the rosary and that I needed time to explore my own reasons for why I should or should not believe in the Christian faith. I sensed from her a disappointment, more self-blame than anything else, as if she did not raise us Christian enough, did not take us to church enough, did not hang enough crosses or pictures of Jesus on the wall. It was not that I did not want to believe. Rather I wanted to believe in something with which my soul could move in deep connection.

During my undergraduate years at the University of Hawai' at Mānoa, after moving from one major to another, I decided finally to major in religion. I wanted to explore why people passionately believed in defending a particular faith, even when it seemed to work against or do little for them. The university had a very cynical way of looking at religion. I appreciated the anthropological, social, and scientific approach to the study of religion, but these did not answer the deeper philosophical reasons for why my mother believed in her faith so much, why she prayed so much. I could not agree to see my mother's faith as a pathology. At that time I felt faith needed to be explored on an existential level, so I decided to enter seminary.

JESUS OF THE OPPRESSED

Studying theology in seminary was a turning point in my life. It is where I encountered the Jesus of the oppressed. It is where I found a common language that I have with my former colonial masters. It is the language that I now use to address the contradictions that I face in the cruel reality of oppression. In a tragic sense, Christianity gave my stories—the ones that were burned by the Spanish and then appropriated by the Americans—a place to hide. Our people had no choice but to adopt the Christian faith. Jesus or death: those were the options. We chose Jesus. But a different kind of Jesus—a brown Jesus, the farmer Jesus, the Jesus of the parched earth of the Ilocos, and the Jesus who organized his people against an oppressive empire.

Reading the gospels from the eyes of my own history gave me a better understanding of how my mother came to believe in Christianity. She did not believe in Jesus because of the promises of the afterlife. She believed in his story because she saw her story as the story of Jesus. Jesus, like my mother, grew up poor in a rural community. His father was a carpenter, and his mother got pregnant at a very young age. My mother grew up in a farming community in Ilocos, and she has lived most of her life there surviving on her own because of the heavy migration of her family to Hawaiʻi. She gave birth to me and my sister while my father was in a war in Mindanao, Southern Philippines. I remember her speaking to the hardships of being a young mother with very little financial help. Jesus grew up in the Roman Empire in the outskirts of Nazareth; my mother grew up in the American Empire, on the outskirts of the Ilocos. I understood then why my mother believed in the story of Jesus. It was her way of believing in her own story as well as the values and sentiments that she grew up with. The comparisons can in themselves become an addition to the Christian texts.

The more I read the gospels the more I realized they were my story and the story of other oppressed communities. In many ways it is almost impossible to read the gospels without being radicalized. A close reading of the gospels compels one to be moved against oppression. It is not a simple faith to follow; after all, it cost Jesus his own life.

Reading about the poor man from Nazareth, I am reminded how misunderstood he was—even until the last moment in his life. Everyone in his community wanted a political revolution through armed struggle. He knew that this was not enough, that an armed uprising would not work against the Roman empire, the largest, most ruthless empire of that time. He knew a different kind of revolution needed to be articulated in order to free his own people. His life and his work generated a revolution from the inner depths of the soul. Changes in our own beings, in how we engage the world and transform realities, are far more powerful than a change in political structure. Jesus knew that simply filling the seats of power with his people did not guarantee meaningful change. What good is a political change when colonial values still reside in the soul?

STATIONS OF THE CROSS IN KALIHI

Reflecting back to my time in the seminary, I realize now that theology is really about the study of the Sacred. Theology can be a powerful entry point into the lives and soul of our community. If I wanted to be a part of the communities to which my mother belonged—the Filipino community, the Kalihi community, the larger Hawai'i community—then I had to take seriously what she saw as sacred. The way to engage our communities is not to turn away, but to enter into the realm of their most deeply held beliefs. There is a reason why our communities would rather listen to a priest or pastor than a medical doctor or professor from the university. It is no wonder the world has always paid attention to people like Dorothy Day, Mother Theresa, Dr. Martin Luther King, Jr., Malcolm X, or Mohandas Gandhi, among others. They were able to shift the paradigm of their own people through engaging how they viewed the sacred. The cultural wars that we have in Hawai'i and other parts of the world are really about values that stem from the sacred. What do we hold as sacred? And what meaning does the sacred have in the way we live our lives? These questions were the inspiration for doing the Stations of the Cross in Kalihi.

In terms of religious affiliation, Kalihi is largely a Christian community made up of many different denominations and varied, though more often conservative, theological viewpoints. Home to many indigenous and migrant communities, Kalihi has always suffered from a lack of institutional help, and at the same time, always garnered media attention for all the wrong reasons—violence, drugs, poverty, etc. Local media are typically silent about the positive aspects of Kalihi—our diversity, innovative health care, and food programs, to name a few.

Stations of the Cross in Kalihi came about after attending several prayer circles with Filipina elders who were cancer survivors. They shared with me that they performed Stations of the Cross every Friday at their Roman Catholic home church. They believed that it was prayer and community that helped them overcome cancer. Seeing them battling physical cancer, I realized that our communities were suffering from other forms of cancer that are just as deadly—domestic violence, houselessness, poverty, lack of heath care, racial/ethnic discrimination, militarization of the Land. I envisioned Stations of the Cross to be a vehicle through which the community could move away from political rallies and academic jargon to a more prayerful and communal mourning. The goal was to grieve for our community, to cry and pray together to acknowledge the cancers and wounds that have affected our Kalihi community. Instead of doing the Stations of the Cross in the Church, we decided to pick "stations" in the geography of Kalihi that have impacted the soul of

Kalihi: Kūhiō Park Terrace (affordable housing), Fort Shafter (militarization), Puea Cemetary (burial site of Joseph Kahahawai, murdered by Thalia Massie's husband in 1932, and a reminder of racial injustice in Hawai'i), Farrington High School (public education), and Kokua Kalihi Valley Health Center (affordable health care), to name a few. We walked silently to these sites, prayed, cried, sang, and lifted up the particular needs of the community.

The first Stations was comprised of about twenty-five people, mostly working mothers and fathers, with some students and community leaders. Each year the numbers have increased, with growing numbers of Kalihi community members who would not normally attend political rallies or university events. 2013 marks the fourth year of the Stations, and the gatherings have grown to about 80 to 100 people. Each year the wounds of the community have been articulated by a different group, and, as a result, the themes for each Station have become more complex, encompassing the diversity of voices in our community.

Stations of the Cross has witnessed many silent wounds spoken out loud. A young woman in her twenties spoke to the horrific experience of domestic violence, and how she came to survive that experience. A group of young men spoke about the inferiority complex Filipinos learn in public schools, and how that stunted their own personal ambitions. A Micronesian woman spoke about the military bombings that displaced her family.

There are wounds that spoke to a silent hope as well. Sāmoan and Micronesian communities have come together to grieve a young Sāmoan man's death. Filipinos and Native Hawaiians have shared knowledge of the Land in the back of Kalihi Valley. Elders have taught youth medicine stories that speak of the wonders of the world. During these walks around Kalihi, the pilgrims name their own pains and traumas, hopes and joys.

The stories shared become Holy Scriptures even for these brief moments. What matters in these moments is that the community comes together to share its stories. If we do not tell our own stories, someone else will. And this is the greatest violence that has afflicted our communities. Can you imagine living a life in which our scripts have already been written?

Stations of the Cross is only one of many steps toward healing and social transformation. It is an attempt to engage us in a deeper, more reflexive way of addressing that which we refuse to see, or cannot see because it is too painful to put into words. When our communities can represent their identities without performing, and be witnessed without judging, then we can begin a process of building bridges to each other's Soul. When we are able to reach each other through our soul consciousness, we can begin to be moved from our own woundedness and see the tangibility of healing.

FROM WOUNDEDNESS TO MENDEDNESS

The more I immerse myself in the world of theology and the powerful language of faith, I begin to find words like "solidarity" and "ally" as "safe" words, meant only to distance ourselves from each other when the going gets tough. In the struggle for equity—whether it's queer, indigenous, or class-based struggle—words like "solidarity" and "ally" fail as the starting point within communities of struggle. More and more I am moved by the location of trauma and woundedness as a starting place for decolonization and anti-oppression work. I can only stand with other oppressed peoples when I understand my own oppression. I stand with the oppressed only because I too am oppressed. My soul and body move only because in order for me to heal the Other, I too must heal.

My own woundedness has given me the courage to walk side-by-side with people who have invited me to their struggles. Only when we acknowledge that we cannot heal without one another can we begin to foster a revolution based not on guilt but on love.

I do not yet know what words or concepts can replace "solidarity" or "ally." What I do know is that to build a grounded, more sustainable, and transformative movement, our relationships with each other must be redefined so that our humanity is reaffirmed and our relationality made central. In a world that is increasingly privatizing every aspect of life, we must resist illusionary walls and social constructions that divide our communities. We cannot compare each other's oppressions. No one is more or less than the other. If we see each other as connected through a spiritual umbilical cord, then we must always attend to the physical and spiritual malnourishment of each other—it is to each other that we turn.

Our fragmented lives make it difficult because we see our own woundedness as something that needs to be healed privately. We get trapped because we fail to see that woundedness is not something that we should avoid, but rather an experience that allows us to move with empathy, to bridge with others, and to support each other's healing. In this way, we recover our humanity and remind ourselves of our relationality. In this way, we remind ourselves of the promise of resurrection through the collective act of prayer.

We need to pray together, especially among different faith traditions. It does not matter how we pray because prayer is always a reflexive ritual of history. When we pray with each other we share each other's trauma—what happened—to dream collectively a future that is not fragmented and exclusionary. When we pray together we name our laments—what is happening—so that our collective tears can baptize us in the name of struggle. When we pray we summon a language of hope—what we want to happen—and when we hope, there is always a possibility for redemption.

RESOURCES FOR FURTHER INFORMATION AND INSPIRATION

1. Michael James's website: *Michael D. James: Popular Education 2.0.*, at http://mjcritical-teaching.blogspot.com.
2. Dorothee Soelle, *The Window of Vulnerability* (Philadelphia: Fortress, 1981).
3. Paulo Freire, *Letters to Cristina: Reflections on My Life and Work* (New York: Routledge, 1996).
4. Aurora Levins Morales, "False Memories: Trauma and Liberation," *Medicine Stories: History, Culture and the Politics of Integrity* (Cambridge: South End, 1998): 11–21.
5. Marcela Althaus-Reid, *Indecent Theology* (New York: Routledge, 2001).

EVE

DARLENE RODRIGUES

The oldest Shortraker Rockfish caught off of Alaska was thought to be about 100 years old. NOAA scientists also found that the fish's advanced years had yet to take a toll on its reproductive abilities. "The belly was large," NOAA researcher Paul Spencer told the Associated Press. "The ovaries were full of developing embryos." [1]

For women everywhere with or without embryos and juicy eggs

You are a 60-pound wonder and 44 inches long
with 100 years wrought on your bone
with a bellyfull of babies ready to spawn
Caught in the trawl
Swept in the pull of our nets and our never sated hunger.

You make me ask what is newsworthy
Why men always wonder at our ovaries
And our wombs that develop babies.
Why they puzzle at our ability to still produce even after a certain age.
Why any female becomes a unique specimen of our species
When we go a different path or choose a different fruit.

Why not wonder at your stories from decades of trolling the sea.
What a slow sweep of your memories would dredge.
What it was like to live through two world wars
The Valdez oil spill
The Chernobyl disaster
The invention of the microwave and TV.

When they slit open your bellyfull of eggs
Did it reveal how the rise of warm water
Has been changing your life?

Or what you thought about giving your
Young to a sea that is being poisoned slowly?
What grand epic you would unfold if
We only knew to listen.

We could heed the advice to your spawn in dark times.
How to choose less perilous paths to swim.
How to survive after years and years of growing uncertainty.
How did you wait out the years to etch line-by-line on their
ear bones, awaiting their curving and lengthening
While listening for the crash of coming doom.
What would you tell us, land-bound females
As we give over our seeds to this grim world.

I want to bind up your wishes with mine
Because we navigate through riverways—
The war on terror, the war on drugs, the war on homelessness.
We who swim every day through the seep of violence
Whose lives end at the point of a drone-baited hook,
or the short end of nuclear radiation.

I want women in Guåhan, Afghanistan, America, and Hawai'i to be like you,
With years wrought on our bone
Who still marvel the scientists by our viability and persistence.
To be that Eve who slips silently in the depths of a sea
Undetected by the net of greed and brutality.
Who takes the fruit of knowledge,
Begetting children who never turn a blind eye to truth.
One who swims freely even in the deep, the darkness and the silence.
And for many ages goes fiercely.

NOTE

1. Associated Press, "Fisherman Catch Big, Old Alaska Rockfish," *NBCNEWS.com*, 6 Apr.
    2007.

PUʻUHONUA,
CREATING PLACES OF HEALING

MARK PATTERSON

When I was young growing up in Mākaha, there was a homeless drunkard named Raymond who was always sitting at the front entrance of the 7-11 next to Cornets store. Once or twice a month, my grandmother would go to the store to pick up Raymond and bring him to our house. Grandma would feed him and make him clean the yard. When he was finished she would let him wash up, clothe him, and feed him again. Grandma would give him money, and then Raymond would leave, walking back to 7-11. Shortly thereafter, he would be sitting at 7-11 smelling like alcohol again and begging for money. Finally, after witnessing several cycles of my kupuna's compassion, I questioned my grandmother and asked her why she did what she did for Raymond. My grandmother would smile at me and simply say, "Bumbye you understand."

TRAUMA-INFORMED CARE AT WCCC

This is a story about the Trauma-Informed Care Initiative at the Hawaiʻi Women's Community Correctional Center (WCCC), where we are working within the visionary framework of creating a puʻuhonua—a place to live a forgiven life, a place for transformation, a place that nurtures healing within the individual, family, and community. Taking a community-building approach, we use a *Mind, Body, Spirit, and Place* perspective to address trauma and to work toward community healing and well-being.

I am often asked why I do what I do. For twenty years, I was a correctional officer at Hālawa Correctional Facility and at the Oʻahu Community Correctional Center (OCCC). I then became warden at WCCC. How does a twenty -year veteran adult correctional officer walk into WCCC and start speaking about trauma-informed care and sanctuaries of healing for prisoners?

When I first became the acting warden at the Women's Community Correctional Center, it was important for me to truly understand Hawaiʻi's female offender population. So, I researched, studied, and found out that at a national level, female offenders' crimes were mostly drug-related and non-violent. Female offenders typically followed pathways that separated them from their peers. Common factors, or points along their paths, included 1) undereducation, 2) few employable skills, 3) a lack of positive relationships over time, and 4) substance abuse. Additionally, I learned that with respect to their substance abuse, a large number of women who become addicts have suffered from some kind of significant trauma.

Violence, and the trauma that it causes, is pervasive in our society. The literature shows that the vast majority of women in prison are trauma survivors, as are the majority of all women with substance abuse and/or mental health problems. An understanding of the impact of trauma on women's lives, how trauma survivors develop coping mechanisms that can bring them to the attention of law enforcement, and what strategies can help trauma survivors to heal were all key to changing the environment of WCCC.

Healing and reconciliation are crucial to addressing trauma. For many female offenders, healing is complex because it often involves the home and relationships with other family members. The process of healing and reconciliation is about more than the individual woman. With this in mind, the concept of pu'uhonua, or sanctuary, for these females to seek a safe haven, began to become clear. When I became warden, I remember seeking counsel from my high school spiritual guide, Kahuna Pule David Ka'upu, who provided me with a modern interpretation of the ancient pu'uhonua. Kahu Ka'upu talked about creating a place for forgiveness. Kahu said, "When the female offenders reach the walls of WCCC, they are forgiven for their sins; within the walls they are taught how to live a forgiven life." His guidance has become foundational for me at WCCC.

Working with female offenders and their children requires and produces heaps of compassion. The facts are staggering: usually by the time a woman is convicted and sent to WCCC, she would have already lost custody of her child or children. Indeed, by the time a female offender walks into WCCC, she would have already spent a year in one of the other CCCs on O'ahu, Kaua'i, Hawai'i, or Maui, going through detox. "Waking up" while sentenced in WCCC, the woman realizes she has lost everything. For those women who still have contact with their children, the contact is often limited due to strained relationships between her and her children's caregiver.

At WCCC, we work at reestablishing familial bonds between mothers and their children during the incarceration period. This is important, because children and family are important for the woman's successful transition back into the community. Restorative justice circles are conducted by community organizations, and begin the journey of healing between the family and the incarcerated women. In addition, community faith organizations sponsor events within the prison that allow mothers and their children to participate in activities and share a meal to maintain the familial bond. It is a well-known statistic that over half the children of incarcerated parents will end up in the criminal justice system.

* * * * *

When I was young, dinner was an important part of our day. It began with the setting of the table. Fork on napkin, place on left side of plate; spoon on right; glass on right above spoon. There were ten of us who sat at the table. My father was at the head, and instead of a fork, we placed chopsticks where he sat. To his right was my mother. Between them was my baby brother on the high chair. My younger brother, Matt, and I sat to her right. To my right was my older brother, Kama. At the other end of the table, sitting across from my father, sat the eldest sibling, Kaleo. To my father's left was my grandmother and to her left were my two older sisters, Ulu and Brenda.

Dinner started at six, exactly at six; you didn't want to be late. My grandma or mom cooked the meal. My older brothers would have a hard time making it in on time, especially when surf was up. The latecomers ended up washing dishes. The boys always had to be presentable, with at least a T-shirt on. Dinner began when one of us, picked by dad, said the prayer. Discussion topics would vary depending on dad's questions and who they were directed at. We had to ask permission to leave the table when we were finished. Clearing the table and washing the dishes was a rotated duty managed by mom. This was the structure I was raised in.

Every crime committed today is preceded by a choice. Each choice is preceded by an experience. Each experience comes from a personal journey. Each journey starts from an all-too-familiar environment. We call that environment: home.

Home. What was once a safe place has become a place of complex social dynamics that has, within our most recent history as a people, produced both the victim and the predator—the best of who we are and the worst of who we are. It is a heavenly place and it is a place of hell. Abuse born within the home is a factual reality. It is that which cannot be spoken of. It is our greatest shame. It has been proven to be a lifelong disease. And as a result of trauma in the home, a life journey of rebellion begins. A search for substances to ease the pain. Entering the criminal justice system.

In ancient times, my ancestors lived in villages—clusters of homes for survival and defense. Each home had a purpose, each person had a gift. A gift that sustained the whole, the village. When an offence was committed within the village, processes to rebuild relationships were already in place, to maintain the balance of gifts necessary for the survival of the whole. When offences became greater than the village could handle, areas outside the village were created to sustain the gift. These sanctuaries would house the gift until ready to return to the community. When the individual returned, he or she was accepted back into the community and their gift was utilized again for the betterment of the whole.

In today's world, we have forgotten how to be a village. We have learned how to be selfish. We no longer need our neighbors to survive. And when offences are committed, we simply send the offenders away to places where the light of their gifts is smothered.

And upon their return they are shunned, ignored, a gift no more.

TAKING A BAT TO THE CRIMINAL JUSTICE SYSTEM

Sometimes I wake up in the morning and I just wanna take a hard swing at the criminal justice system with a BAT. This BAT of mine has become an acronym of my work and leadership at WCCC. In order for our staff to be successful in all that we do where we are "AT," I must invite the community to come into WCCC to share with the women. I must be an advocate for programs and initiatives that address their lives Before ("B") they end up at WCCC, in order to prevent young girls from coming to prison in the first place. This includes partnerships with community organizations that work in family court, Child Protective Services, Hawai'i Youth Correctional Facility, Juvenile Detention Center, Home Maluhia, etc. Through these partnerships, we aim to help young women understand the reasons for their entry into the system, and we think about how we can work together to get them out.

In order for our staff to be successful in all that we do where we are "AT," I must also be an advocate for programs and initiatives that address their Transition ("T") out of or after WCCC, in order to stop women from coming back. These partnerships with community organizations include providing support for them in getting jobs, additional schooling, substance abuse relapse prevention, family reunification, and continual spiritual healing. Advocating for and supporting community organizations that assist the women in transition benefit both the women and the government in an inclusive wraparound service approach that attacks the criminal justice system.

About 600 women are currently incarcerated in Hawai'i prisons and jails. They represent several thousand women who are currently in the larger criminal justice system—either on probation, awaiting trial and parole, etc. If you add the two together, we are talking about several thousand children. We haven't even begun to talk about the thousands of women who are not yet in the criminal justice system, who are suffering from the same trauma and addiction behaviors but have yet to commit a crime or be caught. These numbers are unimaginable, yet they are a reality. Every woman and child mentioned above represents a family in crisis.

FROM MODALITIES OF PUNISHMENT TO MODALITIES OF CHANGE

We need to move away from modalities of punishment to modalities of change. Recently I visited the new Juvenile Detention Center in Kapolei. As a professional corrections officer, I was very impressed with the correctional state-of-the-art design and security software. The front entrance included metal detectors, x-ray machines, and private security officers, and was overlooked by a one-way mirrored central control that reminded me of the TSA checkpoint at the Honolulu International Airport. Of the four jails and four prisons in the Department of Public Safety within Hawai'i, none of them has a front entrance security screening process as rigid as the new Juvenile Detention Center.

This example reveals how we create environments that contradict our ability to truly care for our troubled youth. We did not create a place of healing for our children; instead, we built a state-of-the-art Juvenile Correctional Facility, straight out of western thinking and influence. If we build an environment like that, we are going to create people like that. Instead, we need to create environments where people can feel safe enough to change internally. Over 90 percent of female offenders are going to be released. What state of mind do we want them to be in when they return to their communities?

And the problems begin way before people reach the prison, so building better prisons is not enough. How can we create places of healing outside the prison, before the prison? Places of healing, safe places—to feel vulnerable, to trust. When you're going into relapse, or going into hard times, you need to be able to go to a place where you can revitalize your spirit and become pono with yourself. Can Family Court be a place of healing? Can the Department of Education be a place of healing? Can the Juvenile Detention Center be a place of healing? I don't even know what this would look like. But I do know that we need to be a village again. Like an ancient village, public and private agencies have gifts. We need to manage these gifts together, strategically, to align them in ways to collectively change the criminal justice system.

It is wrong for us to believe that changing prisons alone will solve everything. We need to think bigger, and partner with others to think about ways to heal our communities. For example, Hina Mauka, a community-driven Substance Abuse Treatment Center under the leadership of Alan Johnson has adopted more trauma-informed care in its treatment approach. They believe they are a place of healing. Another example—The Pū'ā Foundation, under the guidance of Executive Director Toni Bissen, is the lead community organization involved in the WCCC trauma-informed care initiative. The foundation's goal is that in a world of differences, it chooses to make a difference. Another example—Ah Lan Diamond is currently leading restoration efforts to return Waimea Valley to its historic role as a puʻuhonua. The partnership created between WCCC and these three organizations has goals to treat clients and offenders, and their families, and provide them with experiential opportunities within the valley that can enhance internal transformation and create a sacred place for them to come to. It is our cultural belief that the land will heal the hands that work it, and then the land and its people will flourish.

* * * * *

When we started training WCCC staff and community volunteers in trauma-informed care, I began sharing the story of my grandmother and Raymond. It was my intent to tell them of their kuleana to care not only for each other, but to those among us who have nothing. We are all connected. Together with understanding and compassion we are stronger and can make a difference. Stronger children, stronger families, stronger communities. Grandma, I understand.

RESOURCES FOR FURTHER INFORMATION AND INSPIRATION

1. TEDx, "The Criminal Justice System: A Place of Healing: Mark Patterson at TEDxHonolulu." You can watch this online at http://www.youtube.com/watch?v=8uCC3DedyfU.

2. Wellspring Covenant Church, "Kids day with care givers June 2013/Prison Monologue." You can watch this online at https://vimeo.com/71799573.

3. Office of Hawaiian Affairs and the Department of Public Safety, "OHA Puʻuhonua Summit: Creating a Place of Refuge." featuring Ted Sakai (PSD), Kamanaʻopono Crabbe (OHA), and Toni Bissen (Pūʻā Foundation). You can watch this online at http://vimeo.com/52980300.

4. Kimberlee Bassford, "Prison Monologues Opening 2012." You can watch this online at http://www.youtube.com/watch?v=3m1JtTbPFNo.

5. "A Road to Puʻuhonua" discusses the concept of puʻuhonua from the paʻahao point of view. You can watch this online at ʻŌlelo.net, at http://olelo.granicus.com/MediaPlayer.php?view_id=30&clip_id=32625.

6. Darby Penney, "Creating a Place of Healing and Forgiveness: The Trauma-Informed Care Initiative at the Women's Community Correctional Center of Hawaii," *National Center for Trauma-Informed Care*, 2013. You can read this online at http://www.nasmhpd.org/docs/NCTIC/7014_hawaiian_trauma_brief_2013.pdf.

HE WELO

HĀWANE RIOS

Thriving
Temple
Unwavering
Boundless
Energy
Essence
Clarity
Unity
Frequency
Vibration
Highest
Upmost
Sacred
Brilliant
Majestic
Birthright

KA WEHENA / THE RISING

As I step out into the darkness, a peaceful calm comes over my being. Shades of blue paint the expansive sky, getting lighter as I journey to the top. A cloudbank comes to greet the summit with a gift of lei for an old friend. The cool mist of Lilinoe dances playfully with the breeze of Līhau. A gust of wind awakens my spirit and sends an electric chill through my feet, landing at my very core. The first rays of sun touch the great realm of Kanaloa and shine ever so slightly, like the dew on the wings of an ʻiwa bird in the morning. Kūkahauʻula spreads his warm red kapa cloak over the majestic mountain and embraces cherished Poliʻahu with a kind of love that is both rare and true. As I lift my arms to the mighty Wākea in silent prayer, while grounding deep into the great Papawaliʻinuʻu, a divine energy trembles on the earth and reflects in the sky. My eyes wander to the last of the gleaming stars above that whisper the stories of creation, and I am forever changed. E ala e ke ʻāpapalani e. ʻO Mauna a Wākea ke ʻāiwaiwa laʻa kapu o Hawaiʻinuiākea.

KA PILINA / THE CONNECTION

The profound connection I feel to Mauna a Wākea is so deep, so clear and unwavering, that it is almost indescribable. My childhood memories are filled with moments of looking to this sacred mountain in awe of its incredible vastness and unprecedented beauty. I was raised to honor the mother earth and her marvelous bounty; to know the powerful relationship between human, earth, sky, sea, and creature; and to understand that we are not separate but one with the universe. These teachings allowed me to open myself to the wonder of the spirit world and to tap into the pure and all-encompassing interconnectedness of which my ancestors were masters. Like all of us, my spiritual journey began long before my soul came back and manifested in this body form. I am humbled to have come down bringing the gift of sight with me, a gift that many in my family line have carried with them for generations. I am no longer afraid to talk about what I see and hear in the spirit world, for this is a part of my history, my culture, and genealogy. However, when I speak about this, I do so in trust and with the utmost respect and gratitude to the realm that has shaped me in every way.

KA HOʻINA / THE RETURN

The first time that I can recall an encounter with the spirit in full detail was when I traveled to Kauaʻi at the age of ten. I can still remember sitting up in my bed and looking around me with elements of confusion and fear. When I finally settled into the magic happening around me, I realized the magnitude of the moment and chose to accept it with gratitude. As time passed and I grew older and more influenced by the weight of society, I became fearful, and asked that this gift be taken from me. I was told that only when I was ready, open, and clear of the fear and doubt would I be able to see again. Years passed, and I grew further away from my center and true self. I allowed myself to get so enraptured by the human experience and drama of it all that

I almost forgot the teachings I was brought up with. I am grateful for that time of my life for it allowed me to explore and venture down paths that led to many of my most intense and insightful life lessons. Each of these experiences has taught me great things about perseverance, forgiveness, and courage. The path back to the center, to the mauli, began when I planted my feet on the summit and bowed down to the power of the elements. A promise and commitment to the mountain was made and has since then guided my every step as a kanaka Hawaiʻi of this land.

KA HOʻOHIKI / THE PROMISE

In 2011, my family became petitioners in the contested case hearing for the proposed Thirty-Meter Telescope to be built on the Northern Plateau of Mauna a Wākea. My younger sister, a seer of the Moʻo realm, was asked by the great Moʻoinānea of Waiau if we as family could try one more time to protect and save the mountain. There were specific and clear instructions as to how we should proceed. We were to do this with the highest frequency of love and compassion. As a passionate young woman, this instruction was difficult to grasp at times, especially when standing in the face of adversity and criticism. However, my family kept strong in what was just, true, and in complete alignment with our spiritual guides and ancestors. Our growth as individuals, as a family, and as a community is deeply transcendental and rooted in sacred ceremony.

This ceremony has brought boundless gifts of insight to many, and created connections to native people around the world. I am humbled to have been given the chance to stand next to healers of different nations, histories, and beliefs; seers from the forests of Brazil to the cold peaks of Mount Shasta; and mediums of all ages, sizes, and colors. To gather in a circle with people that know the relationship of oneness is to elevate to a higher understanding of life.

Learning the art of coming back to center, I slowly began to open myself up to my own spirit, in turn lifting the fear to which I once held so tightly. Standing upon Puʻu Kūkahauʻula at sunset, looking to its immeasurable shadow in the distance, I witnessed the opening of a portal of crystal energy that descended from the sky and rose from the earth. The prophecy of Kapihe—"E iho ana ʻo luna, e piʻi ana ʻo lalo, e hui ana nā moku e kū ana ka paia"—took on a new depth of meaning for me at that moment.

I was led to a place on the mountain not far from the main road going up to the summit. In mid-ceremony, I hiked across the sharp and uneven rocks to find a platform with large stones standing erect surrounding the area. There was a hole in one of the largest stones and in an instant I felt the urge to kneel down and exchange hā, breath. When I opened my eyes, I saw seven men of the spirit world standing beside the stones, each one holding a staff, each one ancient and wise. I asked who they were and they told me that they were of the highest star counsel of Kāne, what I like to call the Kāne Repairers or Ke Ao o Kāne. They gifted messages of the star realm and shed light on the great power of the temple Mauna a Wākea and her connection to all things. They took me to explore the brilliance of the cosmos, the expanse of the universe, and the many incandescent worlds. There are no words that can begin to express my ample gratitude and respect for these beings. Ke Ao o Kāne have given me one of the greatest gifts, a glimpse into the relationship my ancestors once had with the sky, earth, and spirit.

KE HOʻĀLA / THE AWAKENING

These experiences on the Mauna led me to the most pivotal time in my life thus far: my journey to the eldest atoll in our island chain, Hōlanikū (known as Kure Atoll). Upon graduating from the University of Hawaiʻi at Hilo with my Bachelors Degree in Hawaiian Language with an emphasis in Performing Arts, I took a trip with the Ola Nā Iwi course to Pihemanu (also known as Kuaihelani and Midway Atoll) in the Northwestern Hawaiian Islands, or Papahānaumokuākea. During the week we were there, I finetuned some of the "tools" in my spiritual toolbox, recentering and grounding my piko, calling in my spirit guides with purpose, and closing myself off to possible incorporations or mediumship. Pihemanu allowed me the time and space to surrender to the enchantment of mother earth and her many children. The energy of the beings of the sky realm that manifested in bird form renewed old perspectives of wildlife and taught me of our inherent connection to all living beings. I was able to see their cycle of life within the week I spent there; life, death, and birth. I was able to see the path of the sun standing on one place of the atoll and was there to feel the vibration of the sun and the moon on the horizon at the same time. Each moment gifted new truths of life that I had only sparsely given myself the opportunity and freedom to experience. My short time on Pihemanu opened a new path, and I was ready and willing to follow it wherever it chose to go.

I remember quite distinctively creating an affirmation while on Pihemanu that I would one day return to Papahānaumokuākea. I didn't know how, only that I would somehow, some way. Upon returning to Hilo, I felt an incredible yearning in my very core to set my eyes on the atolls of the Northwest and to learn from these ancient lands. A few months went by, and I once again became accustomed to the hustle and bustle of life and its many turns. Then one day I received an email from a dear friend and fellow traveler to Pihemanu about the need for an emergency hire out on Kure Atoll, the eldest island in our archipelago. I had some conversations with a few people who had made it out all the way to Kure and I was moved by their stories. As I read the email, I felt a jolt in my naʻau strongly pulling me out of all that was familiar and comfortable into an unforeseen, seven-month journey.

I had only three days to give my final decision and then a few weeks to gather myself and all the gear and necessities that I needed. I was headed into a winter field camp with little or no experience about real hard labor or working with wildlife. And there would only be five of us on the team for the whole time! I never knew if I would even have the strength, courage, or perseverance to endure such an adventure. While the anxiety, fear, and doubt coursed through my body, the underlining, clear voice of wisdom within carried me through.

My family asked me where I wanted to go for ceremony before I left, and the first place that called to me was the great Mauna a Wākea. A few of us made the familiar journey up the mountain and headed to the Ke Ao o Kāne site. We made our way across the uneven terrain and unstable rocks to that place where, for the first time, I had experienced such a strong connection to the spirit world. I could feel the presence of the ancient ones surround me and trusted their guidance to move forward on this journey, with no question. I felt something that I had only felt a few times before: total and complete certainty. When we finished our ceremony, we hiked to Lake Waiau to collect water to take on the journey. We chanted, sang, and gave hoʻokupu to set the foundation and call in the guardians of protection. I stood and secured my roots deep into the earth, then lifted my hands up to the sky to gather in the clarity that rested above. The vibrations healed any of the fears and doubts I once had. I carried my constant and true love for the tallest mountain of our land to connect to the lowest of our islands, which was once a mountain itself. This was the physical form of my path inward then outward, a path that carried a kind of balance for which I had always searched.

KA HULIHIA / THE CHANGE

The time spent on our eldest of lands gifted me with the most profound lessons and experiences. Like most long journeys, the beginning transitions were not always easy and often were very uncomfortable. This place was like a mirror; it showed and reflected some things that I was ready to see, and many things that I was not ready to see. I was given the opportunity to face some very real and harsh realities about the person I had become through my decisions and actions. I replayed in my head many different scenarios of situations

I had no control over; I found myself reliving conversations and quarrels I once had. Eventually I decided to make a positive shift, and much of my time alone went into concentrating on the beauty of forgiveness and the power of release. As each full moon washed me clean of past attachments to habits that no longer served me, my connection to nature and spirit grew so strong that they were inseparable. I was in a place where there was a balance and reverence for the wildlife and the land, and where money and fortune held no real power. It was the first time in my life that I truly understood what solitude really meant, and it was not loneliness. It was oneness.

Lessons came with the tide, and surged as the moon waxed and waned. When the winter birds started coming in to mate and nest, the whole island was filled with dance and song. The amount of healing that occurred just by watching and listening to them was such a great gift. I could sit for hours and be continually filled with the sound of the resonant tone of the earth mother that was reflected in the elements. Each moment there led me to understand better the connection our ancestors once had with the earth. It simultaneously gave me hope because I now know such connection is still possible. The more time passed, the more I opened myself to the gifts of sight and hearing in both the physical and spiritual worlds. The most beautiful sound became the sound of my own inner voice, my naʻau, my unique intuition. There came a time when this voice was so strong and so loud that I had no other choice but to follow the agreements of the soul with complete trust. And yet I was and will continue to be deeply humbled in the gratitude I feel for our eldest land. Kau kehakeha Hōlanikū i ka makani Hāliʻimālō. Ola i ka wewe kapu o ka moana nui ākea.

KE KUMU / THE SOURCE

In writing this piece, I chose to open and share parts of my very deep and personal journey inward and my experiences of the spirit world. I consciously make this choice to be vulnerable because it is not just the right time to do so but the most imperative time. We are living in an era when the health and well-being of our entire planet and all of its inhabitants are threatened daily by our decisions and actions as human beings. Many of our young ones are growing up looking down at tiny screens for entertainment instead of exploring the greatness of the outdoors. There are many times that I myself am completely distracted by our new technologies and various ways of communication. I find myself rushing through tasks and thinking ahead about what I have to do next. In those moments I tell myself to take a breath, ground, go outside, look up to our great mountain, and remember the sacred union once again.

I have learned that to rekindle the relationship with the earth is to simply go to the earth. It is gifting yourself a moment to lay down on the land and communicate with the sky. It is going outside to plant a seed and make a vow to nurture and watch it grow. It is savoring the sweetness and the brilliance of a starry night. It is taking your children or relatives to the mountains or the beaches that shaped you. It is lifting your arms up to the sun and letting the rays reflect your own inner light. It is knowing, really knowing, that you come from generations of ancient gifts, of strength, of love, and of divine connection. One of the most beautiful lessons I learned in this wonderful journey is that you need not travel far to return to center, for you possess within your spirit all of the wisdom needed to guide you. The earth mother, Papahānaumoku, the great healer and teacher, is all around us and resides within us. She is a living and breathing source that connects everything within to everything without. Let us all ignite that source within, ke kumu ola, heal together as a people, and forward in unity. Ola.

KA WELONA / THE SETTING

Standing with my feet on the most ancient sands of all of Hawai'i, I watch as the sun reaches the end of its path, leaving glimmering truths on the lagoon. A flash of green illuminates my eyes for just a moment as the last tones of a chant leave my lips. Thousands of wings decorate the purple expanse and slowly transform into gleaming stars. Oceans of wisdom wash over me like a prayer, and just like the tide I breathe in my power, then release my strength onto the shore, to find that with every wave a new truth is born. Then I see her in the distance, what seems to be the magnificent Mauna a Wākea nestled in the clouds. With arms extended she becomes a sail navigating through the realms of the cosmos, her body the vessel that carries the eternal song. She begins to hum gently with the eastern winds, beckoning me to sing the refrain I was created for. With grace she waits for the last sound to walk its path. Glancing to the sea of reflections, she becomes a mirror of all. I turn to dance in the brilliance of her shadow to find that I was always her and she is forever me. Ua ao, ua ola, ua noa, noa hōnua. 'Āmama ua noa a lele wale ē.

To all of my relations,
na Hāwane Rios
no Pu'ukapu, Waimea, Moku o Hawai'i

RESOURCES FOR FURTHER INFORMATION AND INSPIRATION

On Mauna a WāKea:

1. "Issues: Sacred Summits," *Kahea.org.* You can find this online at http://kahea.org/issues/sacred-summits.
2. The film *Mauna Kea Temple Under Siege*, Nā Maka o ka ʻĀina, 2006.
3. *Pōhakuloa*, a short film by Ruben Carrillo for Kamakakoʻi (OHA), 2013. You can watch this online at http://vimeo.com/63867248.
4. Hawaiians on both sides of the Mauna a Wākea debate:

    • Kealoha Pisciotta, "Not the Whole Story about TMT," OpEd piece from *Hawaii Tribune-Herald,* May 9, 2013. You can read this online at http://kahea.org/blog/not-the-whole-story-about-tmt.

    • E. Kalani Flores and B. Pua Case, "Mauna a Wākea is our Piko," *Ka Wai Ola o OHA* 30.7 (July 2013): 27.

    • Chad Kālepa Baybayan, "Modern exploration is consistent with past practices," *Ka Wai Ola o OHA* 30.7 (July 2013): 27. These are two parts of a "Room for Debate" op-ed page in *Ka Wai Ola o OHA.*

On Papahānaumokuākea, the Northwestern Hawaiian Islands:

1. *Papahānaumokuākea Marine National Monument* website, at http://www.papahanaumokuakea.gov.
2. Kekuewa Kikiloi, "Rebirth of an Archipelago: Sustaining a Hawaiian Cultural Identity for People and Homeland," *Hūlili: Multidisciplinary Research on Hawaiian Well-Being* 6 (2010): 73–115. You can read this online at http://www.ksbe.edu/spi/Hulili/Hulili_vol_6/5_Rebirth_of_an_Archipelago.pdf.

ALOHA

HALEY KAILIEHU

DEFENDING HAWAI'I WITHOUT MACHINE GUNS

JAMES KOSHIBA

We love Hawai'i. The signs of that love are smoothed over the rear windows of our trucks and cars—"Maui Built," "Moku Nui," "HI Life"; all declare our island pride. Like all loves, however, this one can tip toward fear and anger when the things we treasure appear threatened. Debates over what's best for Hawai'i—wind, geothermal, urbanization, the Superferry, and more—thus devolve into open combat, fracturing our otherwise tight-knit communities. Even our bumper stickers evince this tension, urging us to "Live Aloha" while pledging to "Defend Hawai'i"—with a machine gun.

Some might say that public discourse in Hawai'i is no more polarized, or even polite, compared to other states. Yet this raises the question of whether an island people, so closely connected and interdependent, can afford to adopt a continental style of civic debate. One thing is certain: the number of conflicts and their urgency will only increase in the years ahead. Precious natural resources will become more precious under the strain of population growth; government budgets will be stretched thin as obligations to retirees come due; the things we love about Hawai'i will continue to be under pressure, from inside and out.

As these pressures mount, we would benefit from a new way of fighting for what we believe in. We could use a new kind of activism that accounts for the unique dimensions of island living and honors island values of humility, aloha, and kuleana. We need a way of fighting over the things we love, over Hawai'i, that holds space for both peace and justice once the fighting is done.

But what would such an island-style activism look like in practice?

AN EXAMPLE OF ISLAND ACTIVISM

I was wrestling with this question a few years ago, when I was invited to participate in an "Environmental Justice Tour" of the Wai'anae Coast of O'ahu organized by the advocacy organization KAHEA. The tour took us to landfills, power plants, waste spills, and illegal dumps scattered from Nānā-kuli to Kaʻena Point.

Following the tour, we sat with a group of kūpuna, the Concerned Elders of Waiʻanae, each one an accomplished activist and community leader, for an intimate discussion. I wanted to ask for their thoughts on island-style activism, but I didn't have the words at the time. Instead, I asked, "How do you get people to join you in your activism, particularly your non-activist neighbors, family, and friends?"

Each kupuna offered sound advice, but one, Auntie Alice Greenwood, shared a powerful story. The year before, Alice had been homeless, living on the beach and caring for her hānai son. There were many challenges living on the beach, but Alice found one aspect of houseless life especially painful: each day, she saw young children playing unsupervised in the filthy beach park bathrooms.

Now, a typical beach park restroom on Oʻahu is already a dicey affair. Imagine the filth of a restroom serving beach-goers *and* a community of several hundred homeless residents. Alice agonized over what to do. Should she tell parents to keep their keiki out of the bathrooms? Or chastise those who dirtied the bathroom? (It tended to be a known handful of people.) She decided to do neither. Instead, without fanfare, she committed to wake every morning at dawn, and clean the bathroom herself, top to bottom.

When her neighbors on the beach realized what she was doing, they thought she was crazy, and politely told her so. "Alice, no sense—the bathroom going be all pilau by lunchtime." "Alice, you one kupuna. Let somebody else do 'um." Each time, her response was the same: "I *have* to do this. Kids play in here sometimes."

After a few weeks of cleaning every day, some of Alice's homeless neighbors offered to pitch in: "Take a break today, Alice. I got it." Still there were the cynics, "You guys cannot last." After a month, a shift system had emerged, with people rotating cleaning duties. Even the hardest cynics took turns standing *outside* the bathroom, hosing off people's feet *before* they entered the bathroom, reminding them, "We *gotta* keep this place clean. Kids play in here sometimes."

Without any resources or authority—indeed, without demanding anything of others—Alice moved her entire community. The power of her action could be described as leading by example, but it was also more than that. Alice took responsibility for a problem that was not of her making, an unpleasant task that few others wanted to tackle. It was this act of responsibility-taking and sacrifice—beyond any reasonable expectation—that jarred the conscience of others and moved them to action.

EXPERIMENTS IN ISLAND-STYLE ACTIVISM

When I met Alice, I was staff at Kanu Hawaii, a new, grassroots non-profit working to "build social movement for a more sustainable, compassionate, and resilient Hawai'i." After listening to Alice, I began to see Kanu's work in a new light, as a series of experiments in island-style activism.

From the beginning, Kanu Hawaii asked people to "join" the movement by making a *personal commitment* to a change in their own life that modeled sustainability, compassion, or resilience. Some joined with simple commitments: walking or biking to work once a week to cut emissions, buying locally grown food to shape a more resilient economy. Others were more ambitious, involving their entire family in monthly service projects, growing their own food, downsizing their cars. Kanu's online community enabled members to join others' commitments with a click, or write their own. Commitments were published online as part of each member's public profile.

The idea of building a movement rooted in personal commitments spread quickly. In Kanu's first two years (2008–2009), nearly 10,000 people "joined" and shared their commitments online. "I will . . ." became the unofficial slogan of the organization.

Initially, I understood "I will . . ." as a call to lead by example and shorthand for a pledge to change. After meeting Auntie Alice, though, I came to read "I will . . ." as a statement of *kuleana*: "I will take responsibility for changes I wish to see in the world, even when it's not my job, and even if that change seems beyond my control."

In 2009, once a few thousand people had "joined" Kanu, we began to search for ways to take the spirit of "I will . . ." into advocacy. We launched campaigns that called people to group action: an Eat Local Challenge, an Energy Conservation Month, a Live Aloha Campaign, and more. Many of these campaigns aimed at changing personal behavior, but three aimed at politics and public policy. It was these three campaigns that offered the richest lessons in island-style activism.

ENERGY AND CLIMATE POLICY

In 2009, frustrated with the slow pace of lawmaking around climate change, we launched our first policy campaign urging the State Legislature to pass bills related to clean energy. Several environmental advocacy groups were organizing rallies and protests at the State Capitol. We wanted to organize a political demonstration in the spirit of "I will . . ."

Instead of marching on the Capitol, our members spent a day in the underground Capitol parking lot checking tire pressure on more than 300 cars belonging to lawmakers and their staff. We left reminders on the windshields if tires were low, e.g., "Your left rear tire is underinflated. Keeping tires properly inflated will save you a full tank of gas and prevent almost 250 lbs of greenhouse gas emissions each year."

We took turns going upstairs to visit with lawmakers, hands blackened by the work below, to swap incandescent light bulbs for more energy-efficient CFLs. And while there, we delivered a message to each lawmaker: "We are here today, checking tire pressures and changing bulbs because we care deeply about energy and climate issues. We are willing to do our part to tackle this important problem. We ask you, our leaders, to do your part by passing these important bills." The message included a list of the bills we were following.

This was our first attempt to use an ethic of "I will . . ." for activism in politics and policy, an arena where activism tends to focus on "I want . . ." and "You will. . . ." It is, of course, impossible to trace legislative action to any particular group or influence, but there were some indications that Kanu's work had an effect. Four out of the five energy bills we targeted passed, and a few lawmakers referenced our unique demonstration in their floor speeches.

FURLOUGH FRIDAYS

Later that year and into 2010, parents of public school students across Hawai'i were in an uproar over "Furlough Fridays." Negotiations between the Hawai'i State Teachers Association (HSTA) and the Governor had produced a teachers' contract that cut seventeen days from the school year. Instead of falling on holidays or planning days, the HSTA had negotiated on the basis that any cuts would mean fewer *instructional* days. This bargaining tactic, and the parties' failure to find a different solution, left Hawai'i with the shortest school year in the country in a State where students already lagged behind peers on the continent.

Despite the public outcry, the Governor and the union refused to reopen talks. The public turned to the Legislature in the hopes that partially restoring budget cuts would get the parties back to the table, but leaders in the House and Senate pointed to the Governor and the Teachers Union as the ones to blame. The Governor and Union blamed each other, but also pointed to the Legislature for cutting the education budget in the first place.

Families scrambled to find alternatives. Parents at some schools pooled their money and offered to pay teachers to teach on Furlough Fridays. Some teachers offered to volunteer their time, noting that they normally worked on holidays and weekends anyway. Teachers were told by union leaders that this would weaken the union's bargaining position, and told by Principals that it would expose teachers to personal liability.

As frustrated parents began to organize, Kanu played a support role. We chose more traditional protest techniques: a rally at the Capitol; a statewide petition; sign-holding outside of HSTA; a sit-in in the Governor's Office and a camp-out at Washington Place. Rallies and sit-ins attracted local and national media coverage, and Kanu collected more than 10,000 petition signatures in two months to support parent efforts, but still the parties did not budge.

Even at the time, this campaign felt like a departure from activism rooted in "I will. . . ." Its methods were designed to force expedient change by amassing public opinion. In hindsight, we should have been more creative in our activism. For instance, we might have organized volunteers, including teachers, to offer educational activities on Furlough Fridays *on school grounds*. We would have faced arrest, but the action would have juxtaposed the good will of volunteer educators against arguments over liability and bargaining strength, laying bare the adult interests standing between kids and school. In the end, the Furlough Fridays dragged on through the end of the 2009–10 school year.

REVIVING POLITICAL ENGAGEMENT

A third learning experience was Kanu Hawaii's campaign to revive voter engagement during the 2012 election cycle. In the span of fifty years, Hawai'i had gone from having the highest voter turnout in the US to the lowest in the country. We launched a campaign to address the concern that the people's voices, already fading in volume, were being drowned out by the rising volume of money in politics.

We reached out door-to-door and online to re-engage people in the political process. Volunteers knocked on doors to gather input for a "crowdsourced" candidate questionnaire, and registered people to vote. With the help of No Vote No Grumble, we were able to concentrate outreach in low-turnout communities along the Wai'anae Coast, Windward O'ahu, Waimanalo, and the University of Hawai'i at Mānoa.

Volunteers knocked on 2,000 doors in low-turnout communities, registered more than 2,500 new voters, and drew 26,000 individuals to read-up about candidates before election day. In the end, 88 percent of those we contacted turned out to vote, compared to a historical turnout of 40–50 percent in the surrounding community. The entire effort was run by a group of mostly 20- and 30-somethings who learned grassroots organizing by doing it, and spent nights and weekends reaching out to increase the vote.

While out canvassing, we were asked more than once, "Why are you doing this when you could be at the beach or watching TV?" And, "If people don't vote it's because they're too lazy or apathetic, it's not your job to get them to vote, is it?" To which our standard response was, "Hawai'i has the lowest voter participation in the nation. We want to be sure the people's voices are heard."

PRINCIPLES OF ISLAND STYLE ACTIVISM

Activism today is synonymous with the rally, the boycott, the protest and petition—tactics used to amass just enough power (or the apearance of it) to force change, regardless of what fellow citizens or leaders themselves may believe. Reflecting on Kanu Hawai'i's campaigns, I see a different approach. When it worked best, Kanu's activism embodied an "I will . . ." ethic; it aimed at changing hearts and minds, as well as policies and institutions. I drew the conclusion that there is great, untapped power in activism rooted in "I will . . ."

Though what passes for activism today is mostly coercive, there is a long tradition of activism in Hawai'i designed to change consciousness along with institutions. Indeed, the Hawaiian cultural and political renaissance of the late-twentieth century was sparked by such actions: a daring landing amidst bombs still falling; the tuning of a guitar in the old "slack-key" fashion; navigating by the stars. Each of these acts had and continues to have political, economic, and institutional consequences, but they were intended first and foremost to speak to the heart, mind, and na'au. Gandhi called this "*satyagraha*," an "insistence on truth." Martin Luther King called it "soul force." Thich Naht Hahn calls it "interbeing." All point to the power of individuals to transform society through selfless acts that raise nagging moral questions.

Kanu's experiments helped me see the elements of effective island-style activism:

1) Sacrifice: Demonstrators must be willing to experience discomfort in order to raise a moral question. Meaningful sacrifice doesn't require risking life or limb. It can be as simple as doing that which no one else wants to—cleaning a beach park bathroom, going door-to-door on a weekend, or getting your hands dirty checking tire pressure.

2) Responsibility: The sacrifice should convey a willingness to take responsibility for a community problem, above and beyond what others would expect. When a problem seems intractable because parties blame each other—the dirty bathroom, the school furlough—it presents an opportunity for provocative responsibility-taking. If people ask, "Why are you doing this when it's not your fault?" as they did when we went door-to-door for voter engagement, it's a sign that you're on the right track.

3) Service: The action must be more than mere street theater. It must produce tangible, direct benefit for others. The impact of changing light bulbs and checking tire pressures at the State Capitol amounted to measurable reductions in emissions and oil, whether or not the policies we advocated passed. If what you are doing produces tangible good for the community, regardless of the political statement it makes, it helps place the act itself above question.

4) Integrity: Behind powerful civic actions lie powerful values. Being clear on what these values are, and ensuring that your actions are consistent with those values, down to the smallest detail, creates the conditions for resonant messages. At every Furlough Friday event we organized, we offered childcare. At every meeting for environmental campaigns, we brought reusable plate ware, mugs, and water bottles instead of disposables. Going door to door, we practiced asking and listening, and avoided telling or selling, modeling the kind of democratic leadership we hoped for.

5) Self-replicating: Ideally, an action is simple enough for others to copy on their own. Self-replicating actions become social movements. The tire pressure demonstration at the State Capitol prompted calls from neighbor islanders who wanted to replicate the demonstration at their County Councils.

None of our campaigns at Kanu Hawaii met all these criteria. But as we developed a clearer understanding of what made a demonstration compelling, we strove for these elements more and more consistently. I continue to believe that deliberate use of these elements in civic action can be the basis for a new and powerful island-style activism.

CONCLUSION

Of the elements above, I believe sacrifice and responsibility are most essential. When we see people willing to suffer for something they believe in; when someone takes responsibility for a problem that is not their fault or within their control—such actions have transformative power. Self-sacrifice and responsibility-taking are the building blocks for political actions that shake awake the conscience of a community, sparking change in allies and adversaries alike. They can yield lasting change in our policies and institutions as well.

I am not suggesting that we abandon the use of political and economic force. The use of force may be necessary in some situations, and it's been used successfully in nonviolent movements of the past. Nor am I suggesting that we avoid conflict altogether. Indeed, one of the great dangers of island living is that we can be "too nice," avoid conflict, and let injustice slide in order to keep the peace.

What I am suggesting is that the use of *soul force,* as King called it, is notably missing from our arsenal today. And the absence of soul force is a dangerous deficiency for an island society. If coercion and force become the only ways we settle differences in the pursuit of change, then we risk tearing at the fabric of the very community we love.

The cultural pressures of the continent will continually urge us toward heavy-handed uses of political and economic power—the sound bite, the political ad, the big-budget PR campaign, the casting of opponents as demons—to win our fights with each other. Creative, nonviolent activism must have a permanent home in Hawai'i, a place to nurture and grow, and a training ground for those willing to practice it. We must build a heart for island-style activism that is resilient and enduring.

If we cannot, then one day soon we will have only machine guns to defend Hawai'i from ourselves and from each other. Then, we islanders, for whom navigation is so essential, will have truly lost our way.

RESOURCES FOR FURTHER INFORMATION AND INSPIRATION

1. Parker Palmer, *Healing the Heart of Democracy: The Courage to Create a Politics Worthy of the Human Spirit* (San Francisco: Jossey Bass, 2011).
2. Thich Nhat Hanh, *The Art of Power* (New York: Harper One, 2007).
3. Homer Jack, *The Gandhi Reader: A Sourcebook on His Life & Writings* (New York: Grove, 1994).
4. Martin Luther King, Jr., *A Testament of Hope: The Essential Writings & Speeches of Martin Luther King, Jr.* (New York: HarperCollins, 1991).
5. The Kanu Hawaii website, at http://www.kanuhawaii.org.

CEREMONY

NO'U REVILLA

Ladies and gentlemen, are we are gathered here today to join together in unholy matrimony these freshwaters of Hawai'i to this state of Hawai'i?

Do you, state, take these waters from our lives, to have and to own from this day forward, for development and profits, in sickness and drought, to divert, privatize, and distribute 'til poetry, sustainable practices, and informed protest do you part?

And do you, freshwaters of Hawai'i, take this state, to be your deeply unfortunate husband? To permit his narrow mind and slippery fingers their illusions, as if he could actually contain you, as if his green-green pockets could hold your roaring body, as if he could "I do" you?

And he hasn't met your salt water cousins yet.

His people don't have a word for the place where fresh waters and salt waters meet, eat, and genealogize, so on your wedding night, as you're remembering the cold, dark mountains you come from, your cousins will be rising and rising to find you, and your deeply unfortunate husband will be taken out to sea.

CONTRIBUTORS

Jeffrey Tangonan Acido is a 1.5-generation Ilokano-Filipino immigrant to Hawai'i. He is completing his PhD in Education at the University of Hawai'i at Mānoa. His research interests are in intersections of Critical Pedagogy, Popular Education, Liberation/Postcolonial Theology, and Ethnic Studies. In the near future he hopes to build a Center for Popular Education and Ancestral Wisdom in Hawai'i.

U'ilani Arasato has been writing poetry for about four to five years. She is a new mother and a growing student. She's continuing her education in order to be a Senior English teacher for Wai'anae High School.

Kamanamaikalani Beamer is an Assistant Professor in the Hui 'Āina Momona program, split between the University of Hawai'i at Mānoa School of Hawaiian Knowledge and School of Law. In the Richardson School of Law he is based with the Ka Huli Ao, Center for Excellence in Native Hawaiian Law. He received a bachelor's degree in both Philosophy and Hawaiian Studies in 2002, and a PhD in Cultural Geography in 2008. He is a former 'ōiwi Ake Akamai doctoral fellow as well as a Mellon-Hawai'i post-doctoral Fellow, and a codirector of the First Nations' Futures Fellowship Program. His research publications and interests focus on indigenous agency, Native Hawaiian land tenure, and the land and resource law of the Hawaiian Kingdom. He teaches courses on resource management, land tenure, and the Hawaiian Kingdom. He is a farmer, father, and husband.

Makena Coffman is an Associate Professor of Urban and Regional Planning at the University of Hawai'i at Mānoa. She teaches graduate courses in environmental planning related to climate change mitigation and adaptation in the Asia/Pacific region, energy and environmental policy, and planning methods. She specializes in economic-environment modeling, holds a BA in International Relations from Stanford University, and a PhD in Economics from the University of Hawai'i at Mānoa. She is a Research Fellow with the University of Hawai'i Economic Research Organization.

Donovan Kūhiō Colleps was born and raised in 'Ewa Beach, O'ahu. He is a PhD student in English at the University of Hawai'i at Mānoa, and writes poetry and fiction.

Sean Connelly is an interdisciplinary designer, integrating architecture, urban design, conceptual art, and the watershed. He is a graduate of Castle High School, and received his degrees in architecture and urban design at the University of Hawai'i at Mānoa. He is currently studying architecture and urbanism at Harvard University.

Elise Leimomi Dela Cruz-Talbert has been a researcher and community advocate on diverse issues related to health and social justice. She firmly believes that to promote health for all people in all places, we must be able to identify health disparities, build community capacity for health promotion, and push for data-driven policies. Raised in Kāneʻohe, Oʻahu, Elise went on to receive her BS in Biology, Genetics and Development from Cornell University, and her Masters in Public Health from the University of Hawaiʻi at Mānoa, where she is currently a doctoral student in Epidemiology. Her doctoral research involves measuring the relationship between neighborhood food environments and health outcomes.

Noelani Goodyear-Kaʻōpua teaches at the University of Hawaiʻi at Mānoa as an Associate Professor of Political Science specializing in Hawaiian and Indigenous politics. Raised in Kalihi and Heʻeia on Oʻahu, her academic work is one part of a lifetime commitment to aloha ʻāina—politically-engaged, loving care for Hawaiʻi. Her previous research projects have involved documenting Hawaiʻi-based transformative social action, including her first book, *The Seeds We Planted: Portraits of a Native Hawaiian Charter School* (U of Minnesota P, 2013), and the edited collection, *Ea: Hawaiian Movements for Life, Land and Sovereignty* (Duke UP, 2014), co-edited with Ikaika Hussey and Kahunawai Wright and in partnership with documentary photographer Ed Greevy.

Consuelo Agarpao Gouveia is a Kumu and the Elementary Curriculum Specialist for Hālau Kū Māna New Century Public. She received a Master's Degree in Curriculum and Instruction for K-12 with an emphasis in Literacy from Grand Canyon University, and will pursue a Doctorate Degree in Administration or Special Education. Consuelo earned her Bachelor's Degree in Elementary Education from the University of Nevada at Las Vegas. She has taught grades Pre-K to twelfth, and has even taught at UNLV's Preschool, which specializes in servicing kids with special needs from birth to age five. Outside of school, Consuelo loves to spend time with her ʻohana and her three boys: Aiden (8), Tanner (7), and Logan (4).

Tina Grandinetti is a proud graduate of Mililani High School and the University of Hawaiʻi at Mānoa. She recently spent fourteen months living out of a bright blue backpack, traveling to various places in Asia, the Middle East, Europe, and the Pacific, driven largely by a desire to understand the shared struggle of indigenous peoples around the world. She dreams of a world in which indigenous knowledge is respected and valued, and in fact believes that this may be the only way to create a future worth living in. Currently, Tina is happy to be home pursuing her Masters in Political Science at the University of Hawaiʻi at Mānoa, and beginning to understand her place in the global indigenous movement.

Hunter Heaivilin is a Kailua boy currently pursuing a Masters of Urban and Regional Planning at the University of Hawaiʻi at Mānoa. He is a Permaculture designer and educator helping direct the Asia-Pacific Center for Regenerative Design.

He is infatuated with island resilience and climate adaptation agriculture. When not gleaning in Honolulu, or caught between the pages of a textbook, he can be found in one valley or another tending to his livestock menagerie.

Sania Faʻamaile Betty P. Ickes teaches histories at University of Hawaiʻi at Leeward Community College. Her doctoral dissertation explores the relationship between decolonization in the Tokelau homeland and identity formation and social change in the Tokelauan diaspora in Hawaiʻi and New Zealand. She also serves as the Executive Director for Te Taki Tokelau Community, Inc., which operates Te Lumanaki o Tokelau i Amelika School. She volunteers as a Tokelauan language teacher for the school's PK-1 class.

Kathy Jetnil-Kijiner is a poet, writer, and journalist born in the Marshall Islands and raised in Hawaiʻi. Her poetry is a blend of storytelling and activism.

Bonnie Kahapeʻa-Tanner was born and raised in Kāneʻohe and lives with her husband and two keiki in Kaʻalaea. Stepping aboard the voyaging canoe *Makaliʻi* for the first time in 1995, she immediately felt a strong connection and began training with the crew. In 1999, she was a crew member in the epic "E Mau, Sailing the Master Home" Voyage, honoring grand master navigator Pius Mau Piailug. Upon the completion of the voyage, Mau had only one request of the crew: to share their experience and new knowledge with others. She established and leads the Kānehūnāmoku Voyaging Academy, which focuses on perpetuating the legacy of Mau Piailug via educational programs, and has partnered with numerous public charter schools and non-profit organizations. A licensed Captain through the US Coast Guard-Merchant Marines, Bonnie has more than twenty years experience working as an educator on the ocean.

Kainani Kahaunaele is the makuahine haʻaheo of Kaniaulono, Hāʻenaala, and Kūaea Hāpai, and wahine aloha of Halealoha Ayau. She is a multi Nā Hōkū Hanohano Award winning vocalist and haku mele who recently earned her Master's degree in Hawaiian language and literature focused on mele hula of Niʻihau. Her CDs *Naʻu ʻOe* and *ʻŌhai ʻUla* showcase her deep aloha for our akua, ʻāina, ʻohana, and kuleana connections through original mele.

Joseph Keaweʻaimoku Kaholokula is an Associate Professor and Chair of the Department of Native Hawaiian Health in the John A. Burns School of Medicine and the University of Hawaiʻi at Mānoa. He is also a member of Hale Mua o Kūaliʻi, a Hawaiian cultural group dedicated to the perpetuation of Hawaiian cultural values and practices, and leadership development for Hawaiian men. As a clinical health psychologist and behavioral scientist, he has studied the effects of acculturation and discrimination on the health of Native Hawaiians, and helped to develop clinic and community-based health promotion programs to improve the cardiometabolic health of Native Hawaiians and other Pacific Islanders.

Born and raised in Kukuipuka, in the ahupuaʻa of Kahakuloa, Kaʻanapali, Maui, **Haley Kailiehu** is kamaʻāina to the steep cliffs and rugged coastline of Makamakaʻole valley. Descendant of generations of ʻŌiwi artists, Haley's art is shaped by the genealogy and ʻāina of which she was born. Currently, Haley is pursuing a PhD in Education with a focus in Curriculum Studies. Her research is focused on community- and ʻāina-based art as a means of reclaiming ʻŌiwi spaces and places.

Hiʻilei Kawelo, a native of Kahaluʻu, Oʻahu, is the Executive Director of Paepae o Heʻeia. Raised in Kahaluʻu by her skilled fishing family, she has been a student of the art and science of lawaiʻa and to Kāneʻohe Bay her entire life. She is a 1995 graduate of Punahou School and also received a Bachelors of Science in Biology from the University of Hawaiʻi.

Keone Kealoha is the cofounder and Executive Director of Mālama Kauaʻi, a non-profit organization focused on building community resiliency and abundance through local, healthy, and equitable food systems. He is currently living the dream and homesteading on the island of Kauaʻi with his partner Katie, Baby Shea, and the rest of the Kealoha ʻOhana.

Emelihter Kihleng was born on Guam to a White American mother and a Pohnpeian father, and was raised on the Islands of Pohnpei in the Federated States of Micronesia, Guam, and Oʻahu, Hawaiʻi. Growing up on these three very different Pacific Islands has greatly influenced her thinking and writing. She lives in Wellington, New Zealand, where she is working on her PhD at Victoria University.

James Koshiba is the cofounder and former Executive Director of Kanu Hawaii, a non-profit organization working to build grassroots movements for a sustainable, compassionate, and resilient Hawaiʻi. He helped lead Kanu Hawaii's efforts for five years, and stepped down from that post at the end of 2012. The views expressed in this essay are his, and do not necessarily reflect the views of Kanu Hawaii, its staff, board, or supporters. James is currently Principal of Social Ventures, a firm that incubates island-grown innovations in environmental, economic, and spiritual sustainability.

Derek Kurisu has been working for KTA Super Stores since 1968, from bag boy to Executive Vice President today. He continues to innovate ways that local businesses can give back to and enrich local communities, creating the successful Mountain Apple Brand product label, and producing two Big Island family television programs. He has served numerous other community organizations, including the Kiwanis, the Hawaii Farm Bureau, the University of Hawaiʻi at Mānoa College of Tropical Agricultural and Human Resources, and various state educational programs. He invests time with senior citizens and students throughout Hawaiʻi through speaking engagements and cooking demonstrations.

Dawn Mahi grew up all over Kailua and Kāneʻohe before her family moved to Washington State. After many years there and a year in Nicaragua she finally came home. She is the Lei Hīpuʻu Coordinator at Kokua Kalihi Valley Comprehensive Family Services, exploring Pacific cultural connections and weaving community strengths and provider services into a coordinated lei of support for families. Her background and interests are in community development, talk story, public health, and liminality.

Born and raised on Maui, **Brandy Nālani McDougall** is of Kanaka Maoli (Hawaiʻi, Maui, Oʻahu, and Kauaʻi lineages), Chinese, and Scottish descent. She is the author of a poetry collection, *The Salt-Wind, Ka Makani Paʻakai* (Kuleana ʻŌiwi P, 2008), the co-founder of Ala Press and Kahuaomānoa Press, and the costar of an amplified poetry album, *Undercurrent* (Hawaiʻi Dub Machine, 2011). She is an Assistant Professor of Indigenous Studies in the American Studies Department at the University of Hawaiʻi at Mānoa.

Mailani Neal is currently a junior at Kamehameha Schools Kapālama Campus. She has been a boarding student since seventh grade, and lives in Kailua-Kona on Hawaiʻi Island. Mailaniʻs favorite activities include running, hiking, and surfing, and she hopes to pursue a career in astronomy.

Ryan Oishi currently teaches at Kamehameha Schools. He has several poems published in *Tinfish 18.5*, and along with Aiko Yamashiro, Emelihter Kihleng, and Mark Guillermo, was a co-editor of *Routes*, a collection of poems and stories about TheBus that was published by Kahuaomānoa Press in Fall 2009.

Jamaica Heolimeleikalani Osorio is a kanaka maoli wahine poet/activist/scholar, born and raised in Pālolo Valley (Oʻahu). Jamaica's artistic experience ranges from poetry writing and performance to fiction and essay writing and music, while her academic interests span ʻike Hawaiʻi, ethnic studies, literature, politics, and critical race theory. Jamaica is a three-time national poetry champion, poetry mentor, and a published author. She is a proud graduate of Kamehameha, Stanford (BA) and New York University (MA), and has finally moved home to begin her PhD studies in English (kanaka maoli literature) at the University Hawaiʻi at Mānoa.

Eri Oura is a queer womyn of Japanese ancestry, born and raised on the island of Oʻahu. She recently received a master's degree in Political Science from the University of Hawaiʻi at Mānoa, concentrating on indigenous politics and feminist theory. Eri is a community organizer and educator in the movement for social justice. She has worked as a youth project coordinator for Hawaiʻi Peace and Justice, and is active with the International Network of Women Against Militarism.

Faith Pascua is foremost a student, a spoken word artist, and a mentor. Faith currently attends University of Hawai'i at Leeward Community College for her Associates of Arts in Teaching. She is heavily involved in Pacific Tongues and Youth Speaks Hawai'i, where she teaches other youth to "own" their stories through spoken word and performance.

Mark Patterson is the Warden of the Women's Community Correctional Center (WCCC) in Hawai'i and has held that post for the last six years. With over twenty-five years of public safety experience both in Hawai'i and Nevada, he began his career as an adult corrections officer. Raised in Mākaha and a graduate of the Kamehameha Schools, Mark attended New Mexico Military Institute, and holds a degree in criminology from Florida State University. His vision for WCCC is to create a Pu'uhonua—a sanctuary, a place of healing and transformation. His strategy includes taking a community-building approach through partnership formation, utilizing a mind, body, spirit, and place perspective, and incorporating a trauma-informed systems of care framework.

Prime / John Hina grew up in Honolulu and was a part of the hip hop graffiti scene in the early '80s. His organization, 808 Urban, has been creating murals and mentoring teens since late 2006.

No'u Revilla was born on the island of Maui. She is a Kanaka Maoli poet and performer and is currently pursuing her PhD in the English Department at the University of Hawai'i at Mānoa.

Hāwane Rios was raised in the small ranching town of Waimea, Hawai'i. She attended the Kamehameha Schools Kapālama Campus then went on to further her education at the University of Hawai'i at Hilo, earning her bachelor's degree in Hawaiian Language from Ka Haka 'Ula 'o Ke'elikōlani College of Hawaiian Language. Upon graduation, Hāwane traveled to the last atoll in the Hawaiian chain, Hōlanikū/Kure, to do island restoration and wildlife conservation work for seven months. During her journey, her first CD single, *Poli'ahu i ke Kapu,* was released, and earned her a Big Island Music Award in the Hawaiian Language Category. The proceeds generated from this song will be donated to the Mauna Kea Defense Fund. Since then, Hāwane has released two more singles and continues to compose and perform her music throughout Hawai'i. Hāwane is a young leader and activist in her community who believes deeply in the healing vibration of music and the power of awareness and unification that it can bring. I ka piko o ke aloha.

Darlene Rodrigues, a 2nd/3rd generation Bisaya living on O'ahu, descends from a long line of rice farmers, chance takers, and pineapple pickers. Her poetry and essays have appeared in *Bamboo Ridge, Amerasia Journal, disOrient,* and in the anthologies *Babaylan: Writings by Filipina and Filipina American Writers* and *Words Matter: Conversations with Asian American Writers.* She works for the Hawai'i People's Fund as the Community Grants Program Coordinator.

Cheryse Julitta Kauikeolani Sana is currently the Farm Manager at MAʻO Organic Farms in Lualualei Valley, Waiʻanae. MAʻO is a community-based social enterprise that is *indigenizing* Hawaiʻi's local agriculture and education systems to restore ancestral abundance. Having graduated from the Youth Leadership Training Program (YLT) and receiving her BA in Hawaiian Studies from Hawaiʻinuiākea School of Hawaiian Knowledge at the University of Hawaiʻi at Mānoa, she is leading other young adults to succeed and bring prosperity for themselves, their families, and their community.

Dean Itsuji Saranillio grew up in Kahului on the island of Maui. He has published in numerous journals and anthologies, including *Positively No Filipinos Allowed*, *Asian Settler Colonialism*, and *Formations of U.S. Imperialism*. Currently, he is an Assistant Professor in the Department of Social and Cultural Analysis at New York University.

Lyz Soto, Cofounder of Pacific Tongues, and mentor with its award-winning program Youth Speaks Hawaiʻi, is working towards a PhD in English at the University of Hawaiʻi at Mānoa. She has performed in Hawaiʻi, Aotearoa, and the continental United States. Her chapbook, *Eulogies*, was published in 2010 by TinFish Press.

Innocenta Sound-Kikku is a powerful Chuukese woman activist from the beautiful island of Lukunor, Chuuk, in the Federated States of Micronesia. On Oʻahu, Innocenta continues her creative organizing work with Micronesian women by developing culturally accessible and appropriate approaches and materials for the Chuukese community. Professionally, she currently works at Kokua Kalihi Valley Community Health Center as a Program Manager for Lei Hīpuʻu, working with young moms and their children to develop and strengthen their parenting skills. She is an active leader in the health care reform movement in Hawaiʻi, as an officer of the Micronesian Health Advisory Council, and an active member of the Micronesian Community Network.

Cade Watanabe was born and raised on the Hāmākua Coast of the island of Hawaiʻi. He is a graduate of the University of Hawaiʻi at Mānoa, and since 2006 has been a community/political organizer with UNITE HERE! Local 5—a local labor organization representing 10,000 hotel, health care, and food service workers throughout the State.

Jill Yamasawa is an AVID elective teacher in Kapolei, Hawaiʻi. She enjoys dancing, traveling, cooking, and spending time with loved ones. Her book of poems, entitled *Aftermath*, was published by Kahuaomānoa Press in 2010.

Aiko Yamashiro was raised in the powerful embrace of the Koʻolau mountains, in Kāneʻohe. Her ancestors came to Hawaiʻi from Japan, Okinawa, and Guam. She graduated from Castle High School in 2003 and is currently blessed to be a graduate student and teacher at the University of Hawaiʻi at Mānoa English Department, and a board member of the Hawaiʻi People's Fund. Her interests include decolonial and anticolonial literature of Hawaiʻi and the Pacific.

Matt N. Yamashita lives with his wife and three children on the island of Molokai. He has a BFA in Film/TV Production from Chapman University, c. 2000, and owns and operates Quazifilms Media. Matt is also active in the community, serving on various non-profit boards and participating in renewable energy and community strengthening efforts.

Aubrey Morgan Yee is a doctoral student in Alternative Futures at the University of Hawaiʻi at Mānoa, a writer and strategist for foundations working on resiliency and food security, a serial entrepreneur, a photographer, a mother, a wife, a daughter, and a friend to many. Hawaiʻi is her one and only home. She aims to use her expertise in the field of alternative futures to work on shaping preferred futures for Hawaiʻi by helping individuals and organizations to embrace and harness the immensely creative and liberating possibilities created by uncertainty in a time of rapid change.